INDIGENOUS PEOPLES, CIVIL SOCIETY, AND THE NEO-LIBERAL STATE
IN LATIN AMERICA

INDIGENOUS PEOPLES, CIVIL SOCIETY, AND THE NEO-LIBERAL STATE IN LATIN AMERICA

Edited by

Edward F. Fischer

Berghahn Books
NEW YORK • OXFORD
www.berghahnbooks.com

First published in 2009 by

Berghahn Books

www.berghahnbooks.com

© 2009 Berghahn Books

Originally published as a special issue of *Social Analysis*, volume 51, issue 2.

Library of Congress Cataloging-in-Publication Data

Indigenous peoples, civil society, and the neo-liberal state in Latin America / edited by Edward F. Fischer.
    p. cm.
Includes bibliographical references and index.
ISBN 978-1-84545-597-2 (pbk. : alk. paper)
    1. Indians—Government relations. 2. Indians, Treatment of—Latin America. 3. Indians—Social conditions. 4. Civil society—Latin America. 5. Neoliberalism—Latin America. I. Fischer, Edward F., 1966–.

E65.I476 2009
323.119708—dc22

2008041448

British Library Cataloguing in Publication Data

A catalogue record for this book is available from the British Library.

Printed on acid-free paper

CONTENTS

ACKNOWLEDGMENTS

This volume brings together anthropologists, historians, and activists to address the complicated and multi-faceted role that civil society plays in indigenous politics in Latin America. The contributors bring on-the-ground ethnographic approaches to the topic that are especially well-suited to describe the multiple ways that grass-roots indigenous activism works through civil society. It has been a pleasure to work with these authors, each of whom advances our understanding in novel and often surprising ways. Their sharp analyses and rich descriptions make this volume an important contribution to the field.

The late Kingsley Garbett first proposed the idea that this collection be published as a special issue of the journal *Social Analysis*. Without his support and vision, this project would never have come about. After Kingsley's death, Bruce Kapferer took over the editorship of *Social Analysis*, and his sharp eye helped direct many useful revisions to see the publication through to completion.

This volume would not have been possible without the collaboration of a number of colleagues. Conversations with Jan Rus and Peter Benson helped me formulate key parts of the introduction and shaped the direction of the work as a whole. Jan never fails to inspire the best in authors, and this work is no exception. I trust Peter's sensibilities implicitly, and his support helped me finalize this endeavor. The introduction and shape of the volume as a whole were also influenced by exchanges with Marta Casaús, Demetrio Cojtí, Alberto Esquit, Tim Smith, Kedron Thomas, and the anonymous reviewers. Special thanks go to Roddy Brett, Daniel Reichman, and Sarah Lyon for their valuable feedback. As always, Norma Antillón and Laurie Fleming deserve more recognition than I am able to offer for their logistical and editorial support.

At Berghahn, Shawn Kendrick's editing of both substance and style greatly improved all of the chapters; she elevates editing to an art form. Also at Berghahn, Ann Przyzycki and Marion and Vivian Berghahn provided invaluable assistance.

Finally, Mareike Sattler, my wife, not only put up with my usual writing neuroses but did an outstanding job of compiling the index.

Ted Fischer
Nashville, Tennessee

INTRODUCTION
Indigenous Peoples, Neo-liberal Regimes,
and Varieties of Civil Society in Latin America

Edward F. Fischer

Civil society is a slippery concept, and therein lies much of its appeal. By meaning many things to many people, it is one of those frequently invoked yet strategically ambiguous ideas that have real traction, not only in the rarefied world of professional journals, but also in the arena of public policy and political practice. Much of the recent literature on civil society has come from political science. But anthropology (ethnography in particular) has a lot to offer by documenting the on-the-ground diversity of civil society. The leitmotif that emerges from the chapters in this collection is that civil society takes many forms, with multiple, sometimes contradictory, social and political valences. Focusing on its complexities and vernacular forms moves us toward a more nuanced view of the potentials and pitfalls of civil society.

References for this section begin on page 16.

The allure of the concept of civil society also stems from its triangulation of traditionally progressive and traditionally conservative stances. It invokes the noble empowerment of marginalized peoples as well as the retraction of government obligations. It conjures possibilities for voluntary associations and grass-roots organizations as well as increased power of unelected officials and economic interests. Civil society's surge in importance has allowed Latin American indigenous communities access to funding, national and international awareness, and in some cases increases in de facto and de jure autonomy. At the same time, the rise in the importance of civil society goes hand in hand with the rise of neo-liberal political and economic reforms that threaten the material bases of indigenous culture and expose populations to the fickle fashions of First World funding and constraints on time and energy.

To what extent, then, does civil society serve as a space for what Foucault (1991) calls governmentality? Civil society allows the expression of collective will, of hopes and aspirations for the future, along with a sense of choice, self-determination, and empowerment. But this space of expression and agitation also fits into social and political relations in a way that buttresses claims of inclusion and representativeness while still upholding a particular status quo. Working through what Fischer and Benson (2006) have termed "limit points," civil society can co-opt and corrupt movements of resistance and utopian narratives by providing a foreshortened yet feasible alternative. At the same time, trying to co-opt resistance is a risky business: as Giddens (1984) observes, such elements may begin to structure the system itself in ways not foreseen. In this light, civil society also provides a radically democratic position from which marginalized peoples can exert influence on policies and practices. This is not an either-or proposition. The complexity of civil society resides in its quantum-mechanical aspect: simultaneously a point of resistance and of hegemonic collusion, civil society is formed from a contradiction that cannot be reconciled. The ethnographic challenge, then, is to represent this complexity without trying to force a synthesis of the thesis and antithesis.

In recent years, the concept of civil society has received a lot of attention from political scientists, economists, and sociologists but less from anthropologists. To be sure, ethnographers have observed and analyzed the impacts of civil society institutions on the communities they study, but they often do so outside of the paradigm of civil society studies. If we conceive of ethnography not just as a methodology but as epistemology—as the dialectic construction of knowledge through an engagement with 'the field'—then it is all the more necessary for the study of paradigm-bending vernacular forms of civil society. Kapferer (2000: 189) sees fieldwork as "an attitude and a means to break the resistance of the anthropologist's own assumptions, prejudices and theories, wherever the site of origin, concerning the nature and reason of lived realities." Indeed, herein resides the power of ethnography—a means of breaking down preconceptions and forcing an engagement with the lived reality of practice. And it is through such an approach that we sometimes come to unsettling conclusions about social forms that we are apt to celebrate.

The contributors to this book all employ an ethnographic approach that challenges received wisdom about civil society by showing the complex and variable outcomes of vernacular civil society in countries across Latin America. Addressing the multiple potentialities of civil society growth and critically assessing its potential for sustained change, these contributions speak not only to Latin American anthropology but also to the changing shape of global systems of political economy.

Indigenous Civil Society and New Social Movements

There was a moment in the 1980s and 1990s when there was great optimism about the potential of 'new social movements'—movements that were based on issues of identity rather than class and that stressed plurality of identity over unity of ideology (Laclau and Mouffe 1988; see also Buechler 1999; Escobar and Alvarez 1992). In the present collection, we too are concerned with identity politics and ethnic activism while also seeking to emphasize the importance of material conditions and macro-political economic contexts. Whereas the new social movements of Europe and the United States are in many ways post-materialistic (or anti-materialistic), the indigenous movements of Latin America are clearly rooted in conditions of material poverty and exploitation (even if many of their leaders are the more affluent among a marginalized population). Nonetheless, globalized new social movements in the North have deftly focused on human rights—specifically, the right to have rights, which opens the door to ethnic rights and indigenous identity politics.

In focusing on cultural aspects, the literature on new social movements sometimes neglects the political-economic structure that conditions new forms of organization and activism. The rise of indigenous civil society in Latin America must be understood as situated in a particular political-economic context: the debt crisis of the 1980s leading to neo-liberal reforms, and neo-liberal reforms opening up new spaces and creating conditions for new forms of activism.

Political-economic changes and the rise of indigenous consciousness over the last 20 or so years have invigorated civil society. Just as many governmental economic protections have been dismantled, civil society institutions (especially those focused on indigenous and environmental issues) have taken on increasing power in influencing state policies. This is a sort of proxy populism, allowing (or forcing) elected representatives to respond to constituent demands. While superior to benign disregard or active disdain for public opinion, it can be the case that the most vocal and the most media savvy—and not necessarily the most needy—get the attention, a point to which I return below.

Indigenous civil society organizations in Latin America have been especially effective in forging international alliances that help pressure the state from without, just as grass-roots action applies pressure from within. In many ways, the international Left legitimates indigenous civil society even as it seeks to be legitimated by an association with authentic indigenous protest. At their best, such alliances strengthen indigenous civil society in Latin America by mobilizing the material resources and media access of international networks. Yet there can also be a heavy-handedness of good intentions that can become oppressive, even racist, in visions of indigenous futures built on distant moral projects and romanticized dreams.

Civil Society and the State

Civil society is often defined by what it is not: not of the government, not of the private sector. While at its broadest it can encompass everything from knitting circles to the Catholic Church, in practice it most often refers to organized NGOs (non-governmental organizations). Keane (1998: 45) provides what I find to be a particularly useful definition of civil society as the "non-legislative, extra-judicial, public space in which societal differences, social problems, public policy, government action, and matters of community and cultural identity are developed and debated." Whereas we generally think of civil society in terms of 'institutions', which is to say formal organization, there is also a fertile realm of spontaneous, non-organized civil society.

Theorizations of civil society often draw heavily from the literature on social capital.[1] Social capital, as outlined by Bourdieu (1984), includes the resources (actual and symbolic) that an individual or group attains through networks of relations. Social capital is intimately linked to cultural capital, and both are convertible—in ways at times explicit and at times hidden—into economic capital (Marx's 'productive capital'). Civil society provides a structure through which social capital can be converted to economic and political ends vis-à-vis the state.

Civil society's relation to the state is complex, for while it is separate from the state, it is the state that guarantees its autonomy. Mamdani (1996: 15) argues that "the constellation of social forces organized in and through civil society" can operate only "by ensuring a form of the state and a corresponding legal regime to undergird the autonomy of civil society."

Early considerations did not draw the stark line between civil society and the state that is now fundamental to our understanding. Aristotle's thoughts on what he termed 'political community' (which, significantly, was translated into Latin as *societas civilis*) describe an ideal in which civil society was the state. The state was based on individuals agreeing to live together by certain principles derived from community values—and, of course, a bit of coercion.

In *Philosophy of Right*, Hegel ([1821] 2006) views civil society as distinct from the state but not from the private economic sector. He saw civil society (*bürgerliche Gesellschaft*, which might also be translated as 'bourgeois society') as including the economic sphere (ibid.: § 182):

> In civil society each member is his own end, everything else is nothing to him. But except in contact with others he cannot attain the whole compass of his ends, and therefore these others are means to the end of the particular member. A particular end, however, assumes the form of universality through this relation to other people, and it is attained in the simultaneous attainment of the welfare of others. Since particularity is inevitably conditioned by universality, the whole sphere of

civil Society is the territory of mediation where there is free play for every idiosyn-
crasy, every talent, every accident of birth and fortune, and where waves of every
passion gush forth, regulated only by reason glinting through them.

Hegel saw England, with its flourishing capitalist enterprises, as the embodi-
ment of a civil society based on rational self-interests and utilitarianism and the
breakdown of family and community ties bound by tradition. This sort of civil
society eroded traditional political society, and it was to be the role of the state
to mediate these drives by expressing a unified, rational collective will through
politics. Capitalist civil society destroyed ancient traditionalism but could not
replace it with the collective morality of the state. Eventually, civil society
would become subsumed to the state. Hegel argued that the state of nature
(needs, narrow egoistic self-interest) must be mediated through civil society
(including the economy) before becoming political. Civil society thus educates
and tames self-interest. In this way, Hegel sees civil society as molding the
convergence of individual and collective will through the state.

It is this Hegelian view that gives rise both to contemporary conservative
and to liberal views of civil society. There is the tradition that started with the
conservative Hegelians and continues through modern neo-conservative views.
The Cato Institute, a libertarian research foundation headquartered in Washington, DC, defines civil society as a way of "fundamentally reducing the role of
politics in society by expanding free markets and individual liberty" (quoted in
Edwards 2004: 2). Conservative authors such as Don Eberly (2000: 17) note that
"civil society not only mediates on behalf of the individual, and works to curb
atomization; it inculcates core democratic values." These in turn are 'seedbeds
of virtue' of the sort Tocqueville described, fertile ground for the pursuit of
enlightened self-interest. Eberly maintains that while many conservatives see
civil society as a replacement for government, many liberals view it as a mechanism for making government work better and connect more firmly with the
populace. In this sense, they are more closely aligned with the young Hegelians,
whose progressive views of change inform the so-called New Left.

Such genealogies lead Partha Chatterjee (2004) to argue that civil society is
a product of Western modernity that is meant to replicate Western modernity.
Those who do not "conform to the (Western bourgeois, secularized Christian)
principles of modern civil society" are excluded and relegated to the realm of
the traditional (ibid.: 61). He proposes "political society" to discuss that space
wherein political (electoral) mobilization not grounded in Western civil society
exercises power. Such political society allows the poor, both rural and urban,
to come together to shape the state and its responses through various means,
legal and extra-legal.

Chaterjee's inclusive, libratory vision builds on, while critically challenging,
the Gramscian tradition of civil society studies. Gramsci (1971: 208) reintro-
duced civil society debates into twentieth-century social science, and, unlike
Hegel, clearly defined it as neither of the state nor of the private market sector: "[B]etween the economic structure and the state with its legislation and
coercion stands civil society." While Gramsci is often remembered for viewing

civil society as potentially disruptive and anti-hegemonic (see Hardt 1995), he placed great weight on its use as a mechanism through which hegemonies were constructed (particularly in public spheres such as schools and the media).

Gramsci's views on civil society see in it the multiple potentials we focus on here. While he regards civil society as the socio-cultural sphere through which state power is legitimated and buttressed, the site of hegemonic formation, he also highlights the more radically democratic potential of civil society—the disruptive potential of organic intellectuals to critique the state of things—and its capacity as a site of resistance against the state. This multi-faceted view is especially useful in understanding civil society as a political space and institutional framework with the capability to resist as well as reify state-sanctioned relations. The chapters in this book speak to the range of potentialities realized through indigenous civil society organizations in the varied contexts of Latin American countries.

Civil Society and Governmentality

While civil society promotes association, it is ecumenical with regard to the content and aims of those associations. Civil society can fractionalize as well as unify—or do both simultaneously. Indeed, associations of ideologically like-minded individuals provide a context in which extremism can easily flourish. The middle ground can become easily skewed, allowing ideas and discourses to move to an extreme without disturbing unspoken assumptions. Civil society can promote racism and sexism and exclusion as easily as inclusion. It can also provide a venue for despots and criminals to pursue their aims (Keane 1998).

Gramsci saw civil society as supporting the powers that be while providing a venue for resistance to power structures. A Foucauldian perspective focuses on the former rather than the latter possibility, while extending the concept of power beyond the formal apparatuses of the state and into the fluid relations between individuals. Foucault (1991) argues that civil society underwrites the state; indeed, he denies the separation of civil society and political society. Like Hegel and Gramsci, Foucault sees civil society institutions serving an educating function, but where Hegel celebrates this as moving natural subjects in line with idealized and mutually beneficial goals of the state (Hegel's enlightened, benevolent state), Foucault shows how the education that Hegel celebrated creates and fixes identities—all the better to govern with.

For Foucault, the enclosures of civil society produce disciplined subjects, exerting more subtle control than out-and-out subjugation. Here civil society feeds into Foucault's (1991) theories of governmentality, or the mentalities of government (in the particular sense of governing individuals' conduct as well as the expansive sense of political governance). In Foucault's view, government is the "conduct of conduct" and involves governing the self as well as governing others (see Dean 1999). He perceptively argues that governing (*gouverner*) is most effective when it colonizes modes of thought (*mentalité*). In this way, individuals are led to govern the self, internalizing mechanism of self-governance, or rather choosing of their own 'free' will identities that lend themselves to governance. Such 'political rationality' operates outside of state institutions and can come to permeate private relations as well as public ones. Indeed, in its economic guise, political rationality thrives on the contraction of the state, as is the case in neo-liberal regimes in which market forces are invested with the qualities of natural law and the decentralized power outsources much of the state's disciplinary work to the governed themselves. Such governmentality works through mechanisms that shape our wants and aspirations, for which, especially as responsibilities devolve back to individuals, we are held to be self-responsible.

NGOs and civil society organizations bring economic thought and market forces to bear on governance and governmentalities. By concentrating energies on the feasible and fundable alternatives of realpolitik, they structure realms of possibility and condition and foreshorten dreams of possible futures. Here ethnography provides a crucial complement to Foucault by showing the nuanced and disruptive permutations that civil society organizations may take on the ground.

Many have argued that social capital breaks down with the hyper-individualization of post-Fordist consumer societies (Putman 2000). But following Skocpol (2003), we may also see civil society not so much as the spontaneous eruption of grass-roots sentiment but as the product of institutional structures that condition participation. With the neo-liberal contraction of the state, the role of civil society has changed to advocacy and championing special interests, often played out in the courts rather than the legislature. By professionalizing advocacy through lobbying, there is no need for participation. And this civil society marketplace has produced a whole new way to articulate with the government.

Hardt (1995: 27) argues against the late-twentieth-century celebratory literature on civil society: "[W]hile recognizing the democratic functions that the concept and reality of civil society have made possible, it is also important to be aware of the functions of discipline and exploitation that are inherent in and inseparable from these same structures." Drawing on observations by Gilles Deleuze that in the postmodern era we have moved from a disciplinary society to a society of control, Hardt contends that as the logic of capitalism has permeated ever more spheres of daily life, civil society has withered away. He claims (ibid.) that the era in which we live is best characterized not as postmodern but as a "postcivil society." Whereas Fordist regimes defined roles that were based on fixed relations, in this age of flexibility there are no fixed identities or roles. As Deleuze and Guattari (1987) note, the spread of post-Fordist capitalism results in the hyper-segmentation of social units while also smoothing over the divides by infiltrating all social spheres, both public and private. Where capital achieves a true subsumption of labor, "instead of disciplining the citizen as a fixed social identity, the new social regime seeks to control the citizen as a whatever identity, or rather as an infinitely flexible placeholder for identity" (Hardt 1995: 31).

Applying these ideas to the circumstances of Latin America, Yúdice (1995: 17) looks to the tension between neo-liberal reforms and the rise of grass-roots movements, which are opposed to each other "yet contribute to the relinquishing by the state of the obligations to provide citizenship rights." Neo-liberal reforms can open new spaces for indigenous politics (Fischer 2001), but to what extent is this just a diversionary tactic of governmentality? Gustafson (2006: 374) suggests that the problem is in the framing of such questions. Looking at how civic regionalism is variously mapped in Santa Cruz, Bolivia, he concludes that the projects were "neither wholly that of the hegemonic state operating against resistant locals nor entirely the one of neo-liberal governmentality flowing out of transnational nowhere."

In looking at the emergence of "neoliberal multiculturalism," Hale (2004) writes of the *indio permitido* (or 'authorized' Indian), a pernicious situation in which indigenous groups are allowed some realm of expression that is confined to areas deemed non-threatening to state power. Those 'authorized' Indian groups that play along are praised and held up as examples of the inclusiveness of the state; those that do not are excluded and branded as divisive, even terrorists. While Hale's view of state power is decidedly Gramscian, his understanding of the motivations of the *indio permitido* resonates with Foucault's writings on governmentality and the ways in which power relations are defined with respect to enumerated populations.

In shaping desires, such internalizations of power relations become intertwined with notions of self-determination. At the same time, a concern with what is feasible and within reach often focuses efforts on 'limit points': goals that foreshorten the possibilities of radical change by concentrating attention and energy on what is viewed as attainable (see Fischer and Benson 2006). Indigenous leaders who seek radical reform are often marginalized for being idealistic and unrealistic—racist, even. And in these circumstances, the contours of civil society governmentality are especially stark.

Civil Society in Transnational Space

At the international level, a new breed of NGOs emerged in the 1990s to form what has been termed a 'global civil society'. There are about 40,000 international NGOs and 20,000 international NGO networks, 90 percent of them formed since 1970 (Edwards 2004: 23). Holly Cullen and Karen Murrow (2001) point out the role of NGOs in implementing and monitoring international accords in the absence of other mechanisms, which in turn raises questions about NGO accountability. We often assume that NGOs represent the people, that they are democratic by nature, but in fact they can be elitist. Cullen and Murrow conclude that many NGOs do have credibility and work hard to strengthen grassroots support—a form of legitimacy—but that this is a constant struggle.

It is often assumed that NGOs have the power to confer democratic legitimacy in situations where there is not much to be found (international law, Latin American governments, etc.). However, a Ford Foundation study of civil society and governance "found that associational life does contribute democracy and state accountability, but not as much as was thought, and only when certain conditions are met—alliances and coalitions between associations, for example, inclusive membership, and independence, including as much domestic funding as possible" (Edwards 2004: 84). In addition, Bebbington and Thiele (1993) show how NGOs become vehicles for the political aims of both the international Left and Right and how such funding influences the direction that these organizations take.

Increasingly, NGOs and other civil society actors operate in a world order dominated by what Kapferer (2005) characterizes as "wild sovereignty." Realigned political and economic interests in the globalized world have unleashed virulent, wild forms of corporate and political-military sovereignty. While opening up space for civil society–based resistance, this situation also insidiously promotes forms of governmentality as a survival strategy.

Appadurai (2002) argues that transnational relations can actually work to deepen local democracies. Local forms of organization may produce a sort of counter-governance from below, with justifications based on the kinds of censuses, ancestral claims, and other population-defining technologies that are so central to the more nefarious forms of governmentality. Such forms of civil society organization may be viewed as a sort of "countergovernmentality … governmentality turned against itself" (ibid.: 36; see also Hanson 2007 on forms of counter-governmentality).

Focusing on the "transnational apparatus of governmentality," Ferguson and Gupta (2002) take on the supposition of verticality that envisions the state atop civil society. They argue that in this current age of "transnational governmentality" states may still claim a superior position in relation to civil society, but that the horizontal, transnational linkages of NGOs effectively challenge such claims. And while governmentality works through the IMF (International Monetary Fund), the WTO (World Trade Organization), and other such international non-state mechanisms, it also allows the disruptive potential of transnational grass-roots organization.

Neo-liberal Forms of Citizenship

The forces of globalization have certainly eroded traditional state authority, especially through communications and transportation technologies, and this has allowed indigenous groups and their advocate NGOs to tap directly into international networks. The Zapatistas of Chiapas have effectively circumvented state controls by appealing directly to the international community, arguably playing to the international audience as much as, and at times more than, the national audience. A significant extent of their Mexican national support has come from left-leaning young urbanites—the same demographic in many ways as their supporters in Italy and Sweden.

Ramos (2002: 272) contends that as indigenous groups have "allied with entrepreneurial NGOs," their aims have shifted from collectively advancing a unified native front to pursuing more local and more economic issues, such as community development. She goes on to note that the international stage has provided indigenist groups (the product of "an Americas-style, amplified form of Orientalism") with an effective forum to agitate for change in discriminatory structures of national societies: "[E]thnic groups have found the most comfortable alliance to be not with social classes, not with the state, not with the church, but with supranational powers and private managers of ethnicity" (ibid.: 275). Ramos concludes that "suprastate organisms like the U.N. and extranational entities like NGOs" are providing indigenous peoples with the tools they need to change their circumstances and change themselves (ibid.: 276).

This points to the post-liberal (or neo-liberal) challenge of identity politics. As Sieder (2005), Yashar (2004), Ong (1999, 2006), and others have noted, neo-liberal regimes create new sorts of citizens and new sorts of citizenships. Rather than packaged as a whole, rights and responsibilities of neo-liberal citizenship are divvied up and differentially distributed (a process with a long history, as Baud shows in his contribution to this book). The goal of such structural changes is to produce newly flexible neo-liberal subjects who have to shoulder more risks.

Yashar (2004) looks at Bolivia, Ecuador, and Peru (with some reference to Guatemala and Mexico), focusing on citizenship regimes (the institutional factors that organize political involvement) and corporatist political structures that allowed for a large degree of indigenous autonomy at the local level. With the shift to neo-liberal regimes, which challenged indigenous autonomy, some actors were galvanized into action. Yashar concludes that some movements were more successful at mobilization than others because of the confluence of (1) changing citizenship regimes due to neo-liberal reforms, (2) the presence of political space for association (freedom of association, etc.), and (3) the presence of regional or national NGOs or other groups or networks that allowed mobilization to scale up effectively.

Gywnne and Kay (2004: 17) argue that there is a strong link between neo-liberal policies and democratic governance in Latin American countries. This does not, however, reveal causality; in fact, the international pressures on Latin American countries to liberalize their economies have also advocated democratic reform as part of the same package. This may thus be a case of self-fulfilling prophesies. In any event, democratic openings have allowed an important space for indigenous actors to agitate for governmental reform. In this way, neo-liberal citizenship regimes open up spaces for, and indeed demand, greater civil society participation.

Neo-liberal reforms also shift the risk and responsibility associated with societal change to individuals and associations. Yet neo-liberal privatizing puts the most stress on those who earn the least, sapping them of the time and energy that could otherwise be committed to making their circumstances better. Thus, while neo-liberal citizenship regimes allow for greater participation in the political process and the possibility of grass-roots forms of action, they also place the risks of failure on civil society. Along with this 'civil society heal thyself' attitude has emerged a new discourse of culpability aimed at those deemed incapable or unworthy of the responsibilities of democratic citizenship.

Thus, if neo-liberal reforms have created new spaces for indigenous politics, perhaps this is a case of governmentalities at work, of Hale's *indio permitido*. Are indigenous civil society actors co-opted and corrupted? Even if the goals they achieve are centered around compromised ends, are these not still important improvements? Should not these groups take what they can get? Such questions are asked, Peter Benson (personal communication) points out, against a notion of a real, authentic, fully Indian position. This, in turn, feeds into Foucault's observations about the histories of identities and the ways that populations are defined and governed—except in this case it is defined and governed from below (or at least from an intermediate position) and not from above. From this perspective, one is led to concur with Chatterjee's skepticism toward civil society as a binary between identity-less modern subjects and identity-heavy traditional ones. Indigenous identities articulate differently with the neo-liberal goal of flexible subjects who shoulder risk: being indigenous already entails taking on a great deal of risk.

Part of this risk resides in the fact that in civil society certain types of actors are recognized as legitimate while others are not. Such are the insidious ways, Nancy Postero (2006: 7) asserts, in which "state-sponsored multiculturalism" acts to confine diversity to manageable categories. This confined multiculturalism has flourished under neo-liberalism in Bolivia and other countries. Yet Postero goes on to show that Guaraní leaders were able to use these manageable categories to make further demands and redefine the terms of relations between the state and civil society and indigenous peoples. This may be the exception rather than the rule, but it is important to recognize that in certain circumstances indigenous groups can find tools and resources in neo-liberal programs.

In this vein, Warren and Jackson (2002b) outline how indigenous peoples have translated their own social practices into the idiom of civil society in order to make demands on the state. "The neoliberal project," they write, "relies on a cultural project, which is concerned with packaging these reforms in a palatable manner through appeals to solidarity and a celebration of civil society" (ibid.: 33). In this way, the cultural project of neo-liberalism actually needs the opposition of civil society to give it legitimacy bestowed by open dissent. As Don Kalb (2005: 177) observes, the third-way, neo-liberal alliance of the 1990s "claimed the cumulative convergence of the projects of market-making, democracy-making, the strengthening of civil society and the provision of prosperity for many into one mutually reinforcing set of forces." And just as decentralization can help indigenous NGOs, it can also reinforce local power structures (Sieder 2002, 2005; see also Fischer and Benson 2006)

Yet this leads us to another problem with perceptions of civil society in an international context. While the participation of NGOs in certain settings might suggest that democratic legitimacy has been accorded, the authority to represent is often contested, and the democratic workings of the grass-roots base are frequently problematic (see Cullen and Murrow 2001; Jackson 2002; as well as the chapters in this book by Colloredo-Mansfeld, Pitarch, Rappaport, and Sawyer). Furthermore, indigenous vernacular modernities that emphasize collective action contest the very bedrock of Western frameworks of individualistic liberalism (see Gow and Rappaport 2002).

The Latin American Context

Latin America has long been a laboratory for economic experimentation (and social engineering, as Pitarch notes in this book). In the post–World War II era, there was import substitution industrialization, an earlier inverse version of the

Washington consensus, which was much more costly in terms of international debt. Crushing debt ignited financial crises in the 1980s and 1990s, and a neo-liberal agenda of market-driven reforms was widely promoted as the solution. While the region still had large populations on the brink of severe poverty at the end of the 1970s, the years of heavy borrowing to support import substitution actually had showed modest but healthy rates of GNP per capita growth. In contrast, the neo-liberal turn saw tight restriction on macro-economic policy and a push for reducing deficits and debts—austerity programs that weighed most heavily on the poor (Gwynne and Kay 2004). It is in this economic context that civil society in Latin America has flourished out of opportunity as well as need.

Politically, neo-liberal reforms challenged the corporatist structure of Latin American political systems, pushing for decentralization and deregulation and opening up venues for new kinds of public-private and public-NGO collaborations. Thus, NGOs began to offer new outlets for popular organization—outlets that were less combative and more focused on incremental change within the system. As a field of governmentality, civil society effectively channels discontent toward manageable ends of the *indio permitido* sort.

At the same time, given the 'shallow' democracy characteristic of Latin American reforms, civil society organizations face great challenges working within a system that does not function as it is supposed to. Increasingly, we recognize the necessity of institutional frameworks to spur economic development (see, e.g., de Soto 2000) and to create social capital, one of the primary assets of civil society. Seligson (2005) reveals the need for such an institutional framework, pointing out that social capital is not a natural given of a population, yet he goes on to note that broad democracy-building programs have had only a very limited impact. In countries such as Guatemala, democracy building must contend with institutionalized policies and perceptions of racism (see Casaús Arzú, this book). One effective route for indigenous civil society organizations has been to turn to international law. For example, governments signing on to Convention 169 of the International Labour Organization (ILO), including those of Mexico, Guatemala, Colombia, Ecuador, and Bolivia, are obligated to halt various sorts of assimilationist policies and respect the rights of indigenous peoples. Using the provisions of ILO 169, indigenous sectors of civil society in Latin America have been able to apply pressure effectively from outside the normal channels of national politics as well as from within. The results have been varied. Sieder (2002) shows that Mexico's adoption of multicultural discourse (albeit in what she terms a form of "inclusive authoritarianism") stands in contrast to the rejection of such discourses and practices in places such as Guatemala. Indigenous organizations have also made strategic alliances with supporters and NGOs in other countries and, as Sawyer shows in her contribution to this collection, may also use foreign national law to further local agendas.

Van Cott (1994, 2000) points to the historical importance of indigenous autonomies in creating the conditions for effective indigenous political organization. Similarly, Bebbington and Thiele (1993) highlight the importance of local networks of social capital and the national-level institutional framework they must articulate with. Yet such localized bases have faced difficulties translating their concerns into national projects. Colloredo-Mansfeld (this book) shows how local agendas can hinder the formation of national cohesion. Latin American indigenous movements depend on civil society and NGO associations because their interests are not adequately represented by political parties. (Although one could say that this has changed given the turn to the Left in recent elections in several countries; Brazil, Venezuela, Bolivia, Ecuador, and others are experimenting with new roles for the state and civil society actors and working out the larger balance between public obligations and non-governmental capacities.) Now that indigenous leaders have had some success, they are at times being adopted and co-opted by political parties or, as Cojtí Cuxil (this book) argues, are effecting significant incremental changes within the system.

In countries such as Guatemala, recent histories of state-sponsored violence had the effect of galvanizing human rights concerns through civil society organizations (Brett 2006; Fischer 2001; Warren 1998). Perhaps as a result of the persecution suffered by such groups, indigenous organizations in Guatemala have taken pains to distance themselves from explicitly class-based politics and to focus on issues of culture and language (Dickins's contribution to this book shows how some indigenous groups have adopted the class-neutral language of development projects). In this context, it is significant that the lack of violence in Ecuador and Bolivia has led to crucial alliances between indigenous, peasant, and other civil society organizations and to exceptionally strong national indigenous movements that are working through robust civil society institutions (Zamosc 2004; see also Postero 2006).

This Collection

The contributors to this book show civil society in its many vernacular guises. No single model emerges from these case studies; rather, the lesson we glean is that civil society not only has ambiguous potential but often contradictory results, simultaneously channeling resistance and conditioning governmentalities. Indigenous movements in Latin America have been able to use the space of civil society to agitate for very real changes—not revolutionary but incremental. At the same time, civil society structures promote compromise and working within a system that rewards good (not too revolutionary) behavior. And let us not forget that civil society's associations of like-minded individuals provide a setting in which extremism can thrive. The middle ground in such a context can easily become distorted, with ideas and discourses resulting in exclusion just as easily as inclusion.

Michiel Baud begins by cautioning us to consider the historical context of the recent emergence of indigenous organizations and civil society structures. He points out the paradox that indigenous movements, which are often celebrated for their resistance to the state, usually take for granted (and even embrace) the set of citizenship rights bestowed by the state. Baud argues that "the quest for indigenous rights has become a discursive shorthand for citizenship rights in

general." He observes that where indigenous movements have been successful, they have allied themselves with non-indigenous interests. But this balance
will be difficult to maintain as indigenous movements become concerned as
much with material demands as with identity.

Daniel Goldstein, writing with Gloria Achá, Eric Hinojosa, and Theo Roncken,
maintains not only that vigilante violence is growing in lockstep with neo-liberal reforms in Bolivia, but that civil society itself includes violent as well as
peaceful forms. The authors show how civil society associations arise to combat the insecurity of situations with unstable economic bases and diminishing
state presence. They contend that the way that certain sectors of the population are stereotyped influences the sorts of rights and privileges of citizenship
that they can access. For the most marginalized, even violent forms of civil
organization are aimed at deepening and extending the rights of citizens in a
democratic society.

Suzana Sawyer looks at the formation of civil society institutions, focusing on
the dramatic case of an international class-action lawsuit brought (in the United
States) by indigenous and other Ecuadorian leaders against ChevronTexaco. She
finds that "subaltern subjects were not born resisting." Rather, the creation of a
"class" of resistance was a dialectic process that emerged from the engagement
of a variety of systems (US law, international law, environmental advocacy).
Sawyer's study points us toward a theory of articulation that eschews simple,
romantic views of resistance.

Rudi Colloredo-Mansfeld's contribution shows how local-level, grass-roots
civil society organizations of indigenous peoples in Ecuador have challenged
the formulation of a coherent national project. Writing of the uses of "vernacular statecraft," he reveals that effectiveness at the local level can actually inhibit
the creation of a national institutional framework for more systemic change. He
writes that "for indigenous peoples, a shared cultural identity is a thin political resource, offering few transcendent values." Mechanisms of community
justice, as well as communal work parties, provide the basis for organizing
around immediate problems while larger associational memberships tend to
stress resistance to outside threats over internal cohesion.

In her case study of Colombia's Regional Indigenous Council of Cauca
(CRIC), Joanne Rappaport looks at the way this indigenous organization has
reconfigured itself in the context of changing civil society relations. In Colombia, the indigenous population is small in size but has played a key role in
defining civil society in relation to the state and to armed non-state combat-
ants. Rappaport traces how the movement began with a generic discourse of
indigeneity that became ever more specific as member ethnic groups began to
assert their local and linguistic distinctiveness. This has led to CRIC having to
redefine itself as a source of traditional authority even as it became somewhat
removed from its local bases of support.

Three chapters on Guatemala present very different perspectives on the role
of indigenous peoples, civil society, and the state. Demetrio Cojtí Cuxil, a leading Maya public intellectual in Guatemala, argues that the Guatemalan state
effectively uses the population-defining technologies of governance to engineer

the statistical, if not actual, extermination (through assimilation) of Maya peoples. He shows that the state has ostentatiously promoted a few indigenous officials but contends that this simply hides deep-seated neo-colonialist attitudes that have prevented more profound inclusion. Cojtí concludes that the Guatemalan state continues to promote racist policies of ethnic unity and assimilation and that until this gives way to policies that value diversity, Maya civil society organizations will be limited in their impact.

Marta Casaús Arzú looks at how Guatemala's indigenous elites (including Cojtí) form part of a Gramscian political society. She employs an innovative methodology of discursive analysis that solicits essays from various political actors, which are then coded for opinions toward the Guatemalan state. She finds that the concepts of state, racism, and discrimination are highly correlated, leading to "a tendency to exculpate all social actors and focus on the state as the sole responsible party in charge of defeating these problems." This rings true, given Cojtí's argument, although Cojtí makes a clear distinction between the state and actors working through the state. Here the contradictions encompassed by civil society come to the fore: it can be a sanctioned outlet of acceptable resistance, as Cojtí points out, and it can simultaneously allow Maya elites to take on increasing real power within the state that threatens to overturn the ethnic status quo, as Casaús describes.

Avery Dickins's contribution turns to the local effects of development projects on civil society in a Q'eqchi' Maya community in Guatemala. She paints a vivid picture of *el otro lado*, the far side of the river that runs through town and where outside NGOs have built up an eco-tourism infrastructure. Dickins finds that residents focus their attention on improving the tourist areas while neglecting basic infrastructural development on the lived side of the river. This appears at first glance to be a perverse extreme of governmentality, but Dickins also shows the affective side of the allure of the cosmopolitan Other and the desire to participate in the global economy. She determines, ultimately, that residents are in fact dedicated to their own development projects as well, and that they are able to work within civil society structures to promote their competing visions of the future.

Pedro Pitarch concludes with a provocative analysis of the ways in which indigenous medicine has become a nexus of activism in Chiapas, Mexico. In comparing three indigenous NGOs, he shows how the organizational structure influences the ends as well as the means of activism. Indeed, it turns out that some groups make what Pitarch terms "uncivil" use of civil society organizations. Pitarch documents a case in which non-indigenous advisers reorient a group's goals to support a divergent larger political project. The "ventriloquism" effect that Pitarch describes emerges when non-indigenous leaders adopt an indigenous voice to bolster the legitimacy of their positions.

Taken together, these chapters present a rich and complex view of indigenous politics, civil society, and state policy in the early twenty-first century. They are all striking in both their ethnographic depth and their profound, and often contrarian, analyses. While there is no single story line that unites them, the chapters clearly speak to the formation of civil society, illustrating how civil society institutions (and the historical memory and cultural bonds that underlie them) emerge through the process of articulating with local, national, and international actors. Civil society, it is shown, has multiple potentials—it may even serve uncivil ends. Yet it also provides a space for grass-roots activism and the inclusion of marginalized voices in national dialogues.

Edward F. Fischer is Professor of Anthropology and Director of the Center for Latin American and Iberian Studies at Vanderbilt University in Nashville, Tennessee. His work focuses on ethnic activism and political economy among the Maya of Guatemala. His publications include *Maya Cultural Activism in Guatemala* (1996), *Cultural Logics and Global Economies: Maya Identity in Thought and Practice* (2001), and, with Peter Benson, *Broccoli and Desire: Global Connections and Maya Struggles in Postwar Guatemala* (2006). Most recently he has conducted fieldwork in Germany, examining the relationship of moral values and economic rationalities

Note

1. Edwards (2004) gives an associational view of civil society as including that part of society in between the family and the state that is not the domain of the government or of private firms. He envisions it as a means whereby people can come together to advance common interests through collective action. He writes (ibid: 76) that these forms of civil society "provide societies with sturdy norms of generalized reciprocity (by creating expectations that favours will be returned), channels of communication through which trust is developed (by being tested and verified by groups and individuals), templates for cooperation (that can be used in wider settings), and a clear sense of the risks of acting opportunistically (that is, outside networks of civic engagement, thereby reinforcing cooperative behavior, or at least conformity with 'civic values')." Edwards identifies three areas of civil society: economic, political, and social. Economically, civil society organizations can build up the trust and networks necessary for market cooperation; this is especially important in regions where the regulation of markets is weak. Politically, civil society organizations act as an important balance to corporatist governmental power. Finally, civil society can be an important source of social capital for marginalized peoples.

References

Appadurai, Arjun. 2002. "Deep Democracy: Urban Governmentality and the Horizons of Politics." *Public Culture* 14, no. 1: 21–47.

Bebbington, Anthony, and Graham Thiele. 1993. *Non-Governmental Organizations and the State in Latin America: Rethinking Roles in Agricultural Development*. London: Routledge.

Bourdieu, Pierre. 1984. *Distinction: A Social Critique of the Judgment of Taste*. Cambridge, MA: Harvard University Press.

Brett, Roddy. 2006. *Movimiento Social, Etnicidad y Democratización en Guatemala, 1985–1996*. Guatemala City: F y G Editores.

Buechler, Steven M. 1999. *Social Movements in Advanced Capitalism: The Political Economy and Cultural Construction of Social Activism.* Oxford: Oxford University Press.

Chatterjee, Partha. 2004. *The Politics of the Governed: Reflections on Popular Politics in Most of the World.* New York: Columbia University Press.

Cullen, Holly, and Karen Murrow. 2001. "International Civil Society in International Law: The Growth of NGO Participation." *Non-State Actors and International Law* 1: 7–39.

de Soto, Hernando. 2000. *The Mystery of Capital: Why Capitalism Triumphs in the West and Fails Everywhere Else.* New York: Basic Books.

Dean, Mitchell. 1999. *Governmentality: Power and Rule in Modern Society.* London: Sage.

Deleuze, Gilles, and Felix Guattari. 1987. *A Thousand Plateaus: Capitalism and Schizophrenia.* Trans. B. Massumi. Minneapolis: University of Minnesota Press.

Eberly, Don E., ed. 2000. *The Essential Civil Society Reader: The Classic Essays.* Lanham, MD: Rowman and Littlefield Publishers.

Edwards, Michael. 2004. *Civil Society.* Cambridge: Polity.

Escobar, Arturo, and Sonia Alvarez, eds. 1992. *The Making of Social Movements in Latin America: Identity, Strategy and Democracy.* Boulder, CO: Westview Press.

Ferguson, James, and Akhil Gupta. 2002. "Spatializing States: Toward an Ethnography of Neoliberal Governmentality." *American Ethnologist* 29, no. 4: 981–1002.

Fischer, Edward F. 2001. *Cultural Logics and Global Economies: Maya Identity in Thought and Practice.* Austin: University of Texas Press.

Fischer, Edward F., and Peter Benson. 2006. *Broccoli and Desire: Global Connections and Maya Struggles in Postwar Guatemala.* Stanford, CA: Stanford University Press.

Foucault, Michel. 1991. "Governmentality." Pp. 87–104 in *The Foucault Effect: Studies in Governmentality*, ed. Graham Burchell, Colin Gordon, and Peter Miller. Chicago, IL: University of Chicago Press.

Giddens, Anthony. 1984. *The Constitution of Society: Outline of the Theory of Structuration.* Cambridge: Polity Press.

Gow, David G., and Joanne Rappaport. 2002. "The Indigenous Public Voice: The Multiple Idioms of Modernity in Native Cauca." Pp. 47–80 in Warren and Jackson 2002a.

Gramsci, Antonio. 1971. *Selections from the Prison Notebooks.* London: Lawrence and Wishart.

Gustafson, Bret. 2006. "Spectacles of Autonomy and Crisis: Or, What Bulls and Beauty Queens Have to Do with Regionalism in Eastern Bolivia." *Journal of Latin American Anthropology* 11, no. 2: 351–379.

Gwynne, Robert N., and Cristóbal Kay. 2004. "Latin America Transformed: Globalization and Neoliberalism." Pp. 3–21 in *Latin America Transformed: Globalization and Modernity*, ed. Robert N. Gwynne and Cristóbal Kay. London: Arnold.

Hale, Charles. 2004. "Rethinking Indigenous Politics in the Era of the 'Indio Permitido.'" *NACLA Report on the Americas* 38, no. 2: 16–22.

Hanson, Paul W. 2007. "Governmentality, Language Ideology, and the Production of Needs in Malagasy Conservation and Development." *Cultural Anthropology* 22, no. 2: 244–284.

Hardt, Michael. 1995. "The Withering of Civil Society." *Social Text* 14, no. 4: 27–44.

Hegel, Georg Wilhelm Friedrich. [1821] 2006. *Philosophy of Right.* Trans. T. M. Knox. http://www.marxists.org/reference/archive/hegel/prindex.htm.

Jackson, Jean E. 2002. "Contested Discourses of Authority in Colombian National Indigenous Politics: The 1996 Summer Takeovers." Pp. 81–122 in Warren and Jackson 2002a.

Kalb, Don. 2005. "From Flows to Violence: Politics and Knowledge in the Debates on Globalization and Empire." *Anthropological Theory* 5, no. 2: 176–204.

Kapferer, Bruce. 2000. "Star Wars: About Anthropology, Culture and Globalisation." *Australian Journal of Anthropology* 11, no. 2: 174–199.

———, ed. 2005. *Oligarchs and Oligopolies: New Formations of Global Power.* Oxford: Berghahn Books.

Keane, John. 1998. *Civil Society: Old Images, New Visions.* Stanford, CA: Stanford University Press.

Laclau, Ernesto, and Chantal Mouffe. 1988. *Hegemony and Socialist Strategy: Towards a Radical Democratic Politics.* London: Verso.

Mamdani, Mahmood. 1996. *Citizen and Subject: Contemporary Africa and the Legacy of Late Colonialism*. Princeton, NJ: Princeton University Press.

Ong, Aihwa. 1999. *Flexible Citizenship: The Cultural Logics of Transnationality*. Durham, NC: Duke University Press.

———. 2006. *Neoliberalism as Exception: Mutations in Citizenship and Sovereignty*. Durham, NC: Duke University Press.

Postero, Nancy Grey. 2006. *Now We are Citizens: Indigenous Politics in Postmulticultural Bolivia*. Stanford, CA: Stanford University Press.

Putnam, Robert D. 2000. *Bowling Alone: The Collapse and Revival of American Community*. New York: Simon & Schuster.

Ramos, Alcida Rita. 2002. "Cutting Through State and Class: Sources and Strategies of Self-Representation in Latin America." Pp. 251–279 in Warren and Jackson 2002a.

Seligson, Mitchell A. 2005. "Can Social Capital Be Constructed? Decentralization and Social Capital Formation in Latin America." Pp. 361–377 in *Developing Cultures: Essays on Cultural Change*, ed. Lawrence Harrison and Jerome Kegan. New York: Routledge.

Sieder, Rachel. 2002. "Recognizing Indigenous Law and the Politics of State Formation in Mesoamerica." Pp. 184–207 in *Multiculturalism in Latin America: Indigenous Rights, Diversity, and Democracy*, ed. Rachel Sieder. Basingstoke: Palgrave Macmillan

———. 2005. "Challenging Citizenship, Neo-Liberalism, and Democracy: Indigenous Movements and the State in Latin America." *Social Movement Studies* 4, no. 3: 301–307.

Skocpol, Theda. 2003. *Diminished Democracy: From Membership to Management in American Civic Life*. Norman: University of Oklahoma Press.

Van Cott, Donna Lee, ed. 1994. *Indigenous Peoples and Democracy in Latin America*. New York: St. Martin's Press.

———. 2000. *The Friendly Liquidation of the Past: The Politics of Diversity in Latin America*. Pittsburgh, PA: University of Pittsburgh Press.

Warren, Kay B. 1998. *Indigenous Movements and Their Critics: Pan-Maya Activism in Guatemala*. Princeton, NJ: Princeton University Press.

Warren, Kay B., and Jean E. Jackson, eds. 2002a. *Indigenous Movements, Self-representations, and the State in Latin America*. Austin: University of Texas Press.

———. 2002b. "Introduction: Studying Indigenous Activism in Latin America." Pp. 1–46 in Warren and Jackson 2002a.

Yashar, Deborah J. 2004. *Contesting Citizenship in Latin America: The Rise of Indigenous Movements and the Postliberal Challenge*. Cambridge: Cambridge University Press.

Yúdice, George. 1995. "Civil Society, Consumption, and Governmentality in an Age of Global Restructuring: An Introduction." *Social Text* 45, no. 4: 1–25.

Zamosc, Leon. 2004. "The Indian Movement in Ecuador: From Politics of Influence to Politics of Power." Pp. 131–157 in *The Struggle for Indigenous Rights in Latin America*, ed. Leon Zamosc and Nancy Grey Postero. Brighton, UK: Sussex Academic Press.

Chapter 1

INDIGENOUS POLITICS AND THE STATE
The Andean Highlands in the Nineteenth and Twentieth Centuries

Michiel Baud

In recent years, Latin America has witnessed an eruption of indigenous activism that has increasingly dominated political developments in several countries. This tendency has been especially clear in the Andean region. The implementation of the 'multicultural' 1991 Constitution in Colombia, the emergence of the MAS (Movement toward Socialism) and the presidency of Evo Morales in Bolivia, and the emergence and decline of the CONAIE (Confederation of Indigenous Nationalities of Ecuador) in Ecuador are among the most salient highlights of

Notes for this chapter are located on page 39.

this process. They point to radical changes in the position of the indigenous population in Latin American politics. At the same time, the emergence of indigenous movements has resulted in new combinations of formal as well as informal, extra-parliamentary means of political expression. In this sense, they pose interesting questions about the political position of indigenous societies and the importance of identity politics in present-day political democracy.

In two similar recent studies, Deborah Yashar (2005) and Donna Lee Van Cott (2005) analyze different examples of indigenous mobilization in Latin America and try to connect them to current debates on democracy and citizenship. In Yashar's (2005: 3) view, indigenous movements "have questioned the idea that the nation-state … serves as the legitimate basis for extending and defining democratic citizenship rights and responsibilities." She sees them as fundamentally new movements that have emerged through the quest for new forms of citizenship. New indigenous identities are, in her view, the direct result of changes in citizenship regimes in the region. These changes challenged what Yashar calls "enclaves of local autonomy" that before had gone largely unrecognized by the state (ibid.: 8). The expansion of citizenship replaced and brought into question existing structures of local political authority. To compare the situation in different Latin American countries, she calls on two other criteria: the strength of "transcommunity networks" and "the public space for political association." She makes the case that indigenous movements emerged only where these three factors came together.

Van Cott (2005) focuses on the transformation of indigenous movements into ethnic parties. Like Yashar, she emphasizes the crisis of traditional political parties and the emergence of new political space to explain the rise of ethnic politics in Latin America. Comparing different cases, she focuses on the political consequences of the new visibility of indigenous political parties and the varying outcomes of their struggle.

Both studies are innovative in that they allow for a comparative understanding of the different expressions of indigenous movements in Latin America. Using relative indicators, they are capable of explaining why, in contrast to its neighboring countries, strong indigenous movements have not emerged in present-day Peru. In this respect, these studies offer a new level of understanding about indigenous mobilization in Latin America in the context of changing citizenship regimes in the region.

On the other hand, there are two perspectives that receive little attention from Yashar and Van Cott. National comparisons make sense from the perspective of the nation-state; however, they appear to be less fruitful when we try to explain the background and constituency of indigenous movements. Indigenous activism manifested itself in the first instance as local or regional movements. These local and regional linkages are crucial to understand their emergence. This may explain why indigenous movements have encountered fundamental problems when they start acting on a national scale. In transcending local and regional levels and attracting national and even international attention, they run the risk of losing their dynamism and power base.

This connects to a second matter that may be considered problematic in such comparative studies: the issue of historical depth. Both studies view the indigenous movements and ethnic politics of the late twentieth century as fundamentally new expressions of political participation. They therefore tend to focus on the last decades and to underestimate longer-term historical processes going back to or even preceding the nineteenth century. This not only weakens the explanatory power of their comparative analysis, but also puts undue emphasis on the unique character and strength of present-day indigenous movements. For example, both authors herald the success of the indigenous movement in Ecuador. Yashar (2005: 85) even starts her analysis by stating: "Ecuador claims Latin America's strongest, oldest, and most consequential indigenous movement, CONAIE." She adds: "In a country where civil society is notoriously weak, the strength of Ecuador's indigenous movement is all the more striking." These sentences seem, in light of the political fragmentation of the country and also within the indigenous movement, already hopelessly out of date. This may not be something Yashar could have predicted or included in her work, but it points to the importance of historical timelines. What seems transcendental and unique in one period can end up being of no more than passing importance in the next. In this respect, Van Cott takes a much more culturalist position than Yashar. In her study she frequently alludes to the contrast between Western-style parliamentary democracy and traditional political values. She even uses the word 'contamination' in reference to indigenous participation in political parties, which, as Western institutions, stand in basic contrast to indigenous culture in which "harmony and consensus are valued over competition, and the advancement of the community is valued over the success of individuals" (Van Cott 2005: 233).

This chapter highlights many moments in history that appear to belie this supposed contrast between indigenous and Western forms of politics. It argues therefore that we can understand the emergence of indigenous politics only by looking at the historical development of these movements and especially the long-term relationship between indigenous populations and power-holders. Indigenous leaders position themselves and their movements in a long line of indigenous activism because their organizations, power base, and political participation have deep roots.[1] The present-day movements are linked just as much to historical processes of social and political mobilization as they are to more recent processes of democratic consolidation in the region and globalization in general.

Such an approach draws attention to the importance of the political context in which indigenous movements emerge and their relationship with the state and with political society in general. The issue is not only when, where, and how long indigenous movements (and social movements in general) have existed, but how they relate to other political actors and, above all, to the state. Partha Chatterjee (2004) has pointed to the problematic relationship between civil society and the state in the developing world, today often termed 'the South'. In these societies, the poor are not considered proper citizens and are often ignored by state institutions. But this does not mean that they are outside the reach of the state or even excluded from the domain of politics. Political development and the democratic process have had a profound influence on the lives of the 'subaltern' classes, who, as Chatterjee sees it, today live in a 'political society'. It is here that most political mobilization takes place and where the state has to find and reproduce its legitimacy as providers of well-being to its citizens. In defining these ideas, Chatterjee draws attention to three issues: (1) much of politics is constructed locally; (2) it is done so in direct relation and response to an actually existing state; and (3) its outcome should be considered the result both of the historical development of political society on a local and regional level and of the structures and ideologies of the state.

Chatterjee's historical and dialectical perspective, whereby subaltern politics continuously connects to the state and becomes the prime mover of societal and political change, is an interesting complement to the studies by Yashar and Van Cott. It enables us to understand better the political role of past and present-day indigenous populations and their relation with the Latin American nation-state. It also allows us to understand their autonomous and subaltern background while analyzing its relation to and insertion in national politics. What is sometimes simply called 'indigenous struggle' often contains all kinds of diverse objectives in which the indigenous poor try to defend their interests and obtain citizenship rights. Such a perspective warns us away from a romanticized and, one may say, 'purist' vision with regard to the present-day indigenous movements, but it also draws attention to their significance for the development of the Latin American nation-state. In this chapter, I will try to shed light on these issues, focusing on the historical background and importance of indigenous politics and the changing political role of the indigenous population and its relationship with the nation-state.

The Nation-State and Indigenous Society in the Nineteenth Century

The foundation of independent republics and the subsequent gradual imposition of the nation-state profoundly altered societal relations in nineteenth-century Latin America. This process intensified with the region's insertion into the modern world market and the projects of modernization fostered by its entrepreneurial elites. The political and economic molding of society became an integrated element of the development policies fostered by Latin American states. To eschew this path was increasingly seen as an offensive and even sometimes criminal rejection of the 'sacred' project of modernity. This new vision of society and the processes of economic modernization and political uniformization affected all classes, but the most drastic consequences were felt by the indigenous populations. By the early nineteenth century, popular classes in Colombia had gradually and sometimes painfully taken their place in national politics and had already started to 'bargain' their way into the political arena (Sanders 2004). At the same time, the indigenous populations in the Andes were confronted by an increasingly authoritarian, and at times racist, state. The new elite project in the Andes was, in the words of Brooke Larson (2004), to "coerce" the Indians into civilization and Christianity and, at the same time, to force them to take their place in the project of modernity.

However, it should be recognized that the state and its representatives did not rely on repression alone in order to solve the 'Indian problem', as it was called. They tried to find ways to develop society and to 'elevate' the indigenous masses. Much of modern history of the Andean republics has been shaped by that tension. Larson (2004: 14) explains: "The quandary for Andean Creole elites was precisely how to build an apparatus of power that simultaneously incorporated and marginalized peasant political cultures in the forced march to modernity." Part of their solution was to maintain stark binary discourses of race and space that tried to secure the racial and political order in a dramatically changing society, but the outcome of these activities was varied and ambiguous. Progress was often a euphemism for racial or colonial political projects, but there was also room for more benevolent, developmentalist initiatives.

The results of these state projects were predictably ambiguous and fragmented. State institutions were still weak, and the elite's immersion in their own social and political musings led to ineffective state intervention and non-compliance with the hundreds of republican laws issued by enthusiastic governments. At the same time, many indigenous communities existed far away from the world of the urban elites, and for the major part of the nineteenth century they could hold on to the colonial idea of two *repúblicas*, according to which their rights and obligations were clearly defined under colonial law. Tristan Platt (1982) has suggested that the indigenous population in Bolivia (and probably other Andean countries as well) continued to define its position vis-à-vis the republican state in terms of the colonial images of indirect rule and reciprocity, the so-called *pacto de reciprocidad*. This is not to say that indigenous communities and their leaders were unaware of the political changes that had taken place in the region, but it shows the slow impact of republican law and politics in the countryside and the active role of indigenous populations in shaping the post-colonial states (see, e.g., Méndez 2005).

Only in the late nineteenth century had the Andean state acquired sufficient strength to pursue its political projects seriously. On the one hand, modernizing elites tried to reinforce the state's organizational capacity, influence regional processes of change, and bring about economic (i.e., export-oriented) development. They started to criticize and suppress landowners and political strongmen who used their regional power base to resist state intervention. Simultaneously, and more or less as part of the same project, the program of economic modernization led to increasing pressure on productive sources in rural communities, particularly land and labor. The classic form, heralded by dependency theorists and novelists sympathetic to the indigenous population, was that in which the peasantry was dispossessed of its large landholdings by dubious means, manipulation of the law, and outright coercion, with the result that the former landowners were now forced to work as wage laborers. Although these processes certainly occurred, they were by no means the most frequent and were not as clear-cut in practice as has often been assumed. In large parts of the Andean highlands, the world market entered much more gradually and imperceptibly, its consequences often being tied into traditional forms of social and economic relations. In many regions, especially in the highlands of Peru and Ecuador and to a lesser extent in and around the Bolivian city of Cochabamba, traditional landlords and peasants negotiated new terms of existing patron-client relations, reinventing these relations in different forms and redefining them to adapt to changing circumstances. Silvia Rivera Cusicanqui (1986) has suggested that the success of these negotiations in itself is indicative of the strength and historical cohesion of indigenous societies.

Sometimes indigenous peasants reacted quite actively and even enthusiastically to the opportunities offered by the expansion of the national economy and its connection to the world market. When this strategy was no longer viable, the indigenous population tried to curb the most negative consequences of modernization, either by withdrawal or resistance. Sometimes indigenous communities referred to colonial precedents to defend their rights. In reaction to an increasingly interventionist state, they fell back on the only documents they possessed and the only verifiable proof of their 'immemorial' rights. During this period, simply walking around with colonial documents was deemed by the state to be a criminal offense.

The increasing pressure on their communal lands and the deterioration of their social and economic position led to a plethora of Indian revolts in the early twentieth century that spread across the Andean altiplano, beginning in Peru but rapidly extending to Bolivia and Ecuador (Rivera Cusicanqui 1986: 36–52). Many of these movements had strong millenarian overtones and looked toward an egalitarian society that was inspired by the idea of an egalitarian Inca empire, but also sometimes, as in the Lake Titicaca region, by Adventist missionaries (Albó 1999: 780; Collins 1988: 52–54). Although indigenous resistance inspired the most fear among mestizo populations, violence was not its most common form. Everyday forms of resistance and conflict were much more frequent. The position of local haciendas was quite vulnerable, leading to situations of sometimes stable and sometimes uneasy co-existence between indigenous peasants and haciendas (Larson 2004: 174–176). On more than one occasion, local and regional elites tried to restore their hegemony and put the Indians back in their place. The struggle for indigenous citizenship was therefore accompanied by unprecedented conflicts and violence on a local and regional scale.

Over the course of the latter half of the nineteenth century, the dire situation of the indigenous rural population became an even more pressing political issue. Intellectuals and politicians tried to find a solution for the so-called Indian problem, looking for ways to integrate Indians into the modernizing project of the liberal state. This acquired more urgency with the participation of indigenous populations in revolutionary wars, such as the War of the Pacific in Peru from 1879 to 1883, the struggle between liberals and conservatives in Bolivia's Guerra federal in 1899, and the War of the Thousand Days in Colombia between 1899 and 1902. Military service integrated indigenous soldiers into the political struggle for the nation-state and in this way offered them a kind of implicit citizenship. Around the turn of the century, many urban intellectuals and politicians started to support the indigenous population in its struggle for some kind of political recognition and citizenship. This support may have been partly self-interested, but that does not preclude its enormous societal consequences. It linked the indigenous population to national politics and opened new spaces for its political participation. This process was also stimulated by social and economic change that resulted in urban migration and an increasingly mobile labor force.

Indigenista Politics and Indian Mobilization in the Twentieth Century

The ambiguities of elite attitudes toward the indigenous population were clearest in the policies of *indigenismo*. This was an artistic and political current that arose in defense of the indigenous population in a more or less well-intentioned effort to give Indian heritage a place in the national body politic. Andean *indigenismo* started out as a movement that opposed the conservative, exclusionary politics of the nineteenth century. Partly echoing the liberal criticism of efforts of the Catholic Church (and especially its lower clergy) to suppress the Indian peasant population and to shield it from modernity, *indigenismo* tried to find ways to incorporate the indigenous population into the modern nation-state.[2] Because its project addressed the role of the nation-state and its part in modernization, it is not surprising that *indigenista* ideas at certain times became quite influential in state policies. In Ecuador, it led to the radical government of Eloy Alfaro in 1895. In other Andean countries, *indigenista* ideologues would hold important government positions in the twentieth century. *Indigenistas* were to a certain extent messengers of an incumbent state that was starting to consider the controlled incorporation of the Indians as an indispensable element of the modernization of their societies.

The irony of the *indigenismo* movement was that while it created new spaces for political action, it also reproduced many traditional ideas and prejudices and could be instrumental in containing indigenous participation in Andean politics. *Indigenista* intellectuals and politicians frequently demonstrated their ignorance and idealization of the daily reality in which the Indian population lived. The Peruvian historian, Osmar Gonzales Alvarado (1996: 205) observes for the Peruvian situation: "[T]he creole intellectuals devised an image of the Indians in order to provide them with a tradition (the glorious past of the Inca) and in order to give themselves legitimacy (either for their separation from Spain or to establish themselves as the leaders of national progress)." When the state started to reproduce *indigenista* ideas, it also did so to further its own interests. Using a mix of centralism and virulent anti-clericalism, politicians and state officials used the supposed protection of the Indians to curb the power of the landowning elites (the so-called *gamonales*) and the priests.

There is no doubt that many *indigenistas* were sincerely interested in the fate of the indigenous population and that their activities had an impact. Their opposition to the structural exclusion of the indigenous peasant population and their contact with Indian leaders brought the rural and urban worlds closer together and created social and political alliances between intellectuals and political leaders. However, the daily reality of these relations was fraught with misunderstandings and ambiguities. For one thing, the elites were hardly aware of the changes that were occurring within the indigenous society. While *indigenismo* in Cusco was very strong, its followers did not notice the signs of resistance and violence in the countryside (Rénique 1991). When they were confronted with it, many of these urban sympathizers felt repelled and hastily withdrew their romantic support for the Indians. The social and cultural differences between these groups were so great that only a few people managed to build bridges that withstood the passage of time. Most *indigenistas* concluded in the end that urban Christian decency had to prevail over rural indigenous values (De la Cadena 1994; for a contrasting vision, see Mendoza 2006).

Urban intellectuals and politicians ignored the twentieth-century history of indigenous communities initiating their own projects of modernization and nationalism. Education was one of the fundamental demands of these communities, and their frustration was great when the state could not, or would not, fulfill its responsibilities in creating and safeguarding a system of rural schools. This was clear in Peru where in the initial phase of the long authoritarian regime of Augusto Leguía (1919–1930) a number of pro-Indian laws were proclaimed. These measures provoked widespread enthusiasm among the indigenous population. However, they were only half-heartedly implemented and quickly withdrawn. When rural communities began to send their *mensajeros apoderados* (authorized representatives) to Lima to plead with the president and his advisers, it became rapidly clear that the government was not prepared to accept the Indian negotiators as equals and to recognize their political demands. Many representatives were arrested and accused of organizing rebellions, and gradually the government support transformed into repression (Álvarez-Calderón 2005: 335–337). A revealing incident occurred in 1923 when two indigenous representatives tried to hold President Leguía to his promises to protect their communities, and Leguía furiously snapped at them: "[N]o Indian will raise his voice to me" (Rénique 2004: 100; see also De la Cadena 2000: 89–97). These events were telling proof that the possible alliance between Indians and the ruling party was fraught with obstacles.

These indigenous leaders were seeking acknowledgment of their citizenship rights, which were in principle offered to them by the nation-state. They did so, however, by referring to history, customary rights, and times immemorial. In challenging existing perceptions about citizenship and the position of the indigenous population, their behavior was in many ways revolutionary. But the struggle, presented as an effort to regain the past and defend the foregone, was being waged in 'conservative' terms. Because its discourse was "built on a base of a colonial language of self-denigration, respect for authority, and appeals for protection," Sanders (2004: 42) speaks about "popular indigenous conservatism." The term is worth considering because it points to the conservative direction of much indigenous struggle. At the same time, it questions the often unwarranted progressive optimism of policy makers and academics who see the indigenous struggle automatically as a fight to achieve emancipation and societal change.

On the other hand, the term may be misleading, as it tends to underestimate the strategic use of conservative, traditional discourses for new and sometimes revolutionary objectives. Popular leaders and intellectuals frame their demands in terms that they think will help them to obtain their goals. Their conservatism—if any—is not a sign of isolation and withdrawal, but should instead be seen a result of their interaction with the state and with power-holders, as ideas "forged in dialogue" (Baud and Rutten 2004: 5). These dialogues take place in concrete historical settings, often in local or regional areas of contention that are far removed from national politics. It is therefore necessary to investigate their nature and possible longer-term historical consequences in concrete local and regional settings.

An excellent example of such an analysis is José Luis Rénique's (2004) *La batalla por Puno*. On the basis of lifelong research into the history of the southern highlands of Peru, Rénique analyzes the long-term history of the neighboring Puno province. This province always occupied a marginal position within the Peruvian state, but at the same time it mirrored the main political developments within the country. It was a poor, marginalized region that in the nineteenth century lived under the firm control of local power-holders, called *gamonales* in the local vernacular. Around the turn of the century, new access to the world market and the economic modernization of the national economy changed the context of the region's development. After the demise of the wool economy, the weakened elite was faced with a dense and numerous indigenous rural population that could take advantage of unexpected support from politicians and intellectuals in faraway Lima. The Peruvian nation-state tried to come to grips with an indigenous population that it never really managed to understand. Politicians intensified their attempts to incorporate what was considered a backward indigenous people into the modern nation-state. Urban *indigenistas* professed a new faith in the vitality and creativity of indigenous society and vehemently opposed the archaic domination of the regional elites. In the process, they allied themselves with indigenous leaders who were delegated by their people to defend the interests of their communities.

Rénique describes how modernizing politicians, *indigenistas*, and indigenous leaders came together in an alliance that shaped the region's social history. In the end, political actors—from liberal politicians and *indigenistas* to development organizations, the military, and revolutionaries—continuously constructed and reconstructed representations of Indianness, basically to serve their own ends. Their ignorance could have far-reaching consequences and always threatened to destroy the society they pretended to protect. As Rénique (2004: 265) writes: "The 'struggle for Puno' is the confrontation between national projects that aimed at finding in the altiplano an important place of action." The irony was that the peasant population, which historically was firmly linked to the outside world, maintained its own political perspective and, in so doing, changed Peruvian history: "[T]he rural population calculated its risks and possibilities and took from outsiders what it liked without, in the last instance, forfeiting its own objectives, its own strategies. Its supposed liberators would also be transformed by the experience" (ibid.). The indigenous struggle to gain entrance into the fabric of the nation-state not only changed the Indians' way of being and their political behavior; it also started to change the state, both its ways of governing society and its relationships with different parts of society, now also including the indigenous populations.

In this indigenous resistance we see a fundamental tension. Indigenous groups were confronted with a choice as to the nature of their struggle. They could stake their claims for justice, emancipation, and equality by referring to the past—traditions and colonial rights or titles or achieved customary rights—or they could base their struggle on the present-day Western discourse of democracy, citizenship, and equality. Did they refer to their indigenous organization and original rights from *tiempos inmemoriales*, or did they try to hold the modern state to its promises of equality and justice? In general, indigenous movements fought for political emancipation in the name of past entitlements, a strategy that clearly colored their quest for citizenship.

It is evident that this backward-looking strategy is not the same as conservatism. Indigenous movements may have referred to the past, but they did so to sustain claims for modern citizenship and in the name of democracy. To a large extent, these were struggles for incorporation and integration. They often just asked the state to adhere to its own laws and to open up citizenship to the indigenous poor. Many indigenous rebellions in the Andean highlands were not so much pitted against modernity; rather, they were waged in demand of civil rights and incorporation in republican society. In her analysis of some of the early-twentieth-century indigenous movements in the Peruvian altiplano, Jane Collins (1988: 60) writes: "In building schools and adopting the Spanish language and Western dress, they did not reject their indigenous heritage per se, but denied that it should prevent them from functioning as full citizens of the republic." In many respects, the indigenous movements used the pre-political past in order to gain access to the present-day political system of formal citizenship and the rule of law.

These strategies were influenced by, and constructed in the context of, the rapidly changing circumstances within Andean societies, including not only the gradual and more or less unilinear development of Latin America's modernization and insertion into the world economy but also the conjunctural and rapidly oscillating vagaries of Andean politics, in which different political projects and parties replaced each other, sometimes in dizzying succession. This was clear in the liberal wars in Bolivia and Ecuador and in the temporary support of the indigenous cause in the first years of the Leguía government in Peru. The infamous *pacto militar-campesino* between the indigenous peasantry and the military regime of General Barrientos in Bolivia after 1964 was the most extreme example of the unlikely alliances that these political processes engendered.

Indigenous Struggle and National Politics

Over the course of the twentieth century, the struggle for citizenship moved slowly but inexorably to the level of the national state. While a large part of the indigenous rural population continued to live in quite restricted social and economic worlds, indigenous leaders increasingly took their struggle to the platform of national politics. Whereas originally the goal had been to ameliorate the consequences of economic and political modernization on a local level, in the mid twentieth century the national state became the focus of indigenous mobilization. This was the result of various factors. The imposition of the nation-state had all but put a stop to the autonomy of regional leaders and their clientele and to the free play of regional politics. The export-led development of the economy, albeit sometimes leading to new enclaves, resulted in a scaling up that transcended regional levels and made national issues central to political struggle. This became especially clear after the world crash of 1929, which plunged the Latin American model into a deep crisis. The historian René Arze Aguirre (1987) has stressed that in Bolivia this process was intensified by the Chaco War (1932–1935), which forced the state to acknowledge the citizen status of the indigenous soldiers it needed for the war.[3]

In this way, indigenous political activity became truly national from the mid twentieth century onward. This transformation was symbolized by the many national congresses that were organized. Often helped by the urban *indigenistas* who had acquired important positions within the state apparatus, these congresses gave national—and even international—visibility to the indigenous political cause. The most famous of these congresses was held in Pátzcuaro, Mexico, in 1940. It was sponsored by the OAS (Organization of American States) but was made possible by the socialist regime of the Mexican president, Lázaro Cárdenas. In the Andes, a much more limited but nationally important congress was organized in 1945 under the auspices of Bolivia's newly elected president, Gualberto Villaroel López. The Indigenous Congress in La Paz brought hundreds of indigenous representatives from the whole country to the center of elite domination and state power. Although the Congress is seen by many as an attempt to control the increasingly restless indigenous population, and in the end it did not lead to any concrete measures (Villaroel was assassinated soon after), it brought the indigenous struggle irrevocably to the heartland of the nation-state (Degregori 1998: 187–188). From 1947 onward, the Bolivian countryside was the theater of many uprisings. Despite heavy repression, these events led to the revolution of 1952, which in turn led to the implementation of many laws that had been prepared by Villaroel. It also resulted in large-scale land reform in the country. The irony was that these Bolivian reforms, revolutionary as they were, tended to address the rural population as peasants, not as Indians. After 1952, Indians were accepted in the nation as exploited masses, not as a culturally different population. Nevertheless, the reforms allowed for interesting political processes on a local level. Peasant *sindicatos* became hotbeds of indigenous organization, leading to almost autonomous communities that pushed out state officials and created new neo-traditional authorities (Albó 1999: 799–800).

In Ecuador, where the leverage of the indigenous population was not as strong as in Bolivia, and where the traditional hacienda system had been preserved to a much larger extent, similar processes occurred. *Indigenista* ideas lost influence when the radical liberalism of the government of President Alfaro petered out in the first decade of the twentieth century. Indigenous leaders tried to ally themselves to the incipient socialist movement in order to force the government to embrace social reforms (Becker 2004; Pallares 2002; for similar processes in

Colombia, see Rappaport 1998). At the same time, the indigenous population in the hacienda-dominated highlands was increasingly restless despite the continuing strong cultural and political control on the haciendas (Guerrero 1991). Mary Weismantel (1989) observes that in the Ecuadorian highlands, many hacendados no longer felt comfortable staying overnight on their haciendas out of fear of the indigenous workers and peasants. This may say more about the perceptions of the landowning classes, but it also shows how the social and political situation in the highlands had become tense and volatile in this period.

The increasing political mobilization of indigenous movements took place through more or less enduring alliances between indigenous leaders and different sectors of political society. Indigenous leaders and their allies worked between the lines, personifying temporal alliances and sometimes mediating between different levels of society. Some recent work on social and indigenous movements focuses precisely on these 'people in between'. Sometimes they are 'popular intellectuals', sometimes public employees or local leaders, but what is interesting is that in acting on the fault line of political negotiations and alliances, they symbolize the possibilities, variations, and tensions of these processes. The result of these alliances was, as Rappaport (2005: 59) observes, a long-standing and deep process of leftist penetration into native communities that greatly shaped the political language of indigenous leaders. The shared utopia that Rappaport sees as its result was, however, just as much shaped by indigenous demands as it was by leftist discourse. In this sense, the indigenous struggle provided Latin American socialism with an important stimulus. This was already clear in early Andean socialist debates, and it provided Andean socialism with a specific flavor that has remained its characteristic to the present day.

Ultimately, these processes led to different programs of agrarian reform in which land was distributed to the indigenous and non-indigenous peasantry. Although these programs, such as in Bolivia (1953) and in Ecuador (1964 and 1973), were often criticized because they were not radical enough and hardly touched the large landholdings of the elites, they played a crucial role in the peasantization of the Andean countryside and the political mobilization of its inhabitants. Victor Bretón Solo de Zaldívar (2006: 65) stresses the importance of the agrarian reforms in Ecuador when he describes their consequences, saying that it was "[a]s if the agrarian reforms had destroyed an enormous dyke, causing an immense, unprecedented flood of which we still have not understood the consequences—political, cultural, social, symbolic, and also economic—in all their complexity and magnitude."

The events in these countries also demonstrate the great differences in the historical development within and between the Andean countries in the twentieth century. Especially revealing is the varied relationship between *indigenismo* and Indian mobilization. Liberal *indigenismo* arrived early in Ecuador, where the government of Eloy Alfaro implemented radical legislation in an attempt to modernize the country and to free the indigenous population from onerous and 'archaic' personal obligations. In Bolivia, urban *indigenismo* remained an insignificant factor. Instead, social and political change occurred through communal action and the development of a strong, syndicalist leadership.

The most interesting case is Peru, where *indigenismo* became an important political force in the twentieth century. However, this very success appears to have impeded the country's indigenous political mobilization. Compared to that of its neighbors, Peru's indigenous movement has been less institutionalized and less successful, which can be explained in two ways. First, indigenous culture and Inca symbolism were appropriated very early on by both national and socialist politicians for their own purposes, thus hindering a political struggle for cultural rights by indigenous movements, as occurred elsewhere (see Van Cott 2005: 143–144). This is not to say that indigenous communities did not resist unfavorable state intervention, but their fight was not waged in terms of cultural rights and therefore was not widely recognized as an indigenous struggle. Second, while there was a long history of indigenous protest—from the 'batalla por Puno' in the early twentieth century and the indigenous uprisings around Cusco described by Rénique (1991, 2004) to the famous peasant rebellion led by Hugo Blanco in the early 1960s—the Lima-based governing elite did not appear to notice. The indigenous struggle in the southern provinces hardly affected national politics in Lima. Not until the military regime of Juan Velasco Alvarado in 1968 did the position of the indigenous population became an issue for state intervention. Although this resulted in important political and social reforms, it occurred in a revolutionary process 'from above', which is characteristic of Peruvian history.

Despite these regional and national differences, there is no doubt that everywhere in the Andes the state was assaulted from two sides. On the one hand, there was a coalition between *indigenistas*, social liberalism, and socialism; on the other hand, there was the increasing political presence of indigenous movements. Although the ideology and methods of these two factions were quite different, this period saw increasing and intensifying relations between their representatives. Both groups tried to use the state and its legislation for their own ends. Although this was an ambiguous and contradictory process, it changed the state's position in political and civil society and thus paved the way for more dramatic political changes and a more politically autonomous indigenous movement in the late twentieth century.

Subaltern Voices Take Center Stage

On the eve of the twenty-first century, Bolivian anthropologist Xavier Albó (1991: 299) announced the return of the Indian. What he meant was that since the 1980s (and somewhat earlier in some countries), social movements had emerged "that originated directly or indirectly in their ethnic identity." Eventually, this would lead to the indigenous parties that Van Cott (2005) sees as the defining element of the period. Through these movements and parties, indigenous populations acquired a clear political presence in Andean and Central American politics, allowing them to present their claims and political demands on a national scale. Everywhere in Latin America, emerging political parties placed the situation of the indigenous population squarely on the agenda. In countries such as Ecuador and Bolivia, political reforms offered indigenous movements new "political associational space" (Yashar 2005). Following the 1960s and 1970s, political movements were often organized as confederations to afford some autonomy to the participants and to leave room for a variety of demands. They often started out as social movements with extra-parliamentary activities, such as marches and blockades, but they rapidly became political actors in their own right with political organizations and institutions. In this way, indigenous movements like the ECUARUNARI (the Confederation of Kichwa Peoples of Ecuador), from 1986 CONAIE (the Confederation of Indigenous Nationalities of Ecuador), and the MAS were able to acquire important political experience and political leverage, which allowed them to make the jump to national politics. These parties criticized the subordination of indigenous identity to class identity. At the same time, they became increasingly connected to the indigenous migrant population in the cities, thus becoming truly national parties (Assies, van der Haar, and Hoekema 2000: 7).

The indigenous parties also started to participate in national elections and became formal actors in national parliamentary politics. In Ecuador and Bolivia, these indigenous parties managed to get parliamentary representation. CONAIE presented itself on a national scale during the uprising in 1990 when a nationwide strike paralyzed the country and thousands of indigenous peasants invaded the capital city (Almeida 1993). CONAIE decided to enter electoral politics in 1996 in spite of its frequent rejection of the electoral proceedings in the country. The party that was formed, the Pachakutik Movement for Pluri-national Unity (usually referred to as Pachakutik) functioned essentially as an electoral coalition of indigenous groups and other social movements (Selverston-Scher 2001: 48). It won eight seats in parliament and succeeded in gaining many positions on the local and regional levels. In 1998, it won seven seats in the Constitutional Assembly.

Although the movement wielded a surprising amount of influence, its entrance in the electoral system clearly demonstrated the weaknesses of the movement. Lack of cadres and institutions, accusations of corruption, political inexperience, and a disjunction between leaders and the majority of their followers became increasingly problematic for Pachakutik. Its collaboration with the government of Lucio Gutiérrez cost the movement dearly. When it ended its support in 2004, after just six months in government, the damage had been done. In the October 2006 elections, support for Pachakutik had dwindled to insignificant proportions. This is not to say that its political role has ended, but it clearly shows the weaknesses of indigenous agendas and the problems of the incipient indigenous parties.

In Bolivia, similar processes of growth in the political representation of the indigenous movement can be seen. However, its roots go further back, and therefore the position of indigenous politics in Bolivia appears to be stronger and more stable. After a long history of indigenous resistance and political exclusion, indigenous entry into formal politics occurred in the 1960s when different groups of Aymara Indians started to organize themselves in a loose union, usually called the Kataristas. This movement connected to left-wing intellectuals in La Paz, making it a growing political force (Albó 1987; Degregori

1998: 192–203). In 1993, the Sánchez de Lozada government forged an alliance with this movement and appointed one of its leaders, Víctor Hugo Cárdenas, as vice president (Van Cott 2005: 81–83). Although today most observers consider this a basically opportunistic move, which eventually destroyed Cárdenas's political party, it had great symbolic importance. It also led to new legislation, especially on land reform and the politics of decentralization, which combined indigenous demands with new policies of the World Bank.

In the end, the political balance shifted to the regions of the country where coca cultivations fueled a new economic and political dynamism. The indigenous movements used the new opportunities provided by these laws but at the same time increased pressure through demonstrations and marches, the most famous perhaps being the March for Territory and Dignity in 1990 (Canessa 2006: 246–247). Indigenous political parties that participated in the national elections in 2002 together acquired almost 30 percent of the votes. Afterwards, the MAS, a political confederation of different indigenous social movements, was indisputably established as the most powerful representative of indigenous interests. It became clear in the following years that in spite of this large support, the established political parties were not prepared to relegate any power to this movement. Simultaneously, the MAS started to present itself as the protector of national interests when it turned the exportation of gas and resistance to privatization into central political issues (Assies 2004). Street demonstrations and continuous protests led to the fall of two presidents and eventually to the election of the first indigenous president, Evo Morales, in 2005. One of the most interesting decisions of the newly elected president was the integration of a great number of social movement leaders in his government. This may be seen as a symbolic gesture, making clear his desire to consolidate the interaction between social movements and the state.

This is not the place for a detailed description of the emergence of these movements (see Assies, van der Haar, and Hoekema 2000; Brysk 2000; Van Cott 1994, 2005; Yashar 2005), but it is clear that sometime in the 1970s and 1980s an important change took place in which the indigenous movements took the reins into their own hands and put a stop to the 'ventriloquist' defense of their position by outsiders (see Guerrero 1997). Causes and effects are notoriously difficult to ascertain in historical descriptions, but there is no doubt that the alliance between indigenous movements and *indigenista* sympathizers, which was connected to transformations in the social and economic structure of Andean societies, led to more visibility and stronger political leverage for indigenous demands in the course of the twentieth century (see also Van Cott 2005).

This process can be explained by a variety of factors. First, it can be seen as the historical outcome of longer-term struggles on the local, regional, and national scales described above that allied indigenous groups to sympathizers on a regional and national level. Second, it was the perhaps unintended result of state interventions, often by military reformist regimes, which began in the 1940s (perhaps even 1930s) and intensified in the 1950s and 1960s, in an effort to find solutions for the pressing social problems in their countries. Although these state efforts were couched in terms of *indigenista* sympathies for the indigenous populations, they were certainly also, or even especially, propelled by the fear of social unrest and violent conflict in the Andean countryside. Third, indigenous movements had been able to acquire more or less established links with officials in state institutions, especially on local and regional levels. In this way, they had become accepted partners of the state, especially in its activities on a local level but also nationally, such as when indigenous groups were given the responsibility for bilingual education in Ecuador.

These processes were stimulated by the increasing strength of an international discourse in the defense of indigenous rights in the 1970s and 1980s. This new discourse had in itself a variety of origins, ranging from the liberation theology, to concerned anthropologists who organized an international conference on indigenous self-determination in Barbados in 1971, to international institutions such as the World Bank (Brysk 2000; Hale 2002). At the same time, indigenous organizations increasingly understood the advantages of international linkages. They could use international contacts to present their cases, to protect themselves against abuse, and to connect their demands to other groups. In this way, they managed to insert their demands into what Alison Brysk (2000: 2) has called "transnational normative campaigns." There is no doubt that the success in garnering political leverage on a national scale by present-day indigenous movements in Latin America was partially the result of these international support mechanisms.

These different elements are also reflected in the demands and positions of the indigenous movements. As long as the majority of the indigenous populations lived in the countryside, the demand for land remained the fundamental issue. The indigenous movements originated in a struggle for land rights and local autonomy, and, depending on national circumstances, they used these demands to increase their political leverage. However, they could grow as political actors only by expanding their demands and including the pressing social and economic issues confronted by the rural and urban poor in the region. With increasing migration and urbanization, the main issues became the political exclusion and the social and ethnic discrimination suffered by a large part of the population (Degregori 1998: 176–184). As the indigenous movements extended their program to include all kinds of broader economic and social demands, they also expanded their appeal to urban populations and migrants. Today, they have also been able to connect to urban middle classes and left-wing intellectuals who share their broad opposition to neo-liberal views.

Perhaps the most significant element of this recently developed alliance consists of the new nationalism of the indigenous movements. It has always been an interesting but scarcely noted characteristic of indigenous movements that they never questioned the boundaries or significance of the national state. Apart from some abortive attempts at a pan-Andean movement in the twentieth century, indigenous movements and their leaders have always taken the national confines as the point of departure. This may appear paradoxical in light of a long history of colonial and neo-colonial discrimination and exclusion, but it may just as well be considered the result of a history of constant interaction between indigenous mobilization and the state. The struggle of indigenous movements was not directed against the national state as such;

rather, it tried to compel the state to enforce its own constitutional pledge of citizenship and to comply with its own legislation. An analysis of the rhetoric of indigenous protest shows how indigenous leaders confronted the state and its power-holders time and again with this basic failure to adhere to its own promises. To give just one example, indigenous rebels in the Ecuadorian province of Azuay invaded the house of a local official in 1920. They forced him to read different governmental decrees, sometimes three or four times. Finally, he was dragged into the street and made to read publicly a document prohibiting a number abuses against the indigenous population. In his own words: "They demanded to show them all the documents that were in my possession at that moment, and when I refused to do so, they searched and viewed them one by one, forcing me to read every document to them three or four times. They took the letter in which the Governor [condemns the abuses against indigenous peasants] and forced me to read it in public. At six o'clock on Sunday morning a multitude of men pulled me out of my room and forced me to read the document again" (cited in Baud 1993: 59). Seventy years later, the famous document in which the CONAIE proclaimed a national strike and the beginning of the famous uprising of 1990 began with the words: "In light of the lack of government attention to its obligations owed to our people."[4]

This national, even state-centered, perspective of most indigenous movements acquired new significance in the twenty-first century when indigenous movements became the forerunners of the protests against the privatization of state enterprises, the fears of new trade liberalizations (especially in the shape of the Free Trade Agreement of the Americas), and the frustration of not reaping the benefits of natural resources. More than movements favoring cultural or territorial autonomy, indigenous movements became the symbols of nationalist efforts to look for new ways to strengthen national economies and to improve the situation of the poor. This was especially clear in Bolivia, where MAS became the guardian of Bolivian nationalist pride by defending the country's ownership of its natural resources. This new 'indigenous nationalism' has also allowed these movements to expand their constituencies among the non-indigenous population. Parties such as Pachakutic in Ecuador and MAS in Bolivia succeeded in attracting a large part of the left-leaning constituency in the capital cities of Quito and La Paz. These alliances must be considered the main explanation for the electoral success of these parties.

At the same time, these successful alliances have also caused new problems. Although I do not believe it has anything to do with 'cultural contamination', Van Cott rightly points at the potential risks posed by the negotiations and concessions that political alliances imply. Leaders of indigenous parties became political leaders in their own right. They forged alliances, entered into deals and negotiations, and could not always steer clear of the corruptive influences of politics (Van Cott 2005: 229–234). Their success offered indigenous movements new institutional opportunities, but it also widened the gap between the leadership and *las bases* (the grass roots) (Korovkin 2006).

The relationship between leaders and their constituencies may well become the crucial issue in the maturing of indigenous political parties, not only because it will determine their success in the long run, but also because it will define their political nature. These parties have acquired political leverage as a result of their 'indigenous' program, partly because of internal political processes, partly because of global support for indigenous rights. At the moment that the cultural difference of the 'original' indigenous population was accepted, a whole set of issues emerged, ranging from rights to cultural expression to (partial) political and legal autonomy. Using these mechanisms, the indigenous movements started to address the tricky problem of cultural difference and the consequences for the traditional nation-state in Latin America. But at the same time, they addressed a whole range of social and economic issues. They have thrived on a nationalist program and on radical social and economic demands, which have generated widespread support among sectors of the population that are deeply disillusioned with 'traditional' politics and neo-liberal reforms. While indigenous issues played an important role in the emergence of these movements, the question now is to what extent they will continue to be central.

Ethnic discrimination, exclusionary practices, and racist and anti-indigenous attitudes continue to exist in certain sectors of society, expressing themselves in daily relations and political confrontations (Colloredo-Mansfeld 1998: 186; Degregori 2005), but the political consequences of the emergence of indigenous politics are obvious. The indigenous discourse has been very successful in creating movements and rallying constituencies in the name of ethnic and cultural emancipation. All political parties in the region now accept the need to connect with indigenous populations, and many try to integrate indigenous cadres in their party.

Indigenous politics has never had a one-issue platform, however, and it is clear that the indigenous populations look for parties and leaders who, before anything, can solve their social and economic problems. For the indigenous constituencies, the ethnic question appears only part of the reason that they support these new movements. In his analysis of the Bolivian political process in the 1990s, Andrew Canessa (2006: 247) observes: "One of the key points here was that indigenous issues qua indigenous issues were not of interest to a wider electorate and were apparently not even particularly interesting to the vast majority of people who might be described as indigenous." There is no doubt that today there is a new feeling of being recognized among the indigenous peoples. For the first time in history, they feel represented by a political movement, and they relish the fact that their political leaders represent not only their social and economic but also their ethnic interests and values. Contrary to what has often been suggested, their main objectives do not so much concern 'identity' as they do social and economic problems. Indigenous populations want work, security, and schooling just as they want recognition of their cultural and ethnic rights.

Conclusion: Indigenous Activism and Political Society

This chapter has suggested that we cannot understand present-day indigenous movements without taking into account their centuries-long relation with the Latin American nation-state. From the late nineteenth century onward, indigenous communities and their leaders tried by different means to defend their interests, to adapt to economic modernization, and to appropriate elements of the political discourses emanating from the state. They frequently rose up in rebellion, but they also connected to other sectors and tried by negotiations and alliances to wrest concessions from the republican state. In the process, indigenous communities allied themselves with urban intellectuals and sympathizing politicians, both progressive and conservative. These alliances resulted in local changes but also led to a kind of ventriloquism by which urban, non-Indian intellectuals and politicians acted as the mouthpiece for indigenous demands.

In the course of the twentieth century, the limitations of this localized struggle became clear. Racial discrimination continued and the social and economic plight of the increasingly urban indigenous populations deteriorated. The indigenous movements of the 1960s and 1970s emerged as a political answer to this situation. Their leaders challenged traditional political parties and tried to take advantage of new democratic spaces in order to push the interests of their indigenous constituencies. The fact that they used their own and their followers' indigenous background for political leverage on a national scale was unprecedented, giving a new political significance to indigenous culture and identity. Nevertheless, the denomination of these movements as indigenous runs the risk of ignoring that their political programs were much broader and included a large array of social and economic demands. Indigenous movements have always presented traditional social and economic issues and often collaborated with labor unionism, thus combining backward-looking ('conservative') and forward-looking ('progressive') objectives. In this sense, these movements not only fought for the inclusion of the indigenous masses into the democratic polity but at the same time opened up the debate on how democracy should be defined by asking pertinent questions about the exact meaning of political democracy and citizenship. Indigenous movements proposed alternatives in which Latin American democracies might be transformed so that they will be able to absorb issues of cultural rights and autonomy as well as social and economic equality. In so doing, indigenous politics has radically transformed the nature of the political debate in Andean countries.

The role of indigenous movements in Andean politics supports Partha Chatterjee's (2004) emphasis on the ways in which subaltern groups imposed themselves on the state to defend their interests or to pressure the state to adhere to its own rules. These mechanisms have been visible historically in Latin America since the colonial period (Stern 1982), but they acquired new overtones in the nineteenth and twentieth centuries with the advent of the republican state. The coercive and authoritarian elements of Latin American state formation have obscured not only the developmentalist and sometimes even benevolent policies of the state, but also the different ways in which subaltern politics penetrated and influenced these same state policies.

This political process was clear in the development of indigenous social movements from the late nineteenth century onward. In a context of continuing racism in politics and daily relations, indigenous leaders succeeded in formulating plans and strategies that deeply influenced state policies. These negotiations occurred mainly on a local level until the beginning of the twentieth century, when they gradually transposed themselves onto a national scale. After the early-twentieth-century debates on the desired social and legal position of indigenous populations, new views emerged concerning the role of the state in the emancipation of indigenous populations. Indigenous movements invaded the spaces of public power and emerged as political actors in their own right. Contemporary indigenous movements do not feel subservient to the state; instead, they demand its intervention in the protection of their rights as citizens and autonomous political agents. Supported by a global rights movement, they have turned the idea of popular sovereignty around to defend their rights as *originarios* in the Americas. The results of this process can be seen in Ecuador and Bolivia, where indigenous themes have become issues of national importance and indigenous movements have acquired state power. These achievements may be considered the historical outcome of a long interaction and convergence between indigenous movements and the Latin American state. At the same time, the quest for indigenous rights has become a discursive shorthand for citizenship rights in general.

However, this is not to say that indigenous politics will necessarily continue to dominate political processes in these countries. Indigenous movements could obtain their success in influencing, even sometimes dominating, national politics only by expanding their constituency. In this process, indigenous politics allied themselves to left-wing and anti-globalist movements. By appropriating nationalist issues, indigenous parties succeeded in convincing different sectors of society that instead of threatening national unity, they could become instrumental in its rescue. In an optimist's scenario, this could become a platform for a longer-lasting coalescence between indigenous and national interests and for new forms of multicultural republicanism. Pessimists may point at the lack of concrete social and economic improvements for the indigenous population and the resulting gap between them and their leaders. This process is already leading to defections to other non-indigenous and often populist parties and to the increasingly visible Pentecostal organizations in the highlands (Canessa 2000; Lucero 2006).

Finally, indigenous parties have successfully attracted non-indigenous sectors. They now have to confront the problem of maintaining a balance between the different constituencies and their respective interests. The most pressing issue is how to reconcile demands for some form of cultural autonomy with the universal idea of citizenship rights under the responsibility of national states. This issue has pervaded the indigenous struggle from the nineteenth century onward. The principal problem was and remains "the opposition between the universal ideal of civic nationalism ... and the particular demands of cultural identity, which call for the differential treatment of particular groups on grounds of vulnerability or backwardness or historical injustice or indeed for numerous other reasons" (Chatterjee 2004: 4). Or as Yashar (2005: 5) puts it for the present-day situation: "[Indigenous movements] are demanding equal rights; but they are also demanding recognition of special rights as native peoples."

The indigenous political struggle today tries to incorporate indigenous rights into the general concept of citizenship. In this way it opens the road for new forms of multicultural citizenship. It is, however, important to note that the indigenous struggle for citizenship has always taken place within the framework of existing Latin American nation-states. Although indigenous movements based themselves on their networks of social and cultural cohesion and used the repertoires of indigenous culture and symbolism, they have been fighting for a place within the structure of the republican nation-state. In this quest for citizenship, indigenous parties not only want respect for the indigenous culture, they also—and maybe above all—fight for a solution to the huge social and economic problems that are affecting the lives of millions of Andean people, indigenous and non-indigenous. This political project may present a solution for the dilemma between the universal ideal of citizenship and the particular demands of cultural identity. It may also be the only road for the long-term survival and success of indigenous politics.

Acknowledgments

The author would like to thank Willem Assies, Andrew Canessa, and Ted Fischer for their constructive remarks, which greatly improved this chapter. Of course, the usual disclaimers apply.

Michiel Baud is Director of the Centre for Latin American Research and Documentation (CEDLA) and Professor in Latin American Studies at the University of Amsterdam. His current research interests are indigenist ideologies and their influence on present-day academic interpretations of the Andes, the role of ethnic movements in Latin American politics, the analysis of Latin American modernity, and the construction of collective memories in present-day Latin America. He is the author of *Peasants and Tobacco in the Dominican Republic, 1870–1930* (1995); *El padre de la novia: Jorge Zorreguieta, la sociedad argentina y el régimen militar* (2001); *Intelectuales y sus utopías: Indigenismo y la imaginación de América Latina* (2003). He recently edited a volume with Rosanne Rutten, *Popular Intellectuals and Social Movements: Framing Protest in Asia, Africa, and Latin America* (2005).

Notes

1. The inauguration speech of Evo Morales on 22 January 2006 is a good example. In this speech, Morales placed the success of his party and his presidency in a long historical perspective, mentioning many persons and historical events that he considered central to "500 years of indigenous struggle" in Bolivia (see http://www.comunica.gov.bo).
2. The literature on Andean *indigenismo* is abundant. See, for example, Baud (2003), De la Cadena (1998, 2000), Kristal (1987), Leibner (1997), Mendoza (2006), Prieto (2004), Rénique (1991).
3. For contemporary Bolivia, Gill (1997: 527) also connects military service with citizenship and power. See also Canessa (2005, 2006).
4. This comes from CONAIE's *Documento político* of 14 April 1990, cited in Almeida (1993: 17).

References

Albó, Xavier. 1987. "From MNRistas to Kataristas to Katari." Pp. 379–419 in *Resistance, Rebellion, and Consciousness in the Andean Peasant World: 18th to 20th Centuries*, ed. Steve J. Stern. Madison: University of Wisconsin Press.

———. 1991. "El retorno del Indio." *Revista Andina* 2 (December): 299–345.

———. 1999. "Andean People in the Twentieth Century." Pp. 765–871 in *The Cambridge History of the Native Peoples of the Americas*, vol. 3, *South America*, part 2, ed. Frank Salomon and Stuart B. Schwartz. Cambridge: Cambridge University Press.

Almeida, José. 1993. "El levantamiento indígena como momento constitutivo nacional." Pp. 7–28 in *Sismo étnico en el Ecuador: Varias perspectivas*, ed. José Almeida et al. Quito: Cedime.

Álvarez-Calderón, Annalyda. 2005. "'Es justicia lo que esperamos de Su Excelencia': Política indígena en Puno (1901–1927)." Pp. 312–341 in *Más allá de la dominación y la resistencia: Estudios de historia peruana, siglos xvi–xx*, ed. Paulo Drinot and Leo Garofalo. Lima: IEP.

Arze Aguirre, René Danilo. 1987. *Guerra y Conflictos Sociales: El Caso Rural boliviano durante la campaña del Chaco*. La Paz: CERES.

Assies, Willem. 2004. "Bolivia: A Gasified Democracy." *European Review of Latin American and Caribbean Studies* 76 (April): 25–43.

Assies, Willem, Gemma van der Haar, and André Hoekema, eds. 2000. *The Challenge of Diversity: Indigenous Peoples and Reform of the State in Latin America*. Amsterdam: Thela Thesis.

Baud, Michiel. 1993. "Campesinos indígenas contra el Estado: La huelga de los indígenas de Azuay, 1920/21." *Procesos: Revista de Historia* 4: 41–72.

———. 2003. *Intelectuales y sus utopías: Indigenismo y la imaginación de América Latina*. Amsterdam: CEDLA.

Baud, Michiel, and Rosanne Rutten, eds. 2004. *Popular Intellectuals and Social Movements: Framing Protest in Asia, Africa, and Latin America*. Cambridge: Cambridge University Press.

Becker, Marc. 2004. "Indigenous Communists and Urban Intellectuals in Cayambe, Ecuador (1926–1944)." Pp. 41–64 in Baud and Rutten 2004.

Bretón Solo de Zaldívar, Victor. 2006. "Glocalidad y reforma agraria: De nuevo el problema irresuelto de la tierra?" *Iconos: Revista de Ciencia Sociales* 24: 59–69.

Brysk, Alison. 2000. *From Tribal Village to Global Village: Indian Rights and International Relations in Latin America*. Stanford, CA: Stanford University Press.

Canessa, Andrew. 2000. "Contesting Hybridity: *Evangelistas* and *Kataristas* in Highland Bolivia." *Journal of Latin American Studies* 32: 115–144.

———. 2005. "The Indian Within, the Indian Without: Citizenship, Race and Sex in a Bolivian Hamlet." Pp. 130–155 in *Natives Making Nation: Gender, Indigeneity, and the State in the Andes*, ed. Andrew Canessa. Tucson: University of Arizona Press.

———. 2006. "Todos somos indígenas: Towards a New Language of National Political Identity." *Bulletin of Latin American Research* 25, no. 2: 241–263.

Chatterjee, Partha. 2004. *The Politics of the Governed: Reflections on Popular Politics in Most of the World*. Delhi: Permanent Black.

Collins, Jane L. 1988. *Unseasonal Migrations: The Effects of Rural Labor Scarcity in Peru*. Princeton, NJ: Princeton University Press.

Colloredo-Mansfeld, Rudi. 1998. "'Dirty Indians', Radical Indígenas, and the Political Economy of Social Difference in Modern Ecuador." *Bulletin of Latin American Research* 17, no. 2: 185–205.

De la Cadena, Marisol. 1994. "Decencia y cultura política: Los indigenistas del Cuzco en los años veinte." *Revista Andina* 12, no. 1: 79–122.

———. 1998. "Silent Racism and Intellectual Superiority in Peru." *Bulletin of Latin American Research* 17, no. 2: 143–164.

———. 2000. *Indigenous Mestizos: The Politics of Race and Culture in Cuzco, Peru, 1919–1991*. Durham, NC: Duke University Press.

Degregori, Carlos Iván. 1998. "Movimientos étnicos, democracia y nación en Perú y Bolivia." Pp. 159–225 in *La construcción de la nación y la representación ciudadana en México, Guatemala, Perú, Ecuador y Bolivia,* ed. Claudia Dary. Guatemala City: FLACSO.
_____. 2005. "'Hasta las últimas consecuencias': Gobierno local y conflicto en Ilave, 2004." *European Review of Latin American and Caribbean Studies* 78 (April): 89–99.
Gill, Lesley. 1997. "Creating Citizens, Making Men: The Military and Masculinity in Bolivia." *Cultural Anthropology* 12, no. 4: 527–550.
Gonzales Alvarado, Osmar. 1996. "Entre dos incertidumbres: La apropiación del indio en el discurso criollo." *Allpanchis* 28, no. 47: 179–208.
Guerrero, Andrés. 1991. *La semántica de la dominación: El concertaje de indios*. Quito: Libri Mundi.
_____. 1997. "The Construction of a Ventriloquist's Image: Liberal Discourse and the 'Miserable Indian Race' in Late 19th-Century Ecuador." *Journal of Latin American Studies* 29, no. 3: 555–590.
Hale, Charles R. 2002. "Does Multiculturalism Menace? Governance, Cultural Rights and the Politics of Identity in Guatemala." *Journal of Latin American Studies* 34, no. 3: 485–524.
Korovkin, Tanya. 2006. "Indigenous Movements in the Central Andes: Community, Class, and Ethnic Politics." *Latin American and Caribbean Ethnic Studies* 1, no. 2: 143–164.
Kristal, Efrain. 1987. *The Andes Viewed from the City: Literacy and Political Discourse on the Indian in Peru, 1848–1930*. New York: Peter Lang.
Larson, Brooke. 2004. *Trials of Nation Making: Liberalism, Race, and Ethnicity in the Andes, 1810–1910*. Cambridge: Cambridge University Press.
Leibner, Gerardo. 1997. "Pedro Zulen: Del indigenismo paternalista al humanismo radical." *European Review of Latin American and Caribbean Studies* 63: 29–53.
Lucero, José Antonio. 2006. "Representing 'Real Indians': The Challenges of Indigenous Authenticity and Strategic Constructivism in Ecuador and Bolivia." *Latin American Research Review* 41, no. 2: 31–56.
Méndez, Cecilia. 2005. *The Plebeian Republic: The Huanta Rebellion and the Making of the Peruvian State, 1820–1850*. Durham, NC: Duke University Press.
Mendoza, Zoila. 2006. *Crear y sentir lo nuestro: Folclor, identidad regional y nacional en el Cuzco, siglo xx*. Lima: PUCP.
Pallares, Amalia. 2002. *From Peasant Struggle to Indian Resistance: The Ecuadorian Andes in the Late Twentieth Century*. Norman: University of Oklahoma Press.
Platt, Tristan. 1982. *Estado boliviano y ayllu andino: Tierra y tributo en el norte de Potosí*. Lima: Instituto de Estudios Peruanos.
Prieto, Mercedes. 2004. *Liberalismo y temor: Imaginando los sujetos indígenas en el Ecuador postcolonial, 1895–1950*. Quito: FLACSO Sede Ecuador/Abya Yala.
Rappaport, Joanne. 1998. *The Politics of Memory: Native Historical Interpretations in the Colombian Andes*. Durham, NC: Duke University Press.
_____. 2005. *Intercultural Utopias: Public Intellectuals, Cultural Experimentation, and Ethnic Pluralism in Colombia*. Durham, NC: Duke University Press.
Rénique, José Luis. 1991. *Los sueños de la tierra: Cusco en el siglo XX*. Lima: CEPES.
_____. 2004. *La batalla por Puno: Conflicto agrario y nación en los Andes peruanos, 1866–1995*. Lima: IEP/Sur/CEPES.
Rivera Cusicanqui, Silvia. 1986. *'Oprimidos pero no vencidos': Luchas del campesinado aymara y qhechwa, 1900–1980*. La Paz: Hisbol.
Sanders, James E. 2004. *Contentious Republicans: Popular Politics, Race, and Class in Nineteenth-Century Colombia*. Durham, NC: Duke University Press.
Selverston-Scher, Melina. 2001. *Ethnopolitics in Ecuador: Indigenous Rights and the Strengthening of Democracy*. Boulder, CO: North-South Center Press/Lynne Rienner.
Stern, Steve J. 1982. "The Social Significance of Judicial Institutions in an Exploitative Society: Huamanga, Peru, 1570–1640." Pp. 289–320 in *The Inca and Aztec States 1400–1800: Anthropology and History*, ed. George A. Collier, Renato I. Rosaldo, and John D. Wirth. New York: Academic Press.

Van Cott, Donna Lee, ed.. 1994. *Indigenous Peoples and Democracy in Latin America.* New York: St. Martin's Press.

_____. 2005. *From Movements to Parties in Latin America: The Evolution of Ethnic Politics.* Cambridge: Cambridge University Press.

Weismantel, Mary J. 1989. *Food, Gender and Poverty in the Ecuadorian Andes.* Urbana: University of Illinois Press.

Yashar, Deborah J. 2005. *Contesting Citizenship in Latin America: The Rise of Indigenous Movements and the Postliberal Challenge.* Cambridge: Cambridge University Press.

Chapter 2

LA MANO DURA AND THE VIOLENCE OF CIVIL SOCIETY IN BOLIVIA

*Daniel M. Goldstein, with Gloria Achá,
Eric Hinojosa, and Theo Roncken*

In January 2003, the body of Jerry Rodríguez, also known as 'El Ruso' (the Russian), was found lying in a gutter on the outskirts of Cochabamba, Bolivia. El Ruso had been shot seven times in a manner that police would describe as 'execution style'. In recent months, El Ruso had become rather infamous in Cochabamba as a poster boy for the failure of the state's New Criminal Procedural Code (El Nuevo Código de Procedimiento Penal), passed into law by the Bolivian government in 2001. The New Code was intended to replace the former 'inquisitorial' system, which, due to basic deficiencies in its operation, accorded to police the liberty to (among other things) arrest and detain criminal suspects indefinitely and without leveling formal charges. The procedural guarantees of the New Code mandated greater police attention to the presumption

Notes for this chapter are located on page 60.

of innocence and severely restricted the measures (including, typically, violence and torture, or the threat thereof) that police formerly used to extract confessions from detainees. Given the low budget, lack of training, and widespread corruption within the Bolivian national police force, as well as the relatively small number of police officers on the streets in Cochabamba, the requirements for detention imposed under the New Code are difficult to satisfy, and criminal suspects are frequently released (it is said) for lack of evidence.

According to the daily newspaper *Los Tiempos*, El Ruso was "one of the delinquents who benefited most from the New Criminal Procedural Code (just this [past] year he was in and out of jail on more than 10 occasions)" (*Los Tiempos* 2003). A few hours after the discovery of El Ruso's corpse, a *Los Tiempos* reporter received an anonymous phone call from someone claiming responsibility for the murder. The caller was a representative of Citizens against Crime (Ciudadanos Contra el Crimen), or Triple C, a group of urban residents willing to take the law into their own hands to 'clean up' the streets of Cochabamba. The motivation for this vigilante group was not only to protect themselves against crime but also to protest against the so-called rights of delinquents supposedly protected by the New Code. "We are fed up," the caller told the journalist, "with the robberies of our vehicles going unsolved, and we decided to undertake a cleansing [*limpieza*] against those delinquents who obtain their freedom after being detained" (*Los Tiempos* 2003).[1]

Vigilante violence has become a common method of creating 'security' in the peri-urban neighborhoods or barrios that surround the city of Cochabamba. On literally hundreds of occasions during the last four years, mobs of angry barrio residents have captured and summarily executed suspected criminals whom they have apprehended in their communities (Achá 2003; Goldstein 2004). These lynchings (*linchamientos*, as they are termed locally) are efforts by poor barrio residents to police their neighborhoods against crime and serve as warnings to prospective criminals to avoid that particular community. They also register as moral and political complaints against the prevailing order, which denies the poor and indigenous residents of these communities access to official state policing and judicial services. Fear, generated by personal insecurity, is driving authoritarian behavior by barrio residents and escalating their tolerance for authoritarian forms of crime control and repression—including greater police violence and violation of human rights, generally referred to as *la mano dura*, the 'heavy hand' of the state—in the hope that placing limits on democratic values and a democratic rule of law will enhance their personal security.

What is perhaps most surprising is that this violence and the anti-democratic values it seems to represent are occurring simultaneously with the flourishing of civil society in Bolivia. Since 2000, indigenous Bolivian social movements have been responsible for an unprecedented transformation of neo-liberal society. Despite frequent state violence, they have protested against exploitative foreign investment and the social exclusion of indigenous peoples from the benefits of Bolivian democratic citizenship. The work of popular and indigenous organizations has resulted in the cancellation of a transnational agreement to privatize Cochabamba's water supply (the 'water war'; see Finnegan 2002), the postponement of government plans to export natural gas at unfavorable terms to the United States ('the gas war'; see Lazar and McNeish 2006), the resignations of two presidents, and, most recently, the election of Bolivia's first indigenous president, Evo Morales Ayma, in December 2005. These successes for Bolivia's "popular majority" (Albro 2005) have sparked international attention and, in some sectors, celebration, as they seem to represent the triumph of an indigenous civil society over a state that had long been negligent of, or actively antagonistic to, the needs and rights of Bolivia's indigenous population. Such movements also appear to demonstrate the belief, widely held among social scientists and democracy promoters, that a robust civil society can serve to deepen and extend the benefits of democracy beyond the purely political, expanding the social, economic, and legal rights of all citizens in the process (O'Donnell and Schmitter 1986).

These civil society victories and the rise to power of an indigenous sector in Bolivia have emerged in parallel with the violent authoritarianism displayed by some of the urban poor, as described above. This apparent contradiction resolves itself, however, if we consider 'civil society' to include violent social groups and actors as well as peaceful ones. Indeed, as this chapter shows, the delivery of local 'justice' through violence is one important expression of 'community' (a common gloss for 'civil society' in the Andean context) among these populations.[2] This suggests that despite the country's recent political transformations, the operation of civil society in Bolivia (as elsewhere) may not necessarily be the democratizing, balancing force that many observers might have assumed it to be (see Godoy 2006). If we truly are to understand the nature of civil society in Bolivia and other Latin American countries where 'insecurity' is a principal concern of the urban poor, we must broaden our understanding of what civil society includes. We must recognize that in the neo-liberal democracies of Latin America, the violence enacted by key sectors of civil society (including that of some groups of urban residents) may serve to promote state abuses and to restrict individual rights rather than to deepen and expand them. In addition, despite the recent transformations of the Bolivian state, citizen rights remain unequally distributed in Bolivia, with different groups of social actors enjoying different degrees of rights and thus different, and unequal, forms of citizenship. For those citizens who lack full and equal rights—including access to justice and the rule of law—expressions of authoritarian violence emerge in the domain of civil society in an effort to create 'security', albeit at the expense of the rights of supposed delinquents and the criminally accused. This implied hierarchy of rights, and the violence that certain groups are willing to employ to enforce it, represents another complicating factor that must be considered when evaluating the potential of civil society to contribute positively to the deepening of democratic politics and the expansion of citizenship rights.

Democracy, Violence, and Civil Society

From one perspective, it would appear that democracy has arrived in full force to formerly authoritarian states throughout the developing world (UNDP 2004).

This is particularly the case in Latin America, where, apart from Castro's Cuba, every nation has adopted (formally, at least, and to greater or lesser degrees) a democratic politics and a free market economy. Additionally, by some measures a recognition of the value of democracy seems to have permeated throughout these societies. According to a poll conducted in August 2002, most Latin Americans believe that democracy is preferable to any other form of government (Hakim 2003: 109).[3] Observations such as these have led some commentators to conclude that democracy is now a permanent fact of life in the developing world, and that while the occasional autocrat may still come to power, "the authoritarian option has become unthinkable in most of Latin America today" (ibid.: 111).

But as social scientists and politicians alike now understand, it is not merely the fact of democratic governance but the quality of democracy itself that is most often at issue in many of these transitional nations and that lies at the root of widespread popular dissatisfaction with democracy there today (Camp 2001; O'Donnell 1994; Oxhorn and Ducantenzelier 1998). In theory, democracy can be conceptualized as a kind of "organized uncertainty" (Tedesco 2004: 31), a system for processing conflicts "in which outcomes depend on what participants do but no single force controls what occurs" (Przeworski 1991: 12). The transition from authoritarian to democratic rule, from this theoretical perspective, is marked by the transfer of power from a group of individuals to a set of constitutionally inscribed laws that serve to balance and limit the uncertainty that democracy necessarily entails (Przeworski and Wallerstein 1988; Tedesco 2004). Such a conception of democracy is founded on notions of social, economic, and political equality that guarantee the right of every individual to equal access to opportunity and equal protection under the law. In an ideal democracy, all members of the polity stand as full and equal citizens before the law and share in the benefits of national belonging (Holston 1999b; Holston and Appadurai 1999). The democratic state ensures the maintenance of the legal framework by which citizens' rights are secured and safeguards 'democratic values', including an independent judiciary that guarantees to all citizens equality before the law and protection against unjustified terror, imprisonment, detention, and exile (Diamond 1999; Dominguez and Shifter 2003). The removal of oppressive constraints and limitations on individual rights, democratization theory often seems to assume, will lead to the flourishing of civil society, itself an inherently democratizing force. Through individual and collective popular participation and mobilization, political democracy will transform into social democracy, rights will further expand, and lingering authoritarian tendencies in political society will diminish and disappear.

Although democratic nations throughout Latin America have adopted new constitutions with bills of rights stipulating direct elections and formal guarantees of democratic values, in practice democracy has been at best imperfectly implemented in these nations. Rather than democracy, analysts of Latin American politics have suggested that what in fact has been implemented is a kind of polyarchy, "a system in which a small group actually rules, on behalf of capital, and participation in decision making by the majority is confined to choosing among competing elites in tightly controlled electoral processes" (Robinson

2004: 146). Such a system is the result of neo-liberal economic programs that have everywhere accompanied democratization and that have perpetuated and intensified the pre-democratic concentration of wealth in the hands of a social and political elite (Galbraith 2002; Gwynne and Kay 2000). Critics argue that the resulting "low-intensity democracy" (Gills, Rocamora, and Wilson 1993) provides the appearance of democracy without actually offering real democratic reform or the institution of democratic values, thereby providing a Gramscian legitimation for neo-liberal economic policy while hindering the crystallization of organized political opposition (Comaroff and Comaroff 2001; Tedesco 2004). Citizens within this low-intensity democracy enjoy a highly constrained or "low-intensity" citizenship (O'Donnell 1999), under which they possess the political right to vote but lack the economic, civil, and legal rights that full democratic citizenship is supposed to entail (Caldeira and Holston 1999; see also Van Cott 1994). With wealth so unequally distributed, democratic states in Latin America have had difficulty establishing equality before the law for all citizens, a critical centerpiece of the "democratic dividend" (Neild 2002: 2). The absence in Latin America of such a fundamental democratic principle as equal access to the law has created what Sanjuán (2002: 89) calls "an institutional absurdity: democracies in which the majority of the population lacks citizenship."

It is perhaps not surprising to discover, then, that in such 'poor quality' democracies, many practices and beliefs from the authoritarian past continue to be encountered today, although the justification for them has shifted from fighting communism to fighting crime (Aiyer 2001; Pinheiro 1999).[4] Neo-liberal economic reforms accompanying democratization were intended to create a more productive environment for transnational capitalism by removing barriers to trade and creating a 'flexible' workforce that could provide cheap labor to transnational industries (Harvey 2001; Ong 1999). But these reforms have also resulted in a measurable increase in economic inequality and a dramatic decrease in the standard of living for the rural and urban poor: ownership of land and other resources has become further concentrated, peasants have been dispossessed, and public-sector jobs have disappeared (Gwynne and Kay 2000). This economic crisis has been accompanied by a withdrawal of the state from a declared responsibility for social service provision and social welfare protection for society's most vulnerable, resulting in reductions in health and educational services, food subsidies, and so on.[5]

But it is in terms of access to the law and judicial services that the inequities of the new democracies are most starkly apparent. With the turn to neo-liberal democracy, poverty has worsened in societies throughout Latin America, and crime rates have risen. Perhaps more significantly, fear and insecurity have mounted. For the middle and upper classes, police and judicial services are at least nominally available to investigate crimes, respond to grievances, and resolve conflicts. But for the majority of crime victims, who are themselves typically poor and marginalized, honest and reliable police protection is simply non-existent, and legal resources are distant and inaccessible. Instead, the poor themselves are often criminalized in public discourse and in police practice. In poor urban neighborhoods, when the police appear at all, they may bring violence themselves, as states adopt more repressive tactics in the name of crime control. These measures often include violence and violate the human rights of crime suspects and victims alike (Davis 2003; Frühling 2003; Méndez, O'Donnell, and Pinheiro 1999; Pereira and Davis 2000; Schneider and Amar 2003; Ungar 2002).

Like 'democracies without citizenship', the persistence of human rights violations in a democratic context is contradictory and suggests the emergence of a constrained or 'uncivil' democracy (what is sometimes called in Spanish *democradura*), a condition under which democratically elected governments approximate authoritarian ones in their disregard for basic human rights (Pérez 2003; Prillaman 2000). According to James Holston: "In such uncivil democracies, violence, injustice, and impunity are norms ... Their institutions of law and justice undergo delegitimization; violent crime and police abuse escalate; the poor and the ethnically other are criminalized, dehumanized, and attacked ... and illegal measures of control receive massive popular support" (cited in Pérez 2003: 628). For many citizens confronting such conditions, the only viable option for obtaining security appears to be 'self-help' justice making—lynching—to create some semblance of order in their communities. Even in the absence of direct experience of crime, the fear of criminal violence, perpetuated by 'talk of crime', may drive people to violence and extra-legal measures in pursuit of security (Caldeira 2000; Dammert and Malone 2003; Elbert 1998; Rotker 2002). Where fear of crime is very high, tolerance of more heavy-handed, *mano dura* authoritarian measures to control it is also high (Call 2003; Duce and Pérez Perdomo 2003: 82). In various Latin American cities, people express a willingness to allow police to conduct illegal searches and detention of suspects, and support for the death penalty, formally illegal in most Latin American constitutions, is strongly on the rise (Lagos 2000; Smulovitz 2003). The contradictions are fairly obvious here—people fear the police, who are viewed as corrupt and violent, yet they clamor for a stronger and more violent police presence in their communities.

In the Andes, the contradictions are especially pronounced in urban areas, where a general feeling of fear and insecurity is often pervasive and inescapable, part of the habitus of daily life (Garland 2001). Facing widespread police corruption and violence, urban residents may experience an overwhelming sense of "ontological insecurity" (Giddens 1990) that pervades every aspect of their existence. In middle- and upper-class neighborhoods, such fear may be compounded by racial stereotypes and suspicion of the culturally or linguistically different 'other', who poses a vaguely defined threat to one's physical well-being and social identity (Merry 1981). Fear is widespread among members of all social classes and categories, who perceive the presence of outsiders in their communities as a potential source of crime. Additionally, in a context of rural-to-urban migration, many urban communities lack the social cohesion that once characterized rural villages. Missing is a spirit of community that joins people in common struggle and that enables a collective defense against delinquency. This sense of social disintegration, which typically (though not universally) accompanies urban migration, exacerbates the sense of vulnerability and isolation that urban residents experience when confronting perceived threats to their security.

Contrary to the expectations of democratization theory, then, rather than flourishing with the expansion of democracy and the growth of civil society, basic civil and human rights may in fact be diminished by the drive for security in a low-intensity democracy. In some countries, the expansion of police powers, tolerance of torture and violent punishment, and increasing penalties reflect the lack of respect for human rights by state entities (Huggins 1998; Jochnick 1999; Pereira and Davis 2000). At the same time, popular support for these measures, coupled with increasing incidence of vigilantism, has "a profoundly negative impact on public support for human rights" (Neild 2002: 2). Human rights groups, accustomed to performing a watchdog role against state abuses, now find themselves on opposite sides of justice and security issues from the poor whom they are trying to defend and who may view human rights protections as 'unfair' considerations given to criminals against the rights of crime victims (Caldeira 2000). The very discourse of human rights may itself be conceptualized by poor people as a transnational phenomenon and (like neo-liberalism) rejected as another foreign imposition meant to undermine local autonomy (Goldstein 2007).

This analysis forces us to rethink the nature of civil society in democratic Latin America. As the following discussion of lynching violence in urban Bolivia reveals, in some communities the collective mobilization of social actors identifiable as civil society, rather than serving to promote democratic institutions and values and advance the cause of civil and human rights, instead operates to constrain and limit those rights, while advocating for stronger and more violent state practices to promote 'security'. As Angelina Godoy (2006: 10) points out in her study of popular lynchings in Guatemala, the practice of and demand for *mano dura* forces us to recognize that civil society and unrestricted popular participation may not be an inherently democratizing force. If we define civil society, a notoriously slippery concept (see White 1994), as "a network of voluntary associations and institutions grounded in the exercise of and respect for liberal rights and the rule of law" (Godoy 2006: 129), then lynch mobs clearly have no place in our considerations. But this definitional lack of fit says more about social science classifications than it does about current social reality. If instead, as Godoy (ibid.: 130) suggests, we understand civil society as "an arena in which citizens come together in autonomous, voluntary association for mutual benefit," then violent, illegal groups, which may be antagonistic to basic democratic values and the human rights whose protections they guarantee, must in fact be considered as critical components of contemporary civil society in Latin America.

'Citizen Insecurity' and Civil Society in Cochabamba's *Barrios Populares*

Within indigenous Andean communities, it is tempting to interpret acts of collective violence or vigilantism as aspects of indigenous legal custom unproblematically surviving into the present, their use rationalized in terms of their long-standing histories or 'traditional' status. As Mayer (1991) points out for Peru, however, while collective violence is often viewed as morally justifiable as a last recourse in defense of the indigenous community, it is not necessarily a sanctioned aspect of indigenous law. Nevertheless, in an urbanizing context where official police protection is virtually non-existent, the right to defense of community through collective violence is sometimes justified by residents as custom, a dimension of an autonomous legal system that is said to pre-date the modern state and continues to exist alongside European-derived legality within the post-colonial nation. In an urban setting like Cochabamba, such "legal pluralism" (Merry 1988) is rarely encountered (for a rural context, see Fernández Osco 2000; Ministerio de Justicia y Derechos Humanos 1998; Sierra 1990). In some barrios, however, the language of community justice is deployed to justify vigilante violence, in the absence of any actual mechanisms of adjudication as practiced in traditional rural settings. Indeed, it may be precisely the absence of any shared sense of community or collective identity in many of these urban barrios that contributes to people's willingness to turn to *mano dura* to create 'security'. In a context of enduring poverty and profound insecurity, lynchings and other forms of collective violence represent attempts by insecure barrio residents to affirm a sense of collective identity and local power, and to establish themselves publicly as a community able to defend itself against crime (Goldstein and Williams Castro 2006). Lacking a strong sense of collective solidarity that might be the basis for constructing more peaceful forms of conflict resolution or adjudication in the absence of official state mechanisms, people turn to violence as the "lowest common denominator" (Godoy 2006: 118) of social control, "a form of collective action on criminal justice that does not rely on sustained trust to be successful" (ibid.: 119).

The following sections detail some of the basic social and economic conditions within which *mano dura* emerges as a strategy for creating 'security' in the marginal barrios of Cochabamba. Based on a series of interviews conducted by a team of researchers over the course of the last several years, the following sections explore local perceptions of the sources of insecurity in these barrios and analyze the recommendations that barrio residents consistently offer in response to the conditions confronting them. Through the testimonies cited here, one can recognize the failures of the neo-liberal democratic state and the ways in which a violent civil society operates in these barrios to control 'delinquency'.[6]

Basic Conditions

Formed over the last 20 to 30 years by indigenous migrants leaving the Bolivian altiplano and the Cochabamba Valley in search of better economic opportunities, the peri-urban barrios of Cochabamba's southern zone are characterized by poor living conditions, vulnerability to and fear of crime, domestic and other forms of violence, and high unemployment or underemployment.[7] "No hay fuentes de trabajo" (There are no jobs) is a common complaint among barrio residents. The barrios are inhabited by rural-to-urban migrants who work in temporary and low-paying jobs as small-scale merchants or ambulatory vendors in the city's streets or the Cancha (its large outdoor market), or who spend their time looking for temporary work as laborers, construction workers, or domestics. Others are employed in informal shops, making clothing that is sold in the Cancha. The money that people earn is generally inadequate to support their families or meet their basic needs. In these conditions, frequent thefts of small amounts of material goods are extremely painful. People attest that most property crimes occur in broad daylight, when homes are unattended while residents are at work in the city center.

Interview testimonies from women and men living in some of these barrios emphasized their anxiety about their inability to care for their families and the correlations they observed between poverty and violence: "If there is this insecurity, it is also the result of our great poverty, no?"; "I think that there are delinquents because they have no other option, there's no work to be had." Poverty also correlates with domestic instability, and interviewees indicated a strong recognition here, too, of the economic roots of social and familial insecurity. Some people we interviewed expressed particular concern over the abandonment of or lack of attention given to children in the barrios, as both mother and father work all day in the city center, often leaving very young children unattended for long periods of time. This lack of parental 'control' (to use the term frequently offered by interviewees) was seen by some as a direct cause of delinquency and insecurity: "With this economy in force, we have to leave home to work, the father and the mother, and the children are left abandoned, and there is no control, the street is what guides them … Now we have to work, husband and wife, so there is less control over the children, the young people." Others expressed a different perspective, emphasizing *la parte afectiva* (the role of emotion, of love) in the family: "No, control isn't so important, but the emotional side, to make your child feel that you are protecting him … even though they [the delinquents] are killing you, you are protecting your child, you are making him feel that you are giving him love and security."

Despite the expression of such sentiments, domestic violence is a frequent phenomenon in the barrios of the southern zone, and young people are often subjected to violence both within and outside the home. Interviewees attributed domestic violence to poverty ("The same lack of employment makes couples fight") and alcohol abuse ("Typically the people drink, they come home and they [take it out on their kids]"). The deterioration of familial relations has public consequences, as violence within the home spills out to the streets: "'My mother doesn't want me, so what am I going to do? I have to rob, from my own mother I'm going to rob,' so say the young people." But the streets were described as unsafe for kids and adolescents: "My children are mixed up with these violent people, from early childhood they have grown up with violence"; "Our children don't go out with the intention of smoking or doing drugs, but there are many bad friends, and they sell it to them." Thus, the streets are perceived as spaces of danger, lacking any sort of government investment in parks or activities, leaving young people with no option but to drink locally made corn beer (*chicha*) in public bars (*chicherias*): "In the peripheral barrios there are no cultural activities of the state, or of the municipality, or nothing.

So the young person has to go to the *chicheria* ... because there is nothing else to do." These *chicherias* are generally regarded as sources of vice and crime, localities in which people, especially young people, get drunk and then proceed to act violently or commit other acts of delinquency. But this perception works against youths who want to gather peacefully to dance and socialize, closing off the possibility of non-violent, civil assembly. In the words of one young man: "There is so much prejudice around these topics. And also there is this sense that, well, where there is a party all the kids are bad, all of them are drunks, all are drug addicts ... But it's not like that, no? I think we have to break this stigma ... that young people are always delinquents."

Perceptions of public danger, then, are particularly hard on children and teenagers, whom many view simultaneously as both predators and prey. In this context, youth itself is criminalized, and poor children are especially vulnerable to such labeling. Hence, even while parents expressed deep concern for the safety and well-being of their own children, some were also willing to act on this fear with hypervigilance and sometimes violence targeted against other people's children. Some parents were aware of this contradiction and expressed additional fears with regard to its impact on their own kids, blaming their neighbors' fearful behavior for increasing the pervasive sense of insecurity. Nevertheless, the logic of this perception exhibits a distinctive us-versus-them, insider-outsider quality, in which anyone unknown to you is a stranger and hence a potential threat to your security (Goldstein 2007).

The profound fear that colors daily life in the barrios of Cochabamba is in part attributable to the tremendous growth and proliferation of these barrios during the course of the last 30 years, which has transformed the nature of community life. As described in detail elsewhere (Goldstein 2004), the population of Cochabamba has grown from about 80,000 in 1952 (the time of the Bolivian national revolution) to almost 800,000 today, with most of this population growth occurring in the peripheral zones of the city. Many people described this growth as the obstacle to cultivating a spirit of community in the marginal barrios: "Now we are a population of some 30,000, there is not the custom of gathering together or speaking the same language." Others pointed to individualism in the local population as contributing to the climate of suspicion and mistrust (*desconfianza*; see Goldstein 2002) in the barrio, contrasting it with a remembered or imagined solidarity of rural life: "We have reached the point where we only care about our family life and not at the level of the barrio, no? That's so in the barrios, because in other communities [in the countryside], the people still know one another. But it's not like that in the barrios, in the cities, in the urban areas, no?" Given the difficulties that urban families face in trying to protect their members, some barrio residents felt that it was the community's responsibility to come to their aid—a community that many believe does not exist: "When the family isn't there, the community has to play an important role, and the community has to be supported by other institutions ... But here the community doesn't exist, and ... the children are abandoned."

Many of those interviewed claimed to recall an earlier time when the barrio functioned more as a community and was able to control crime collectively through mechanisms of social control expressive of a certain degree of social cohesion. For some, the difference between that community and the community today resides principally in the increase in the number of residents, which has a direct impact on security and the barrio's ability to control crime: "Before when the population wasn't very great, we were few, there was more control, it was easier to catch the thief." Others blamed the lack of social cohesion in the barrio today on the influence of political parties ("The parties have divided us") and on the lack of "traditional leaders," who functioned with more authority than the barrio leaders of today: "In the countryside ... there was more respect for our authorities. When the *corregidor* [magistrate] came with his whip, you were afraid ... Here [in the city] there's none of that."

Desconfianza and the disarticulation of a community spirit among the barrio residents effectively curtail the possibility of creating and implementing collective instruments that can confront local conditions of insecurity, thus limiting the emergence of what analysts might recognize as a peaceful 'civil society' in the poor barrios of Cochabamba. Interestingly, at the same time that this constrained civil society is the product of insecurity, it is itself productive of greater insecurity in the barrios. As one young man put it when describing the situation facing young people who are denied spaces in which to peacefully congregate and entertain themselves: "If they kick the young people out of these meeting places, for dancing, then they are going to get involved [in crime] ... they are going to do something else. But they [the authorities] don't realize that this mistake that they are making will only make the situation worse." For many of those interviewed, who connected their own perceptions of insecurity with their lack of economic stability and the uncertainties of urban life, the ability to create security appears to be beyond their control. In this context, where civil society is so severely constrained, what perceptions do people hold of the state and the official entities charged with bringing security and justice to their barrios?

Political and Legal Factors

One theme that emerged repeatedly in our interviews with barrio residents was their awareness of the lack of an effective police presence in their neighborhoods and the failure of the police to protect the citizenry from crime: "The police never come when you call them"; "Here [in this barrio] there is a police station. It's a pretty big station. But it's no good for anything because you call them and they don't come." For many in Cochabamba, the lack of police response is directly attributable to the corruption that is presumed to infest every level of the police hierarchy. Many people claimed that only the rich or the middle class get police attention, because they are the only ones who can afford it: "Really, *la denuncia* [filing a police report] is only a palliative, because in the end, he who has money can get things moving, he who doesn't have money, nothing moves ... That's the reality. To investigate, the police ask for money, when there's money they investigate, when there's no money, they don't." A common complaint was that the police are "accomplices of the thieves," that they take money from criminals to release them from custody, and that even "the highest police chiefs are immersed in delinquency." Many poor barrio residents don't even bother to call the police when they are victimized, considering it to be "a waste of time." Many people held comparable opinions about other judicial authorities, including lawyers and judges, who were similarly viewed as inaccessible and corrupt.[8]

Although the accusations of police corruption are widespread, some of those interviewed took a broader view of police failure, attributing it to the overall impoverishment of the police institution. This is a viewpoint reinforced by the police themselves, who often tell crime victims that they cannot attend to them because they lack gasoline for their police cars or personnel to pursue an investigation. Some barrio residents, more sympathetic than their neighbors, recognized that the cops themselves are victims of the poverty of the Bolivian state and its institutions: "Who are the police? They are poor people [*gente humilde*] who are here working, in the end they get 500 or 600 bolivianos [US $60–70] a month … so to maintain themselves they have to accept bribes from the delinquents, too."

Besides inefficiency and corruption, the police also bear the stigma of social, racial, and gender discrimination in their practice, supposedly providing good service to the upper classes and rough treatment to the poor, indigenous, and peasant classes. Among those interviewed, many expressed a strong sentiment that the color of one's skin or one's economic position is the measure by which the police and other judicial entities determine how to administer justice. "In no police station that you can go to right now is there one white kid. They are not going to be detained because they have money and a car." One's place of residence can also determine the treatment one can expect to receive from the police, making innocent people wary of their movements and afraid of the cops, even in their own communities: "If you live in the northern zone they [the police] are not going to bother you … but if you live in the southern zone, obviously, in the southern zone the police can kick the shit out of you, here everybody is a criminal." The irony of this statement is expressed in another man's comment that "in the northern zone, they are all *gente*," an observation that points to the racialized geography of citizenship—who one must be and where one must live in order to enjoy full citizenship rights.[9] Indigenous women are particularly vulnerable to police abuse on the basis of both their race and gender. Even when reporting crimes to the police, they can expect to be verbally or physically mistreated by the attending officers.

Given the great mistrust of police and other justice officials among poor barrio residents in Cochabamba, it is not surprising that many of those interviewed perceived a vast abyss between themselves and the governing elites of municipal and national politics. While this situation has perhaps changed since the election of Evo Morales as president in December 2005, at the time of these interviews, barrio residents had been living under a system of neoliberal democracy headed by political leaders of racial and class backgrounds that were distinctly different from their own.[10] From the perspective of many of those interviewed, the political leaders have absolutely no conception of life in the barrios or of the kinds of problems that barrio residents face: "They have their elite of pure millionaires ... They should have to come down from their money, they should come down here below ... so that they could say, 'This is what goes on down below'"; "The truth is, the authorities know little of the peri-urban barrios ... Without knowledge, what can they do for us?" This ignorance about and distance from the poor barrios means that government authorities fail to understand the difficulties that barrio residents confront in terms of crime and delinquency: "The authorities should realize that the poor people, the people who have to earn their daily bread, that we are worried about this, that the people are robbed, there are thieves ... that enter our homes while we are out looking to earn our daily bread."

Abandoned by justice officials and politicians alike, barrio residents also felt betrayed by local leaders who form clientelistic ties with local politicians in order to advance their own political careers, to secure a job or other resources for themselves within the *alcaldia*, or to consolidate a base for these politicians within the barrios. Some barrio residents complained of the obligations that these clientelistic relations place on them and the inequities that party affiliations introduce into the barrio: "If you want to get a good job, you have to belong to a political party." Local leaders sometimes use party loyalties as a litmus test to decide who may reside in the community and who may not, granting lots for settlement to those who agree to support them politically. In the process, local leaders enrich themselves at the expense of barrio residents. In many neighborhoods, barrio leaders functioning as land speculators (*loteadores*) sold land to individual settlers that was supposed to be preserved as communal land (*áreas verdes*) for parks, schools, or clinics, leaving the communities without spaces for recreation or public services (Goldstein 2004). These illegal practices in turn contribute to mounting insecurity in the barrios: "There were *loteadores* here that took advantage, that began to ... sell the *áreas verdes* ... and those *áreas verdes* have turned into *chicherias*"; "I truly don't know what can be done, it pains me to see these things; we keep doing this [illegal sale of lots], and this automatically influences citizen security, this malicious influence, these conflicts." The dynamics of party politics and the illegal land sales they underwrite contribute to anger, resentment, and fear within local communities, creating an insecurity that further undermines collective sensibilities and inhibits the emergence of a leadership that might be more civic-minded: "Sadly we have found ourselves with vile types in our midst, manipulated by political parties ... and many people have disappeared, I don't know if they are still alive, if they are hiding or if they have been killed ... They don't allow young leaders to emerge here ... the young people are threatened."

The results of this process thus include the gradual erosion of a sense of community solidarity that may once have existed in the urban barrio, limiting the kinds of civil society that can emerge.[11] The various forms of what local people identify as 'injustice' (*injusticia*)—a broad category of experience that includes a range of legal, social, economic, and political inequities, as described above—contribute to a sense of a world gone mad, in which the police are indistinguishable from the criminals and the rewards seem to flow toward bad behavior and away from the socially responsible: "For the poor people there is no justice, there is no justice, to this day, I've never seen it, my friends have perhaps seen it but I never have, there is always injustice, an imperfection working against us. The people that do bad things are the most rewarded ... We who have to make reports to the police, we end up losing more money [through police corruption], after we have been robbed. There is no justice for the society in which we live." In such a system, individualism or else affiliation with some kind of alternative civil society group (e.g., a gang, or a violent self-defense group like the Triple C) seems to be the only logical response, given the need to protect one's self and one's family against the predations of criminals. Some people recognized the venality of the situation: "We fight among ourselves, we are killing ourselves, and the others are filling their pockets ... Nobody says that they [the rich, the government officials] are the ones who are robbing us"; "To the most corrupt we don't say anything and we will never see them in prison. The poor guy who steals 10 bolivianos, him we have to lynch, no?"

Violence and Its Alternatives

From this context of intense social problems, uncertainties, and insecurities emerges a complex combination of sentiments, including rage, fatalism, and impotence among residents of marginal barrios, who feel themselves to be abandoned by state judicial authorities and powerless to correct the problems confronting them. The idea that society is powerless and the state worthless in providing security to the marginal barrios pervades informant testimonies: "It seems to me that our hands are tied, we can't do anything, we are not in power, those in power are the ones who can do and undo things ... But society can't do anything because it doesn't have the power, it doesn't have political power, it doesn't have economic power, so any complaint is in vain." It is not surprising that in such a context, violence emerges as regular means of resolving problems of insecurity: "Sure, the anger is so great, the society ... with all the things that happen, there is no justice, the authorities don't do anything, so, what are you going to do? You catch someone, you lynch him."

Many people described lynching as an inevitable, last-ditch response to uncontrolled criminality in their barrios: "I, too, have this attitude of lynching, because I don't see any alternative." For some, the death of the so-called delinquent was seen almost as a necessity: "The people always have this idea, that only in this way [lynching] are we going to put an end to [delinquency]." Casting it in moral terms, one barrio resident expressed the need for some kind of retribution or payback in that the evil that the criminal act produced gave the community the right, in a sense, to 'collect': "I believe that nobody can hurt another, no? To kill, to lynch somebody. But if they do it, well ... the criminal has also done harm. So he has to pay." Another resident invoked the Manichaean logic of good and evil, so common in discussions of crime and insecurity in other socio-political contexts, to justify lynching violence.[12] As in the 'war on terror', *mano dura* is described here as the only bulwark of 'the good' against 'the bad' in the contemporary context: "So this is what the people say: 'We have to grab him [the delinquent]. The police are never going to stop them,' they say. 'We have to stop them, because there will come a moment,' the people say, 'when there will be more bad than good. Today there is still more good than bad, so we have to catch the bad ... If this [delinquency] keeps growing, the bad is going to do away with the good.'"

Lynching represents the most blatant application of *mano dura* to the resolution of social problems in the marginal barrios, but it is not the only form in which the desire for a 'heavy-handed' approach is expressed. Many people stated their desire to "toughen the laws," calling on the state to impose more effective punishments on criminals and to "implement a social politics that can defend us against this mass of delinquency." Criticism extended particularly to laws seen to be protective of the rights of criminals against those of the victims of crime. As evidenced by the case of the Triple C vigilante group described earlier, many people are extremely critical of the New Criminal Procedural Code, which imposes certain restrictions on police abuses and requires the presentation of evidence for a criminal suspect to be detained. Given the inefficiency of police investigations and the overall debilitation of the police institution, such evidence is frequently lacking, requiring judges to set criminal suspects at liberty. As a result, many of those interviewed concluded that the recent changes to the law have tended to protect the so-called delinquents: "What happens is, our laws are not suited to our reality. If we go to make a denunciation against someone, the next day he is already out of jail"; "There is no justice for anybody ... We don't have law ... The Ley Blattmann [a predecessor of the New Criminal Code] is for the thieves." Similarly, human rights defenders (including the Asamblea Permanente de Derechos Humanos, or Derechos Humanos) are demonized for what barrio residents believe to be their defense of delinquents: "Derechos Humanos comes ... if there is not the required evidence nobody can accuse him [the delinquent], they take him away and immediately the delinquent is back on the street." In many cases, these complaints are accompanied by a demand for 'tougher' laws: "Why do [these things happen] like this? Because they [the delinquents] know there is no law. If there was law, at least they would respect it. Where is it, in India? They put a rapist in the plaza, and they cut off his balls with an axe."

Despite these widely expressed sentiments, some other barrio residents recognized that the source of many of the problems, and a possible avenue to their solution, is the recuperation of what people describe as a spirit of community and collective action. These residents recognize that the disarticulation of community, the individualization of the populace, and the fear and impotence that many people feel in confronting delinquency are in many ways attributable to the lack of collective action organized to provide real security and non-violent remedies in dealing with crime. Some imagined a future in which their barrio is better protected, based upon a community that expresses greater unity in the struggle for self-defense: "We have to find some means whereby the residents can organize, and they themselves can be participants in caring for the property of other residents." Others framed the problem in terms of a loss of collective values at the level of families, neighborhoods, and institutions: "I believe that the essence ... of citizen insecurity is the crisis of values at every level, in the entire structure [of society]." Strong local leadership is another component to which some people pointed as essential to the creation of non-violent measures for dealing with crime and for managing relations with state and judicial authorities, while others mentioned the need for barrio residents to become more knowledgeable about the laws and the workings of the state justice system so as to better defend themselves: "In our environment ... the people are ignorant, they need much orientation ... They don't know the laws, the articles, really I think they are afraid to declare themselves witnesses [to a crime] ... Therefore, we need an organization, in charge of understanding the laws, the civil laws and the penal laws." As with the adolescents mentioned earlier, some people called on their communities to organize to defend their public spaces against *chicherias* and illegal land sales and to provide spaces for recreation and community activities. In all of these testimonies, barrio residents expressed the need for local collective organization and action. Like their more violent neighbors, these residents put no stock in the state's ability to provide security and look to their own collective resources—still unexplored and underutilized—as instruments for the non-violent resolution of conflicts in their neighborhoods.

Conclusion

The assumption of democracy theorists and promoters that a dynamic civil society is an inherently positive force that will serve to deepen citizens' rights in a democratizing context is belied by the proliferation of collective violence in Cochabamba's marginal barrios. Here, it is through extra-legal violence that civil society itself is actually constructed, as individuals and communities come together outside of the state to forge independent associations for their own defense against the forces of 'delinquency'. Many of these same people are also strong critics of the democratic state, its police and judicial systems, and its laws, which they view to be antagonistic to their rights as citizens even as they serve to protect the rights of delinquents. Thus, while barrio residents invoke their own 'heavy-handed' practices of dealing with criminals and suspected criminals (i.e., through lynching), these people also call for the state to employ violent practices of policing and adjudication.

This demand for a return to *la mano dura*, commonly practiced by authoritarian regimes during the era of the dictatorships in Latin America, is an alarming trend for those interested in the spread of democracy around the world. While it is unlikely that security issues will lead directly to a military coup or some other totalitarian seizure of power, what this discussion suggests is that as people become more familiar with and accepting of violence and human rights violations as means to combat crime, the quality of democracy becomes further eroded, setting the stage for a further weakening of democratic protections, values, and rule of law (Call 2003; Pérez 2003). As a result, despite the optimism of some (such as Hakim, cited earlier), 'the authoritarian option' may indeed be 'thinkable' once more in Latin America. Polyarchy, masquerading as democracy, loses legitimacy as crime and violence escalate and the unequal access to law becomes increasingly evident, revealing the differential grades of citizenship that exist within contemporary democratic society. Rather than seek real democratic reform that opens channels of participation and creates institutions of justice in accord with the actual needs of the population, states and citizens alike may push for ever greater authoritarian measures to correct the problems for which democracy is believed to be responsible.

Recognizing that civil society can be profoundly violent and undemocratic further helps us to identify the many ways in which neo-liberal democracy in Latin America has failed to establish and protect the rights of citizens and to acknowledge the consequences of this failure. It is critical to recognize here that we are not speaking of two civil societies, one violent and one peaceful. Rather, civil society must be understood to consist of different social sectors and actors, all of whom share similar values, fears, and social institutions and aim to have their rights as citizens recognized and protected. From this perspective, we can see that the various expressions of civil society, both violent and non-violent, seek to establish and defend citizens' rights, albeit by employing different techniques. Obviously, lynching and other acts of *mano dura* are inherently undemocratic and antagonistic to basic concepts of civil and human rights, and thus it is that violent expressions of civil society can work against the expansion and deepening of democracy and the basic rights of citizens. In their desire to defend themselves, violent actors envision a hierarchy of rights in which one's own rights may be legitimately defended at the expense of another's. This violence, then, although profoundly undemocratic and anti-egalitarian, perversely aims to establish and defend citizens' rights: the right to live free from violence and terror, the right to property and safety, the right to justice—even the right to life itself. Such a recognition further underscores the claim of this chapter that civil society must be understood to include violent actors and groups. Their actions, while clearly destructive to the deepening of democratic rights and values, contradictorily aim to accomplish that which civil society has always been supposed to do: protect the rights of citizens in a democratic society.

Acknowledgments

The authors wish to extend their thanks to Ted Fischer for the invitation to participate in this project and to the anonymous reviewers for their helpful comments. This material is based upon work supported by the National Science Foundation under Grant No. 0540702.

Daniel M. Goldstein is currently studying the competing discourses and practices of security, rights, and democracy, with the financial support of the National Science Foundation, in urban Bolivia, where his research focuses on violence, human rights, and popular politics. With funding from the MacArthur Foundation, he researched and wrote *The Spectacular City: Violence and Performance in Urban Bolivia* (2004). His most recent articles include "Flexible Justice: Neoliberal Violence and Self-Help Security in Bolivia" (2005), "Creative Violence: How Marginal People Make News in Bolivia" (2006, with Fatimah Williams Castro), and "Human Rights as Culprit, Human Rights as Victim: Rights and Security in the State of Exception" (2007). He teaches courses in cultural anthropology at Rutgers University.

Gloria Achá, Eric Hinojosa, and Theo Roncken are social science researchers and human rights activists in Cochabamba, Bolivia.

Notes

1. Some speculate that Triple C was actually a front for elements within the police force who were hostile to the New Code and posing as a group of outraged citizens. Others believe that a rival criminal group was responsible for El Ruso's murder. Whatever the true identity of the Triple C, the target of the vigilantes was clearly the New Code as much as it was El Ruso and his band of thieves.
2. This is not to deny that other strong expressions of 'community' can be found in urban barrios, especially around communal fiestas or other events. For an ethnographic description of this kind of collective celebration and performance of community, see Goldstein (2004) and Guss (2006).
3. Other surveys, such as those conducted by the Latin American Public Opinion Project (http://sitemason.vanderbilt.edu/lapop), have shown widely divergent views on democracy in the region.
4. The recent political transformations of the Bolivian state, particularly the MAS (Movimiento al Socialismo) government's stated commitment toward dismantling neo-liberalism, suggest the possibility of changes emerging in this status quo. See the conclusion of this chapter for further discussion.
5. In most cases, the state's declared responsibility for social service provision was not matched by actual practice in rural communities and urban barrios.
6. For more on these topics, see Hinojosa et al. (2006).
7. For a detailed historical and ethnographic account of Cochabamba's barrios, see Goldstein (2004).
8. It is important to note here that while the accusations of corruption are certainly true, barrio residents' lack of knowledge about the workings of the judicial system and how to access it is also a factor in their feelings of being marginalized by official justice.
9. In popular parlance, to be *gente* (literally, people) means to be educated and of a 'good' social class. The northern zone of Cochabamba, home to many middle- and upper-class families, corresponds to these criteria, unlike the southern zone, where many of the marginal barrios are located.
10. The individual and focus group interviews from which these quotations are drawn were conducted between 2003 and 2005 in the marginal barrios of Cochabamba.
11. Whether a sense of community solidarity once existed in these barrios or is rather a contemporary romanticization of the past is the subject of some debate within the barrios themselves. See the discussion in Goldstein (2004).
12. Any follower of the news from Iraq will recognize the ideology invoked in George W. Bush's 'war on terror'.

References

Achá, Rose Marie. 2003. *Huellas de fuego: Crónica de un linchamiento.* Cochabamba: Acción Andina.

Aiyer, Ananthakrishnan. 2001. "Hemispheric Solutions? Neoliberal Crisis, Criminality and 'Democracy' in the Americas." *Urban Anthropology and Studies of Cultural Systems and World Economic Development* 30 (Summer–Fall): 239–252.

Albro, Robert. 2005. "The Indigenous in the Plural in Bolivian Oppositional Politics." *Bulletin of Latin American Research* 24, no. 4: 433–453.

Caldeira, Teresa P. R. 2000. *City of Walls: Crime, Segregation, and Citizenship in São Paulo.* Berkeley: University of California Press.

Caldeira, Teresa P. R., and James Holston. 1999. "Democracy and Violence in Brazil." *Comparative Studies in Society and History* 41, no. 4: 691–729.

Call, Charles T. 2003. "Democratisation, War and State-Building: Constructing the Rule of Law in El Salvador." *Journal of Latin American Studies* 35, no. 4: 827–863.

Camp, Roderic Ai, ed. 2001. *Citizen Views of Democracy in Latin America.* Pittsburgh, PA: University of Pittsburgh Press.

Comaroff, Jean, and John L. Comaroff. 2001. "Millennial Capitalism: First Thoughts on a Second Coming." Pp. 1–56 in *Millennial Capitalism and the Culture of Neoliberalism,* ed. Jean Comaroff and John L. Comaroff. Durham, NC: Duke University Press.

Dammert, Lucia, and Mary Fran T. Malone. 2003. "Fear of Crime or Fear of Life? Public Insecurities in Chile." *Bulletin of Latin American Research* 22, no. 1: 79–101.

Davis, Diane E. 2003. "Law Enforcement in Mexico City: Not Yet under Control." *NACLA Report on the Americas* 37, no. 2: 17–24.

Diamond, Larry. 1999. *Developing Democracy: Toward Consolidation.* Baltimore, MD: Johns Hopkins University Press.

Dominguez, Jorge I., and Michael Shifter. 2003. *Constructing Democratic Governance in Latin America.* Baltimore, MD: Johns Hopkins University Press.

Duce, Mauricio, and Rogelio Pérez Perdomo. 2003. "Citizen Security and Reform of the Criminal Justice System in Latin America." Pp. 69–92 in Frühling, Tulchin, and Golding 2003.

Elbert, Carlos Alberto. 1998. "Ideología, corrupción y excesos policiales: Pena y Estado." *Revista Latinoamericana de Política Criminal* 3, no. 3: 63–80.

Fernández Osco, Marcelo. 2000. *La ley del ayllu: Práctica de jach'a justicia y jisk'a justicia en comunidades aymaras.* La Paz: PIEB.

Finnegan, William. 2002. "Leasing the Rain." *New Yorker,* 8 April. http://www.newyorker.com/fact/content/articles/020408fa_FACT1?020408fa_FACT1.

Frühling, Hugo. 2003. "Police Reform and the Process of Democratization." Pp. 15–44 in Frühling, Tulchin, and Golding 2003.

Frühling, Hugo, Joseph Tulchin, and Heather A. Golding, eds. 2003. *Crime and Violence in Latin America: Citizen Security, Democracy, and the State.* Washington, DC: Woodrow Wilson Center Press.

Galbraith, John Kenneth. 2002. "A Perfect Crime: Global Inequality." *Daedalus* 131 (Winter): 11–25.

Garland, David. 2001. *The Culture of Control: Crime and Social Order in Contemporary Society.* Chicago, IL: University of Chicago Press.

Giddens, Anthony. 1990. *The Consequences of Modernity.* Oxford: Polity.

Gills, Barry, Joel Rocamora, and Richard Wilson, eds. 1993. *Low-Intensity Democracy: Political Power in the New World Order.* London: Pluto.

Godoy, Angelina Snodgrass. 2006. *Popular Injustice: Violence, Community, and Law in Latin America.* Stanford, CA: Stanford University Press.

Goldstein, Daniel M. 2002. "Desconfianza and Problems of Representation in Urban Ethnography." *Anthropological Quarterly* 75, no. 3: 485–517.

_____. 2004. *The Spectacular City: Violence and Performance in Urban Bolivia.* Durham, NC: Duke University Press.

_____. 2007. "Human Rights as Culprit, Human Rights as Victim: Rights and Security in the State of Exception." Pp. 49–77 in *The Practice of Human Rights: Tracking Law between the Global and the Local*, ed. Mark Goodale and Sally Engle Merry. Cambridge: Cambridge University Press.

Goldstein, Daniel M., and Fatimah Williams Castro. 2006. "Creative Violence: How Marginal People Make News in Bolivia." *Journal of Latin American Anthropology* 11, no. 2: 378–405.

Guss, David M. 2006. "The Gran Poder and the Reconquest of La Paz." *Journal of Latin American Anthropology* 11, no. 2: 294–328.

Gwynne, Robert N., and Cristobal Kay. 2000. "Views from the Periphery: Futures of Neoliberalism in Latin America." *Third World Quarterly* 21, no. 1: 141–156.

Hakim, Peter. 2003. "Dispirited Politics." *Journal of Democracy* 14, no. 2: 108–122.

Harvey, David. 2001. *Spaces of Capital: Towards a Critical Geography.* Edinburgh: Edinburgh University Press.

Hinojosa, Eric, Gloria Achá, Daniel M. Goldstein, and Theo Ronken. 2006. *Inseguridad ciudadana. Percepciones en los barrios populares de Cochabamba, Bolivia: Un estudio preliminar.* Cochabamba: Acción Andina-Bolivia.

Holston, James, ed. 1999a. *Cities and Citizenship.* Durham, NC: Duke University Press.

_____. 1999b. "Spaces of Insurgent Citizenship." Pp. 155–176 in Holston 1999a.

Holston, James, and Arjun Appadurai. 1999. "Introduction: Cities and Citizenship." Pp. 1–18 in Holston 1999a.

Huggins, Martha K. 1998. *Political Policing: The United States and Latin America.* Durham, NC: Duke University Press.

Jochnick, Chris. 1999. "Confronting the Impunity of Non-state Actors: New Fields for the Promotion of Human Rights." *Human Rights Quarterly* 21, no. 1: 56–79.

Lagos, María. 2000. "Between Stability and Crisis in Latin America." *Journal of Democracy* 12, no. 1: 137–145.

Lazar, Sian, and John-Andrew McNeish. 2006. "Introduction." *Bulletin of Latin American Research* 25, no. 2: 157–162.

Los Tiempos. 2003. "Un anónimo se atribuye asesinato de 'El Ruso.'" 5 January, A4.

Mayer, Enrique. 1991. "Peru in Deep Trouble: Mario Vargas Llosa's 'Inquest of the Andes' Reexamined." *Cultural Anthropology* 6, no. 4: 466–504.

Méndez, Juan E., Guillermo O'Donnell, and Paulo Sérgio Pinheiro, eds. 1999. *The (Un)rule of Law and the Underprivileged in Latin America.* Notre Dame, IN: University of Notre Dame Press.

Merry, Sally Engle. 1981. *Urban Danger: Life in a Neighborhood of Strangers.* Philadelphia, PA: Temple University Press.

_____. 1988. "Legal Pluralism." *Law and Society Review* 22, no. 5: 869–895.

Ministerio de Justicia y Derechos Humanos. 1998. *Anteproyecto de Ley de Justicia de los Pueblos Indígenas y Comunidades Indígenas-Campesinas.* La Paz: Ministerio de Justicia y Derechos Humanos.

Neild, Rachel. 2002. "The New Face of Impunity." *Human Rights Dialogue* 2, no. 8: 1–2.

O'Donnell, Guillermo. 1994. "Delegative Democracy." *Journal of Democracy* 5, no. 1: 55–69.

_____. 1999. *Counterpoints: Selected Essays on Authoritarianism and Democratization.* Notre Dame, IN: University of Notre Dame Press.

O'Donnell, Guillermo, and Philippe C. Schmitter. 1986. *Transitions from Authoritarian Rule: Tentative Conclusions about Uncertain Democracies.* Baltimore, MD: Johns Hopkins University Press.

Ong, Aihwa. 1999. *Flexible Citizenship: The Cultural Logics of Transnationality.* Durham, NC: Duke University Press.

Oxhorn, Philip, and Graciela Ducantenzelier. 1998. *What Kind of Democracy? What Kind of Market? Latin America in the Age of Neoliberalism.* University Park: Pennsylvania State University Press.

Pereira, Anthony W., and Diane E. Davis. 2000. "Introduction: New Patterns of Militarized Violence and Coercion in the Americas." *Latin American Perspectives* 27, no. 2: 3–17.

Pérez, Orlando J. 2003. "Democratic Legitimacy and Public Insecurity: Crime and Democracy in El Salvador and Guatemala." *Political Science Quarterly* 118, no. 4: 627–644.

Pinheiro, Paulo Sérgio. 1999. "The Rule of Law and the Underprivileged in Latin America: Introduction." Pp. 1–15 in Mendéz, O'Donnell, and Pinheiro 1999.

Prillaman, William C. 2000. *The Judiciary and Democratic Decay in Latin America: Declining Confidence in the Rule of Law.* Westport, CT: Praeger.

Przeworski, Adam. 1991. *Democracy and the Market.* Cambridge: Cambridge University Press.

Przeworski, Adam, and Immanuel Wallerstein. 1988. "Structural Dependence of the State on Capital." *American Political Science Review* 88: 11–31.

Robinson, William I. 2004. "Global Crisis and Latin America." *Bulletin of Latin American Research* 23, no. 2: 135–153.

Rotker, Susana, ed. 2002. *Citizens of Fear: Urban Violence in Latin America.* New Brunswick, NJ: Rutgers University Press.

Sanjuán, Ana María. 2002. "Democracy, Citizenship and Violence in Venezuela." Pp. 87–101 in Rotker 2002.

Schneider, Cathy, and Paul E. Amar. 2003. "The Rise of Crime, Disorder and Authoritarian Policing: An Introductory Essay." *NACLA Report on the Americas* 37, no. 2: 12–16.

Sierra, María Teresa. 1990. *Lenguaje, prácticas jurídicas y derecho consuetudinario indígena.* In *Entre la ley y la costumbre,* ed. R. Stavenhagen et al. Mexico City: INI-IIDH.

Smulovitz, Claudia. 2003. "Citizen Insecurity and Fear: Public and Private Responses in Argentina." Pp. 125–152 in Frühling, Tulchin, and Golding 2003.

Tedesco, Laura. 2004. "Democracy in Latin America: Issues of Governance in the Southern Cone." *Bulletin of Latin American Research* 23, no. 1: 30–42.

UNDP (United Nations Development Program). 2004. *La democracia en América Latina: Hacia una democracia de ciudadanas y ciudadanos.* New York: United Nations Development Program.

Ungar, Mark. 2002. *Elusive Reform: Democracy and the Rule of Law in Latin America.* Boulder, CO: Lynne Rienner.

Van Cott, Donna, ed. 1994. *Indigenous Peoples and Democracy in Latin America.* New York: St. Martin's Press.

White, Gordon. 1994. "Civil Society, Democratization and Development (I): Clearing the Analytical Ground." *Democratization* 1, no. 3: 375–390.

Chapter 3

EMPIRE/MULTITUDE—STATE/CIVIL SOCIETY
Rethinking Topographies of Power through Transnational
Connectivity in Ecuador and Beyond

Suzana Sawyer

Pablo spoke forcefully as he stood on the flatbed of a large truck seconding as a stage. His words blared through loudspeakers as he rallied a crowd of demonstrators to join his protest chant: "ChevronTexaco, ya viste, la justicia si existe" (You see, ChevronTexaco, justice does exist). It was October 2003, and approximately 500 Amazonian Indians and peasants were gathered outside the Superior Court in Lago Agrio, a ramshackle frontier town in the northern Ecuadorian rain forest. Unperturbed by the morning rains, men and women, young and old, had traveled to Lago Agrio to mark what they called "the trial of the century."[1] Inside the courthouse, the opening proceedings of a lawsuit against Chevron (then ChevronTexaco) had just begun.[2] Filed on behalf of 30,000 indigenous and non-indigenous Amazonian residents, the suit alleged that Texaco had recklessly contaminated the environment and endangered the health of local people during its twenty-odd years of operating in Ecuador.[3]

Past the guarded metal gates, on the fourth floor of Lago Agrio's Superior Court, 100 people packed a muggy courtroom. The Superior Court judge called the court into session. The legal team for ChevronTexaco, having arrived in an armored vehicle under military escort, took their seats across from the plaintiffs' lawyers. Among the spectators, a collection of plaintiffs listened expectantly, periodically relaying news to the demonstrators outside; foreign human rights and environmental activists watched attentively, if skeptically, to what appeared to be highly arcane trial proceedings; and national and international reporters set up their video cameras and microphones, while security police and bodyguards watched over the crowd. All focused their attention on ChevronTexaco's chief lawyer as he proceeded, over the course of the day, to respond to the suit.

* * *

This scenario, composed as it is by representatives of the world's fourth-largest oil corporation and Third World subaltern subjects, captures dynamics many scholars have focused on in recent years—forces recounted in *Empire* (2000) and envisioned in *Multitude* (2004), the academic bestsellers by Michael Hardt and Antonio Negri. According to Hardt and Negri, in their much acclaimed and critiqued work, Empire is an emerging form of power—global sovereignty— that guarantees and further entrenches our present global order. Configured as a network of collaborating powers among the dominant nation-states, the major capitalist corporations, and supra-national institutions (in conjunction with select local and regional powers), Empire is the global sovereign seeking to protect and enhance the interests of a global economic elite. The Multitude, as imagined by Hardt and Negri, is the heterogeneous and heterodox force of the world's marginalized broadly conceived, who share a "double character of poverty and possibility" (2004: 129). In and through the Multitude, differences and singularities simultaneously co-exist as subaltern groups in various forms strive to produce "the common"—a project for global democracy, of collaboration and cooperation, in opposition to Empire. ChevronTexaco exemplifies the method of Empire; the plaintiffs hold the promise of the Multitude.

In this chapter, I reflect on the lawsuit using *Empire* and *Multitude* as shorthand for many contemporary scholarly readings of globalization. That is, I read the ChevronTexaco lawsuit against the grain of *Empire* and *Multitude* in order to think through how the workings of power and processes of globalization in Ecuador converge with and diverge from those described by Hardt and Negri. The lawsuit against Chevron reveals how Hardt and Negri's Empire/Multitude imaginary shares two analytical limitations commonly evident in a differently scaled (although closely related) pair imagery: state/civil society.[4] The class-action lawsuit places in question the assumed physiology of coherence and topography of power implicit in these dyads. The Chevron case suggests that we need to explore the entangled, compromised, and unfinished practices that form what has come to be recognized as Empire/Multitude and state/civil society rather than assume we know their shape and content.

The tendencies that Hardt and Negri examine ring familiar to most social analysts of globalizing phenomena. While disagreeing on specifics, scholars see globalization as a force that is transforming the world order via dramatic social, political, and economic changes: the ethnoscapes of intensified cultural flows (Appadurai 1995), the time-space compression and flexible accumulation of late capitalism (Harvey 1989), the socio-techno networks of global informational capitalism (Castells 1996), to name a few. A number of scholars stress how globalization—understood as emerging from long-entrenched historical processes—has carved out new patterns of global stratification whereby some states, societies, and communities are increasingly enmeshed in the global order, while others are increasingly marginalized from it (Castells 2000; Ferguson 1999; Giddens 1990; Harvey 2006). Prior divides of inclusion/exclusion that formed the boundaries between nations have transmogrified into new hierarchies that cut across all societies and regions (Held et al. 1999; Ong 1998; Sassen 1996). These recast patterns of global stratification link increasingly mobile economic activity as production and finance take on evermore transnational dimensions. Similarly, they enable forms of collaboration and mobilization whose outcomes and effects are not a priori givens (Sawyer 2004; Tsing 2004).

While recognizing these as the forces that give rise to Empire and the Multitude, Hardt and Negri tend to reify each as distinguishably separate and cohesive spheres. What is left out are the messy, lived, embodied processes that implicate, as they give form to, each. As a consequence, and this is part of the problematic I address here, Hardt and Negri have an uncomplicated understanding of the *formation* of the Multitude and an overly determinative understanding of the *effects* of Empire.

For Hardt and Negri, the Multitude—the dispossessed and disaffected, the injured and insulted—are animated by an ineradicable desire for emancipation that compels them spontaneously to rise up against oppression. "There is nothing more natural and noble," they write (2000: 210), "than to resist authority and throw off the chains of tyranny." Indeed "the will to be against" (ibid.) forms the core of the Multitude, its ontological condition. With respect to the Ecuadorian case I will discuss, however, resistance among plaintiffs—even the act of being a plaintiff—did not arise spontaneously. Rather, a collective (let alone oppositional) identity in a tort case had to be actively envisioned, produced, and sustained. As others, most eloquently Ernesto Laclau (2004), have argued, Hardt and Negri lack a theory of articulation. In order to grasp the forces that enable the formation of the Multitude, and by extension civil society, we need a theory of articulation to unravel how positionalities get made and maintained—and ultimately contained—within specific historical conjunctures. A theory of articulation begins from the standpoint that linkages (or connections) among elements are not given but require particular conditions of existence to appear at all; furthermore, they are no more eternal than they are natural (cf. Hall 1991, 1996). In the conjoining—the connected relationality—elements (be they subjectivities, entities, or processes) become themselves transformed (Laclau 2007; Laclau and Mouffe 2001), and often what they seek to affect is transformed in the process too.

As I will argue in this case, subaltern subjects were not born resisting. Rather, this potential Multitude (or Multitude in waiting) came to understand who they were and what they sought (their 'common', as it were) through numerous encounters. The more public encounters were mobilizations in which people directly engaged agents of the state, including members of the Ecuadorian National Congress, the Ministry of Energy and Mines, the attorney general's office, and US and Ecuadorian courts. The less public encounters were numerous meetings among themselves and their variously expanding and contracting networks of national and US-based environmental and human rights NGOs. Contrary to Hardt and Negri, it was not "completely obvious [to the plaintiffs] that those who are exploited will resist" (2000: 210). Rather, through collaborative effort (punctuated at times by irreconcilable tension), subaltern subjects produced a 'common'—a shared identity of being marginalized and injured. But they also produced a new shared identity as citizens of a state in which, over a 10-year period, the marginalized increasingly gained recognition and were becoming crucial actors in a larger movement affecting social, political, and juridical change. Importantly, it was through transnational alliances and connections that the plaintiffs came to inhabit the realm of civil society in Ecuador.

Which brings me to the second concern. Hardt and Negri propose that Empire is the emergent supra-national political network that inexorably supersedes the nation-state as the agent of global power. In other words, Empire eclipses and diminishes the significance of the state. While such tendencies are clearly evident—neo-liberal economic reforms have undoubtedly influenced the actions of the Ecuadorian state over the past two decades—the lawsuit against Chevron similarly appears to problematize the notion that the nation-state is on the decline. Particularly salient is the role of law, indeed, the rule of law—key structures and practices that give the state its form, texture, and boundaries. It was not the absence of law (and thus the state) that nurtured and encouraged subaltern activity. Rather, the practices that affirmed the very existence and further entrenchment of law paradoxically facilitated action. By reconfiguring and reinstantiating law, subaltern subjects sought to call one of Empire's quintessential icons—corporate oil—to account. Importantly, legal structures and the rule of law form the very matrix that congeals the power and legitimacy of the nation-state, corporate power, and popular organizing. Contrary to what Hardt and Negri argue in *Empire*, the lawsuit against ChevronTexaco suggests that the nation-state—and the legal regimes that buttress its existence—are evermore prominent in both enabling the expansive reach of global capital and providing avenues through which a multiply constituted subaltern subject might rein in some of Empire's more egregious tendencies. The lawsuit suggests that the legal institutions on which Empire depends may be more discordant and pliable than Hardt and Negri (2000: 20, 31–32) would have us believe and that the Empire-law lockstep may be more contingent.

More broadly, however, the transborder practices that constitute indigenous and non-indigenous plaintiffs, as well as legal process in the United States and Ecuador, urge us to take transnational networks seriously, nuancing Hardt and Negri's divide between Multitude and Empire and, by implication, classical understandings of civil society and the state. That is, by exploring how lived reality is constituted through global networks (regardless of how unevenly), categories such as Empire/Multitude and state/civil society lose their taken-for-granted or assumed content and character. Denying the presupposed existence of these dyads allows us to examine what James Ferguson (2006: 90) calls the "vertical topography of power" implicit in them. Following Ferguson, I suggest that these categories lean on a spatial imaginary in which the Empire/state floats above, the individual/family huddles below, and the Multitude/civil society mediates between the two. This ordered stratigraphy simultaneously instantiates fixed categories and locates them in a hierarchy of value and complexity. It obscures how each of these spheres is relationally constituted through deeply transnational practices. All dimensions of this hierarchical imagery "operate within a profoundly transnationalized global context" (Ferguson 2006: 93). Systematically exploring the networks of connectivity that produce and transform these binaries allows "the constructed and fictive nature of the vertical topography of power increasingly [to become] visible" (ibid.). Before going on, however, a bit of history is in order.

Legal Wrangling in the US Courts

October 2003 was not the first time that the plaintiffs had appeared before a superior court. In point of fact, the hearing in Ecuador was the product of a decade-long legal battle over jurisdiction in the United States. In November 1993, a Philadelphia law firm filed the same class-action lawsuit against Texaco Inc. (*Aguinda, et al. v. Texaco, Inc.*, 93 Civ. 7527 [VLB]) in the United States District Court for the Southern District of New York for having caused environmental degradation and human illness in Ecuador. The lawsuit alleged (as it still does today) that Texaco made strategic decisions in its New York headquarters to maximize its corporate profits by using substandard technology in its Ecuadorian oil operations. Negligent industrial practices, the lawyers for the plaintiffs claim, spewed toxic wastes into water and soil systems throughout the region, severely contaminating the environment and jeopardizing the lives of local people.

The lawsuit contended that industrial negligence began in 1964 when Texaco first gained rights to an oil concession in the Ecuadorian Amazon.[5] In 1967, the company—via its subsidiary Texaco Petroleum Company (TexPet)—discovered oil. By 1972, Texaco had built the trans-Andean pipeline, connecting Amazonian oil fields to a Pacific port. Over the following 28 years, Texaco produced over a billion barrels of crude and in the process indelibly transformed the northern rain forest with thousands of miles of seismic grids, over 300 oil wells, more than 600 open waste pits, numerous processing facilities and pumping stations, an oil refinery, and the bare-bones infrastructure essential for petroleum operations. The network of roads linking oil wells facilitated the homesteading of the region by over 200,000 poor Spanish-speaking farmers or *colonos* (colonists) (Hiroako and Yamamoto 1980; Pichón 1993). In 1992,

Texaco's rights to operate the oil concession ended, the company pulled out of Ecuador, and its operations reverted to the state petroleum company.[6]

The lawsuit alleges that while a number of Texaco's production practices between 1964 and 1992 are questionable, of greatest concern was (and still is) the effect of large, often soccer-field-size earth pits. Texaco dug these pits (at least two) alongside each exploratory and production well, and then dumped the sludge, formation waters, and unusable heavy crude that surfaced during the drilling process—along with the chemical muds and industrial solvents essential for drilling—untreated into these craters. When an oil well was proven to be productive, additional pits were dug at processing facilities where crude was separated out from the waters, sands, and gases also released from the earth. Unlined and open these excavated pits served as holding receptacles for eventual seepage and overflow.

Even during the early years of Texaco's operations, it was standard industrial practice in the US (and indeed Texas law since 1919) to reinject formation waters and subterranean sands at least one mile below the surface of the earth, and to process chemical solvents until they were environmentally safe. According to the plaintiffs' lawyers, Texaco Inc. chose not to implement this technology in order to cut costs. As one of the lawyers for the plaintiffs, Steven Donziger, observed: "Contaminated water is not the effect of just random spills. It is the result of decisions made by Texaco to install a type of drilling process that would lead to the systematic dumping of toxins. Texaco made a decision to dump these toxins into the Amazon to save money and increase its profits."[7] The decision not to reinject formation waters back into the subterranean strata allegedly reduced the company's per-barrel production costs by approximately $3 and saved the parent corporation roughly $5 billion over the course of its operations in Ecuador.

Although Texaco's practices were sufficiently effective to get and keep oil flowing, the lawsuit contends that they were (and continue to be) harmful to humans and the environment. A growing number of studies document the detrimental and deadly effects of oil contamination on Amazonian populations: high rates of intestinal disease, miscarriages, birth deformities, and various cancers. Physical disorders, the plaintiffs argue, are a direct result of environmental contamination. According to them, now Chevron is ultimately accountable for decisions that condemned many Amazonian residents to living in toxic dumps.

At the time of the initial filing of the lawsuit in 1993, Texaco Inc. summarily denied all charges, claiming complete exoneration and motioning (on multiple occasions) that the case be dismissed from US courts. The multinational corporation contended that a subsidiary-of-a-subsidiary-of-a-subsidiary-of-a-subsidiary was liable for operations in Ecuador and not the so-called parent company. This four-times-removed Texaco subsidiary was legally based in Quito, Ecuador's capital, and it was there, the multinational maintained, that Ecuadorian citizens would have to prove wrongdoing and seek restitution.

Three years after its original filing, the case was dismissed from the New York district court in November 1996. In light of new evidence, the plaintiffs petitioned later that year that the court reconsider its decision. In August 1997, however, the New York district court dismissed the case once more. The following year, in October 1998, the Second Circuit Court of Appeals reversed the lower courts decision and reinstated the case. Three years after that, in May 2001, the New York district court dismissed the case once more. In August 2002, the Second Circuit Court of Appeals heard the case again, but this time it upheld the lower court's decision and ruled that the case should be tried in Ecuador. In May 2003, the case was accepted in the Lago Agrio Superior Court, and plaintiffs gathered to commemorate the beginning of the 'trial of the century' in October 2003.

Producing a 'Class' of Common Resistance

Although the ruling of the appellate court was not what the plaintiffs' lawyers had sought, much had transpired in Ecuador on both the social and legal fronts between 1993 and 2003, making Ecuador a more inviting forum for the plaintiffs and arguably a less predictable one for the defendant (Sawyer 2006). What I would like to suggest is that over the intervening decade, plaintiffs not only forged a 'class' (where there had been none) but also produced a social, political, and legal environment in which the outcome of a lawsuit by poor peasants and Indians against the second largest oil company in the US would not be a foregone conclusion. Importantly, transnational alliances and collaborations were crucial to the practices that forged civil society and the state.

When the suit was first filed in New York in 1993, the idea of a class action was a foreign concept in Ecuador. A collection of people wishing to sue a corporate entity for industrial contamination under Ecuadorian law would each have to do so individually; there was no legal mechanism by which they could sue as a group. Consequently, in order for the New York lawsuit to make sense to people and truly carry the weight of a moral mandate, the 'class' (or grouping) of the class action had to be constructed in the minds, hearts, and actions of the *indígenas* and *colonos* affected by Texaco's oil operations.

Texaco's oil operations had not sparked spontaneous resistance. There was no pre-existing Multitude here, no pre-existing social capital—à la Putnam (2000)—of deep community networks and norms of reciprocity and trust. In fact, forging a 'class' in the northern Amazon was neither inevitable nor easy. Texaco's operations covered a 400,000-hectare area (approximately 66 times the size of Manhattan), and those living in the region shared no loyalties and experienced no common bond. Indigenous peoples, who accounted for one-sixth of the class of plaintiffs (approximately 5,000 out of 30,000 individuals), were divided among five different ethnic groups: Cofan, Siona, Secoya, Huaorani, and Kichwa. The Cofan, Siona, and Secoya were perhaps the most vocal protagonists of the lawsuit among indigenous plaintiffs. But even among them (or between them and the other indigenous groups), there was no sui generis bond of indigenous fellowship and camaraderie. Histories of colonization and modernization from the Spanish conquest to the present had variously isolated and divided northern indigenous groups. *Colonos* living in the northern Amazon constituted a hodgepodge grouping of individuals—people who had arrived in the region at different moments and from diverse parts of the country over the previous 30 years. And while the majority of *colonos* are poor Spanish-speaking peasants, indigenous people from the sierra and the southern Amazon were also often subsumed within this grouping. Consequently, when the lawsuit was first filed in 1993, being a *colono* did not mean that one belonged to an identifiably cohesive group.

To complicate matters further, inter-ethnic relations in the northern Amazon had been tense ever since the arrival of *colonos* (Bustamante 1995; Gomez et al. 1992). Beginning in the 1960s, and once Texaco had built roads, *colonos* moved to the region, often under the auspices of government-sponsored programs to colonize the rain forest's so-called *tierras baldías*, or barren lands (Trujillo 1992; Uquillas 1984, 1989; Zevallos 1989). By and large, *colonos* usurped and homesteaded Indian lands, severely reducing indigenous territory over the decades (Vickers 1984). By the late 1970s and early 1980s, the Cofan, Siona, and Secoya Indians managed to stave off the further colonizing of their lands and acquired legal communal titles. These adjudications, however, secured only a small fraction of what had once been their territorial expanse. In effect, a great deal of indigenous social fabric had already been significantly disrupted through displacement and disease. As a consequence of this history, distrust and suspicion colored much interaction between *indígenas* and *colonos*.

In 1993, Cristobal Bonifaz (an Ecuadorian-born attorney long practicing law in the United States) succeeded in encouraging leaders of the *colonos* and four major northern Amazonian indigenous groups (Cofan, Siona, Secoya, and Kichwa) to join him in New York City to file the class-action lawsuit against Texaco. In Bonifaz's mind, what allowed *colonos* and *indígenas* to join forces was an understanding of common injury. Both groups had experienced the despair and humiliation of having suffered the consequences of Texaco's operations.

But it is one thing to file a class-action lawsuit in New York City—with US-based lawyers staging the scene, directing the action, and footing the bill—and quite another to form and sustain a social movement among historically antagonistic groups. Inhabitants of the northern Amazon (Indian and campesino alike) often voiced a sense of victimization and marginalization in terms of not being seen by either the company or the state. They often felt as though they were made invisible—their humanity inconsequential and their bodies phantom-like (Sawyer 2001). But isolated and individual senses of pain, humiliation, and anger do not make a social movement. So how did they form a class? What practices brought about a civil society?

Given the power of Ecuador's indigenous movement, analysts often surmise that indigenous peoples' sophisticated organization and growing ethnic cachet gave them and their leaders strong and coherent voices to lead the plaintiffs, both nationally and internationally. The Cofan, Siona, Secoya, northern Kichwa, and Huaorani nationalities were, after all, part of CONFENIAE, the regional confederation of Indians in the Ecuadorian Amazon. But when CONFENIAE was formed in 1980, the ethnic groups in the north had already experienced radical dislocation, disease, and death among their population. Some estimates suggest that the Cofan were 15,000 when Texaco arrived in 1964 and had dwindled to less than 1,000 by 1980. Although this demographic decline most probably began before Texaco arrived in Ecuador—as with earlier waves of extractive activity, disease preceded material presence—there is no doubt that it occurred and devastatingly unraveled indigenous social fabric. This scenario reverberated across all the nationalities in the northern Amazon. Thus, despite being in 1993 part of a larger (and at times radical) network of Indian organizations, the indigenous people in the northern Amazon were not resoundingly strong when the lawsuit was first filed. The sense of being defeated and oppressed weighed heavily on these northern groups, despite moments of spectacular bravery and strength (ACOINCO and CEDIME 1991; Trujillo 1981).

Dis-ease—bodily, social, cultural, and environmental—had dramatically undermined indigenous reality. In the hallway outside the courtroom on the trial's third day, Toribio Aguinda (a former president of the Cofan nationality between 1993 and 2002) told me: "We used to live across a vast forest. Today we are contained and contaminated; we are completely contaminated, by what Texaco has done. The Cofan territory is encircled by Texaco [oil] wells. And the waste from those well and their [pumping] station flows into our rivers and streams, and passes through our territory ... Both our bodies and our territory have been disfigured by petroleum." Among the crowd protesting outside the Lago Agrio courthouse, a Secoya elder explained the recent history of his people this way: "Today, the Nacionalidad Secoya, we now live in tiny areas in what was once our great forest. The land and the large rivers have all been polluted and brought to destruction. Texaco and the wells have caused much damage, and have made many of our people ill ... Our people and territory are broken and bleeding."

Indeed, the social upheaval and trauma that the Cofan, Siona, Secoya, northern Kichwa, and Huaorani had experienced made them minority voices in lowland indigenous political organizing since the 1970s. More dominant and vocal were the Kichwa, Shuar, and Achuar of the central and southern Amazon, who sought to assert a strident indigenous politics of opposition to oil (Sawyer 2004). In 1993, a still overriding stance of the smaller northern groups, by contrast, was one of confusion, of being overwhelmed and at times downtrodden. Standing behind a banner that read "Amazonia libre de ChevronToxico" (Amazon free of ChevronToxico) on the street outside the Lago Agrio courtroom, the Secoya elder noted: "Once, we were the guardians and masters of all the splendor of the Amazon. Today we are the guardians of the contamination. We are the guardians of poverty. We are the guardians of disease and illness. We are the guardians of our suffering." Many northern indigenous people were unclear about how to respond to their plight. Over the previous decades (and on through the present), representatives of Texaco had offered them gifts and trinkets as compensation for their apprehension and pain, emotional and physical, singular and collective. While many groups often staunchly rebuked these gestures (especially the Cofan), for others it was hard to resist them when so much neglect had shaped their reality.

Recurrent and chronic health problems sparked initial action among the *colonos* as groups of neighbors along rural roads formed collectives within years of their arrival to voice concern over their ailing bodies. Most prominent among these neighborhood associations were the ad hoc groups that women (often with the active support of members of the progressive church) formed in the early 1970s as a means to lodge complaints with TexPet. As Luz recalled over lunch a few days after the trial began in 2003: "I remember traveling to the company clinic when my son was an infant and meeting other women there whose babies were also covered with scabs and open sores." Like many *colonos*, Luz had moved from the southern sierra to a *finca*, or farm, just north of Lago Agrio in 1971. Soon she became active in organizing women on the road heading north toward the border with Colombia; their efforts grew to be part of the provincial-wide Federacion de Mujeres. "Our children kept on getting sicker," Luz continued, "as the toxins and contamination got worse. Folks from Texaco would tell us that oil doesn't hurt people. But the doctor told my neighbor that her five-year-old son had leukemia. That was when we started to organize ourselves."

Luz and the other women and their children were among the thousands of Amazonian residents who bathed, washed clothes, fished, and cleaned food in rivers whose waters and sediments reeked of hydrocarbons. And their experience contradicted what Texaco representatives told them. Wastes from oil operations contain known carcinogens that bio-accumulate. Crude oil's most toxic components have been shown to affect negatively the reproductive and cellular development of all life forms. Children in particular are susceptible to many of petroleum's ill effects. A number of health studies report an increased incidence of skin and intestinal disease, miscarriages and reproductive abnormalities, and high rates of cancer in the region—most notably stomach, larynx, cervical, and, among children, leukemia (Acción Ecológica 2003; Hurtig and San Sebastián 2002; San Sebastián et al. 2001). One epidemiological report of the northern Amazon indicates that children under 14 years old who live in areas exposed to petroleum are 150 percent more likely to suffer from leukemia (cancer of the blood) than children who do not live in exposed areas (Hurtig and San Sebastian 2004). During the 2003 opening proceedings in Lago Agrio, one of the same epidemiologists testified that "in communities exposed to oil operations, eighteen out of twenty rivers were contaminated with total hydrocarbons between 5 and 250 times higher than the limit permitted for human consumption."[8]

Despite the national and international press (as well as, at times, the lawyers and US judges) repeatedly christening this a "lawsuit by Amazonian Indians" against a US corporation, in point of fact, *colonos* have been the engine of solidarity and perseverance since the case was first filed over a decade ago. With the guidance and support of CONFENIAE and CONAIE (Ecuador's pan-national indigenous confederation) and key national and international environmental rights organizations (specifically, the progressive church, Acción Ecológica, Oxfam America, the Center for Economic and Social Rights (CEDES), and Amazon Watch), *colonos* have led their Indian neighbors and formed the Frente de Defensa de la Amazonia in 1994. During the 1990s, the Frente became a formidable force in the northern Amazon. Early actions focused on organizing monthly workshops in rural communities (initially in coordination with Acción Ecológica and later with CEDES) to educate people about the lawsuit and the US judicial process, the plaintiffs' legal rights in Ecuador and the United

States, and the effects of oil contamination on human physiology and ecological systems. In collaboration with Acción Ecológica, community leaders taught the plaintiffs how to conduct inventories of the presence and effects of Texaco's operations in their communities. In addition, the Frente coordinated direct actions in support of the lawsuit. The plaintiffs and their supporters organized marches, public debates, protests, and occupations to pressure the Ecuadorian executive branch to support the case, to lobby the National Congress to enact protective legislation, to encourage a boycott of Texaco gasoline, and to demonstrate to the corporation and the larger public the moral righteousness of their cause.

Engaging Executive and Judicial Orders

From his ersatz stage, Pablo bellowed to the demonstrators gathered outside the Superior Court in Lago Agrio: "The hour of justice has arrived." Behind him, a huge black banner read "JUSTICIA" in bold lettering. Both Pablo's words and the banner signaled that many who had previously been wary of Ecuador's political and judicial system now increasingly believed that select state officials and courts might treat them fairly. Although discrimination and injustice still abounded in Ecuador, much had also changed. Throughout the 1990s and into the second millennium, social upheaval rocked Ecuador, and the Frente was part of this broad-based social action. Between 1992 and 2003, popular groups—often led by CONAIE—pressed for far-reaching social and political changes. While never achieving complete victory, they rejected the neo-liberal economic agenda that the government had adopted with unprecedented zeal. In addition to ousting three national presidents (Abdala Bucaram in 1997, Mahuad in 2000, and Gutiérrez in 2005), this ever-burgeoning indigenous and non-indigenous movement compelled crucial administrative reversals, constitutional reforms, and legislative changes.

A few instances directly connected to the lawsuit are worth noting, for they were key to creating an identity of common will among subaltern subjects. Similarly, they illustrate some of the multiple practices that tacked between North American and Ecuadorian space to constitute the entities we define as state and civil society. Not only were these tacking practices dependent on transnational forces (non-governmental and legal), they also revealed how the state and civil society were mutually constituted. Neither was the state above nor was civil society below, but rather each was formed transnationally through the actions of the other.

In 1996, the New York district court stood poised to throw the case out of the federal court system. That January and again in June 1996, the presiding judge (Jed S. Rakoff) had received an affidavit and amicus brief from the Ecuadorian ambassador to the United States, Edgar Teran Teran, reiterating the Ecuadorian state's position. From the moment the case was first filed, the standing regime of Sixto Duran Ballen had been vociferously opposed to the class action, presenting the court with affidavits and an amicus brief in January 1994 (two months after the case was filed in New York) asserting that such a lawsuit would endanger national sovereignty and undermine future foreign investment precisely when the state was diligently implementing neo-liberal reforms. On 12 November 1996, Judge Rakoff dismissed the case from the US federal court on the grounds that the United States was not the appropriate jurisdiction in which to hear the case (based on *forum non conveniens*, international comity, and failure to join indispensable parties, i.e., the Republic of Ecuador).[9]

Upon hearing this verdict, the Frente—in conjunction with its solid national supporters (especially CONAIE, CONFENIAE, Acción Ecológica, and CEDES)— threw its mobilizing into high gear. Two of the rationales (inconvenient forum and indispensable parties) were legal arguments that the plaintiffs' lawyers needed to address. But one rationale for dismissal—international comity—was a concern that the plaintiffs could confront immediately. On 18 November 1996 (four days after Judge Rakoff's decision), a group of indigenous and non-indigenous plaintiffs, together with human rights and environmental activists, occupied the Ecuadorian attorney general's office in Quito in hopes of persuading him to officially reverse the Ecuadorian state stance.

Their actions hinged on the internationally recognized legal meaning of comity. As detailed by the Second Circuit Court of Appeals in reviewing the case, international comity is "'the recognition which one nation allows within its territory to the legislative, executive or judicial acts of another nation.'"[10] Under the principles of comity, United States courts "ordinarily refuse to review acts of foreign governments and defer to proceedings taking place in foreign countries, allowing those acts and proceedings to have extraterritorial effect in the United States."[11] This doctrine "is best understood as a guide where the issues to be resolved are entangled in international relations."[12]

In dismissing the complaints in this litigation on international comity, the New York district court explicitly adopted the comity considerations articulated by the Texas district court in dismissing *Sequihua, et al. v. Texaco, Inc.*[13] The *Sequihua* lawsuit—filed only months before the *Aguinda, et al.* class action— similarly alleged environmental and health damages to Ecuadorian plaintiffs as a result of Texaco's oil operations in the Amazon. Applying the factors set forth in Restatement (3d) of Foreign Relations #403 (1986), the federal court of Texas's southern district concluded that "the challenged activity and the alleged harm occurred in Ecuador"; that the conduct at issue was regulated by the Republic of Ecuador and "exercise of jurisdiction by this Court would interfere with Ecuador's sovereign right to control its own environment and resources"; and that "the Republic of Ecuador has expressed its strenuous objections to the exercise of jurisdiction by this Court."[14]

But things in Ecuador had changed since 1994. In May 1996, Ecuadorians had elected a new president, Abdala Bucaram, who had expressed his support for peasant and Indian plaintiffs while campaigning. Indeed, with the Bucaram administration taking power in August 1996, the June 1996 statements and briefs that Ecuadorian Ambassador Teran Teran filed in the district court were the last-ditch efforts of a lame-duck presidency.

Within days after plaintiffs had occupied his office in November 1996, the Ecuadorian attorney general, Dr. Leonidas Plaza Verduga, flew to New York to proclaim to the US federal court that the Ecuadorian regime now supported the lawsuit against Texaco. By then, the plaintiffs' lawyers had petitioned Judge Rakoff to reconsider his decision, given the admission of new evidence.[15] Not only did the state of Ecuador fully support the lawsuit and the US court's jurisdiction, it also wished to intervene as co-plaintiff in the case—which at least momentarily also undermined the rationale for dismissing the lawsuit on the grounds of "indispensable party."[16]

In truth, this was not the first time that representatives of the Ecuadorian state had supported the lawsuit. As early as January 1994, soon after the case was initially filed, the president of the National Congress and presidents of four key congressional commissions wrote a letter to President Ballen, voicing their strong support for the plaintiffs' lawsuit and expressing anger at the Ecuadorian ambassador's actions.[17] In June 1996, the Plenary of the Permanent Legislative Commissions strongly endorsed the lawsuit in a congressional resolution and published their endorsement in the national press.[18] All these congressional actions were the direct result of mobilizations by the Frente. Beginning in 1994, the Frente arranged meetings with key senators, held public debates in Quito, and organized mass protests outside the National Congress, demanding that the legislature renounce the administration's position and back the plaintiffs' cause.

In the whirlwind of Ecuadorian regime change in the late 1990s (Bucaram was thrown out of office in February 1997), the government of interim president Fabian Alarcon, while in support of the lawsuit and the plaintiffs, took a less strident stance despite the Frente's continued actions to mobilize support. And in August 1997, Judge Rakoff dismissed the case from his court once more.

But the fact that the Frente had mobilized the Ecuadorian government to support the case allowed the US appellate court to think twice. In September 1997, the plaintiffs' lawyers appealed the lower court's decision. The appeal had effect. A year later, in October 1998, the Court of Appeals dismissed Judge Rakoff's ruling and sent the case back to his court, asking in particular that the Ecuadorian government once more clarify its position with respect to the case. Again, the Ecuadorian ambassador (this time Ivonne Baki) sent Judge Rakoff a letter expressing that the state did not back the lawsuit. Again in response, the Frente mobilized into high gear. Along with appealing to the National Congress and once again holding large protests in Quito, they organized a non-violent occupation of the attorney general's office. And again, the Ecuadorian state (this time via the minister of foreign relations) reversed the ambassador's statement and declared its support for the lawsuit against Texaco, specifically noting that the northern Amazon was fraught with grave environmental and social problems as a result of Texaco's oil operations.

After prolonged debates, Judge Rakoff dismissed the case once more in May 2001. In the interim, however, the legal standing of the case had crystallized. When the Second Circuit Court of Appeals reviewed the case in 1998, the three-judge panel made clear both during their hearings with the plaintiffs' and defendant's lawyers and in their official ruling that the lawsuit could be dismissed from US courts only if Texaco Inc. agreed to submit to Ecuadorian jurisdiction. The Frente's actions—some highly visibly (such as public occupations and protests) and others relatively invisible (including numerous community meetings, seminars, debates)—were indispensable to the legal process in the US. They kept the lawsuit alive in the US courts; they insured that the case did not become a forgotten memory among the Ecuadorian people; they sustained a vigilant public eye (in both the North and South) on potential corporate or state improprieties; and they created a sense of shared identity among subaltern subjects whose oppositional stance compelled legal change in Ecuador. Importantly, the Frente's transnationally networked practices shaped legal process in the United States, allowing the appellate court to review the lawsuit and condition a corporation's effective submission to a foreign court.

In Ecuador in the late 1990s, intense social pressure brought about the rewriting of the Ecuadorian constitution. New articles of the 1998 constitution state that living in a healthy environment is a collective right (Art. 86) and that communities must be consulted and allowed to participate in state decisions that might affect the environment in which they live (Art. 88). In 1998, Ecuador also signed the International Labour Organization's (ILO) Convention 169, which recognizes the collective rights of indigenous peoples and their right to demand recompense should their territory or its resources be undermined. But supporters of the lawsuit (and those concerned with potential corporate abuse in general) knew that more was needed, should the case ever be tried in Ecuador, especially given that only a small portion of the plaintiffs were indigenous. In particular, CEDES, together with other environmental and legal rights scholars and activists, worked with the Frente toward the introduction of tort law into the Ecuadorian legal system. Joining forces with select senators and representatives in the National Congress, they managed to pass Ecuador's first major environmental law. The July 1999 *Ley de Gestión Ambiental* specifically protects individuals against actions that violate environmental norms, and it allows individuals to file the Ecuadorian equivalent of a class-action lawsuit—an *acción popular*—against entities that have allegedly undermined human health and/or the environment. The 1999 *Ley de Gestión Ambiental* was essential for the lawsuit when it was filed in Ecuador in 2003—indeed, it formed the legal basis for the suit. Along with constitutional reforms and ILO 169, the legislative change made the Ecuadorian court system more sympathetic than ever before to the plaintiffs and their plight.

Circumstances had also changed in the United States. In October 2001, Texaco Inc. merged with Chevron Corporation. When the new company, ChevronTexaco Corporation, moved its headquarters to San Ramon, California, Amazon Watch—an environmental rights NGO on the North American West Coast—expanded the US campaign in support of the plaintiffs. The organization flew peasant and indigenous leaders to the US on multiple occasions. It organized protests in front of corporate headquarters where—on more than one occasion—the Ecuadorians, carrying a poster-sized faux bill from the "Amazon Rainforest Collection Agency," demanded appointments with ChevronTexaco's CEO. Amazon Watch also organized meetings between visiting plaintiffs and residents of San Ramon. Amazingly enough, concerned community and religious leaders from California traveled to the contaminated regions of the Ecuadorian Amazon to see the effects of (now) ChevronTexaco's practices first hand. With their growing concern, they formed an organization, San Ramon Cares, and have brought local pressure to bear on the corporation that calls their town home.

In 2004, 2005, and 2006, Amazon Watch coordinated actions with Amnesty International and Trillium, a socially responsible investment firm. Having garnered the support of large state pension funds in California and New York, this alliance filed a shareholders' resolution. The resolution requests that "the Board of Directors prepare a report on new initiatives by management to address the specific health and environmental concerns of communities affected by unremediated waste and other sources of oil-related contamination in the area where Texaco operated in Ecuador."[19] In both 2004 and 2005, representatives from Amnesty, Amazon Watch, and Trillium, along with two plaintiffs, presented the resolution to the Board of Directors at the company's annual shareholder meetings. On each occasion, two plaintiffs from Ecuador, bearing gifts of contaminated water, spoke directly to ChevronTexaco's CEO, David O'Reilly; these were interventions directed toward the executive of a different order.

Just as social justice and business concerns in the US increased public scrutiny of corporate activity overseas, so intriguing developments on the legal front were bolstering the US court's capacity to extend its power beyond the nation's borders and for Third World courts to do so as well. When the Second Circuit Court of Appeals decided in 2002 that the class-action lawsuit should be heard in Ecuador, it made its ruling dependent on certain conditions. According to the plaintiffs' lawyers, because the case they presented was so compelling, the appellate court, in sending the lawsuit overseas, was obliged to circumscribe ChevronTexaco's defense for plausible deniability. The conditions that the court set were (1) that Texaco Inc. submit to Ecuadorian law; (2) that documents obtained during the 'discovery' period, which up to then had been confidential, could be used in an Ecuadorian trial; and (3) that the decision of the Ecuadorian court could be enforceable in the United States. In the words of Cristobal Bonifaz, the plaintiffs' then chief US-based lawyer: "We won a victory when the New York court forced ChevronTexaco to show up [in Ecuador] and comply. Here we have a situation in which an American court forces an American company to appear before a Third World court and comply with whatever comes out of that court. This case has the potential to establish a new accountability for US oil companies that think they can operate abroad without adhering to responsible environmental practices. On the face of it, this is a 'David versus Goliath' battle. However, the United States court has leveled the playing field by ruling that a small court in a remote town of Ecuador has the same power over a $99 billion multinational corporation as a federal court in Manhattan. This alone is a breakthrough."[20]

All these gestures—openings and closings—are nodes of articulation that produce both Empire/Multitude and the state/civil society not as one being above and one being below but as artifacts of grounded action woven together through transnational connectivity.

Lessons from Empire

Hardt and Negri undoubtedly signal important tendencies that are clearly discernable capacities evident across the globe. Much of what they describe resonates with many of the dynamics at play in the suit against Chevron. Yet the lawsuit also intimates different tendencies at work.

Empire is a book about globalization; Empire is the form that sovereignty takes under conditions of globalization. In the story Hardt and Negri recount, although global capitalism has caused the nation-state's sovereignty to wane, sovereignty per se is not on the decline. Rather, sovereignty has been rescaled from the nation-state to the global level. State institutions clearly persist. But now when governments intervene, they will do so in the name of Empire; that is, they will invoke a consistent juridical logic, what one scholar calls, "the logic of the imperial imperatives of Empire" (Passavant 2004: 3). Empire is, in Hardt and Negri's words (2000: 9), "a new inscription of authority and a new design of the production of norms and legal instruments of coercion that guarantee contracts and resolve conflicts." In their analysis, this "tends to make nation-states merely instruments to record the flows of the commodities, monies, and populations that [Empire] set[s] in motion" (ibid.: 31).

The lawsuit against Chevron suggests, however, that nation-states under Empire do not simply "capture and distribute the flows of wealth to and from the global power" (Hardt and Negri 2000: 310). Nation-states are more than merely "filters of the flow of global circulation and regulators of the articulations of global command" (ibid.). A number of scholars nuance Hardt and Negri's assessment of the future of the nation-state by considering how its sovereignty is being reconfigured. As David Held and his collaborators note, although the nation-state is far from disappearing, "states no longer, if they ever did, retain sole command of what transpires within their own territorial boundaries. Complex global systems, from the financial to the ecological, connect the fates of communities in one locale to the fates of communities in distant regions of the world" (Held et al. 1999: 8). Rather than clearly advancing the decline of the state, other scholars suggest that globalization is re-engineering the power, function, and authority of the state and ushering in new forms of governmentality (Ferguson 1999, 2006; Ong 2006). These scholars suggest that nation-state sovereignty should not be thought of as singular and absolute, but rather as 'graduated' or gradated, juxtaposed in varying degrees with the expanding jurisdiction of non-governmental organizations, corporate formations, institutions of international governance, and international law (Ferguson 2006; Ong 2006). Still others note that rather than diminishing, the power of states is being reconstituted in an effort to engage with the growing complexity of governance in an increasingly "intertwined world of distant proximities" (Rosenau 2003)

As the Chevron case demonstrates, differently positioned actors (be they popular, corporate, or judicial) are affecting the texture of the reconfigured state both within and beyond national borders. Connective concerns allowed the actions of judges in the New York federal court and of subaltern plaintiffs in the Ecuadorian Amazon to ricochet off one another, despite the fact that they rarely engaged directly. These actions, in turn, together shaped the practices that form what is understood as the state, as well as the workings of Empire. On the one hand, judicial rulings in the US federal court compelled mobilization among the plaintiffs—mobilization that changed the Ecuadorian state's official position with respect to the lawsuit and helped introduce critical legislation into Ecuadorian law. On the other hand, subaltern activities in Ecuador compelled further review of the case by different judicial bodies in the US, shuffling it back and forth between the federal and appellate courts. That is, collective action by subaltern subjects on the margins of Empire helped shape judicial process in the United States, "the narrow pinnacle in the pyramid ... of the global constitution of Empire" (Hardt and Negri 2000: 309).

Furthermore, the Second Circuit Court of Appeals in New York did not rule in line with the logic of the imperial imperatives of Empire. Rather than deny the lawsuit a hearing, the court upheld the validity of the case by dismissing it from US jurisdiction and sending it to Ecuador under certain conditions. Echoing Judge Vincent I. Broderick's order over the case before his death in April 1995, the Court of Appeals noted that "dismissal on grounds of *forum non conveniens* would be contingent on Texaco's first agreeing to submit to personal jurisdiction in the courts of Ecuador [and] ... the Court might retain jurisdiction over the injunctive portions of the action."[21] That is, the US federal Court of Appeals ordered Chevron—a corporation that never worked in Ecuador but had assumed all of Texaco's rights and liabilities upon the corporate merger in 2001—to submit to Ecuadorian law. And were an Ecuadorian court—a court that does not have authority over Chevron Corporation—to rule in favor of the plaintiffs, then the US federal court could compel Chevron to comply and carry out any restitution. In effect, the legal decision of an Ecuadorian court could be enforced on US soil.

Similarly, the lawsuit ran counter to Hardt and Negri's political prescription for opposition. Empire, they argue, cannot be overthrown, yet it can be contested and ultimately undermined through the withdrawal of constituent power. Their proposition is that the Multitude confront the machinations of Empire with the tactics of exodus: "Democracy today takes the form of a subtraction, a flight, an exodus from sovereignty" (2004: 341; cf. Hardt and Negri 2000: 210–218). The subaltern subjects suing Chevron, however, have essentially done the opposite. They have intimately and provocatively engaged the very site that instantiates and legitimizes state authority, as well as the interstate system—the law. Struggles over executive reversals and legislative reform became a primary site in which subaltern subjects forged an identity as transgressive beings, an identity that increasingly connected them to each other, to a state, to a foreign judiciary, and to transnational NGO networks. Neither did resistance spontaneously arise, nor, as Hardt and Negri suggest, did it "leap vertically, directly to the virtual center of Empire" (2000: 58). Rather, this struggle became linked through a web-like fashion with other struggles, articulating with them to engender its identity and politics. Laclau (2004: 28) reminds us that "the ability and the will to resist are not a gift from heaven but require a set of subjective transformations that are only the product of the struggles themselves *and that can fail to take place.*" These subjective transformations need not occur. Moreover, in the case of the lawsuit, indigenous and non-indigenous plaintiffs emerged transnationally. Although they embodied a historically entrenched and place-specific identity, they were also undeniably the outcome of networked forces reverberating within and across national borders.

The Chevron case demonstrates that analytical templates—Empire/Multitude or state/civil society—do not mirror separate and distinguishable spheres. Rather, all sorts of connective action and compromised transnational articulations are implicated in the very formation of each. In this sense, then, it is impossible to view the 'state' or Empire as a fixed assemblage of reified and disembodied structures. The form and operations of each are the effect of highly situated and embodied complexes that emerge through specific social practices (Gupta 1995; Gupta and Sharma 2006; Hansen and Stepputat 2001; Mitchell 1991; Nelson 1999). Likewise, it is impossible to view 'civil society' or the Multitude as inherently locally grounded and democratic. The form and operations of each are the effect of globally situated and transnational complexes that emerge through specific social practices. This understanding transforms the implicit topography of power often subsumed with the terms 'state/civil society', and by extension 'Empire/Multitude'. Perhaps, as Ferguson (2006: 103) suggests, what passes as civil society is best "conceptualized not as 'below' the state, but as integral parts of a new, transnational apparatus of governmentality"—that is, as constitutive elements for new forms of knowledge/power concerned with the conduct of conduct, the governing of people, resources, and ideas. "This new apparatus," Ferguson (ibid.) continues, "does not replace the older system of nation-states (which is—let us be clear—far from about to disappear), but overlays it and coexists with it." Such an analytic allows for thinking of civil societies (or the Multitude) "not as challengers pressing up against the state [or Empire] from below but as horizontal contemporaries of the organs of the state" (ibid.), co-existing political embodiments that can quite literally shape the sphere of authority and legitimacy that make up the state as well as the practices of Empire.

Many questions remain as to how the ongoing trial in Ecuador will be resolved. As David Held reminds us: "In a world where powerful states make decisions not just for their own people but for others as well, and transnational actors and forces cut across the boundaries of national communities in diverse ways, the questions of who should be accountable to whom, and on what basis, do not easily resolve themselves" (Held et al. 1999: 81). Any final outcome of this lawsuit is surely to be long in coming. When the present trial ends, the losing side will appeal the verdict first with the Superior Court of Appeals in Lago Agrio and then the Ecuadorian Supreme Court in Quito. As of this writing, however, the Frente—working with a transnational network of US- and Ecuadorian-based lawyers, social justice groups, and environmental rights organizations—has forged a formidable social movement that is influencing legal process in the United States, challenging the norms of corporate action, transforming the relations between formally inimical groups, and embodying novel forms of political engagement in Ecuador and beyond. Simultaneously, the plaintiffs are setting legal precedent and interrupting understandings of globalization.

Acknowledgments

The author would like to thank Ted Fischer for his insights and for the invitation to participate in this volume. I am ever thankful to Paulina Garzon, Pablo Fajardo, and Steven Donziger for their perceptive comments and engagement. Some of the ethnographic material in this chapter will appear in a short chapter titled "Suing Chevron-Texaco" in the *Ecuador Reader* (forthcoming, Duke University Press).

Suzana Sawyer is Associate Professor of Anthropology at the University of California, Davis. Her book *Crude Chronicles* (2004) explores conflicts among indigenous peoples, a multinational corporation, and a neo-liberalizing state in Ecuador. She argues that struggles over resources are simultaneously material and symbolic, remaking (and containing) nature, nation, and citizenship in the process. Her current research examines a class-action lawsuit against Texaco/Chevron from three different angles: critical legal studies and corporate law, science studies and epidemiology, and civil society and social movements. She has published in *Cultural Anthropology*, *Cultural Critique*, *Journal of Latin American Anthropology*, *Latin American Perspectives*, and *Political and Legal Anthropology Review*.

Notes

1. Seeing as how the century had just begun, one might conclude that the plaintiffs' rhetoric was somewhat hyperbolic.
2. In October 2001, Texaco Inc. merged with Chevron Corporation at the cost of $45 billion, creating a new entity, ChevronTexaco. In April 2005, the ChevronTexaco board of directors changed the name of the company to Chevron. Later that year, the corporation bought Unocal for $17.5 billion.
3. For complete legal references and notes on the circumstances surrounding the legal case against Texaco—then ChevronTexaco and now Chevron—see Sawyer (2001, 2002, 2006).
4. Five years before publishing *Empire*, Michael Hardt (1995: 40) proclaimed that "the social conditions necessary for civil society no longer exist" in Western Europe and North America. Latin America (as he more likely suspects) does not fit neatly into his argument for civil society's withering away.
5. In March 1964, Texaco Petroleum Company (TexPet) signed a contract with the government of Ecuador to explore and exploit hydrocarbons in the Ecuadorian Amazon. From 1965 to 1973, Ecuadorian Gulf Oil Company (Gulf) joined Texaco as an investment partner. According to the contract, TexPet was the operator of the consortium and as such assumed all technical responsibility for exploration and exploitation operations. In 1974, as large-scale oil extraction began, CEPE (Corporacion Estatal Petrolera Ecuatoriana), the then state oil company, acquired a 25 percent interest in the consortium. In May 1977, Ecuadorian Gulf Oil Company sold its share to CEPE, resulting in the state company owning 62 percent of the consortium's assets. TexPet maintained its role as operator, the technical partner responsible for the consortium's operations.
6. TexPet ceased managing its concession in Ecuador on 30 June 1990. It relinquished all interest in the concession on 6 June 1992.
7. Conversation with Steven Donziger, 27 October 2003.

8. Miguel San Sebastian, testimony, 29 October 2003, page 3.
9. Ruling of Judge Jed S. Rakoff, U.S.D.J. United States District Court, Southern District of New York, *Maria Aguinda, et al. v. Texaco, Inc.*, 93 Civ. 7527 (JSR), decided 12 November 1996. Memorandum Order, 12 August 1997.
10. As quoted in the Court of Appeals Second Circuit's ruling on 5 October 1998, *Pravin Banker Associates, Ltd. v. Banco Popular del Peru*, 109 F.3d 850, 845 (2d Cir 1997) (quoting *Hilton v. Guyot*, 159 US 113, 164 [1895]).
11. Ibid.
12. As quoted in the Court of Appeals Second Circuit's ruling on 5 October 1998, in re *Maxwell Communication Corp.*, 93 F.3d 1036, 1047 (2d Cir. 1996).
13. See *Sequihua, et al. v. Texaco, Inc.*, Civil Action # H-93-3432, ruling of the United States District Court for the Southern District of Texas, Houston Division, 27 January 1994. See 847 F. Supp. At 63. Although (in the opinion of a few lawyers) poorly research and argued, *Sequihua* was a class-action lawsuit against Texaco Inc. (among other companies) filed in the state court of Harris County, Texas, on 31 August 1993, on behalf of 30,000 Ecuadorians who lived in the Amazon region. On 27 October 1993, the *Sequihua* lawsuit was removed to the federal court in the Southern District of Texas, Houston Division.
14. Ibid.
15. Plaintiffs' lawyers moved for reconsideration under Rule 3(j) (later renumbered as Rule 6.3) of the Local Civil Rules of the Southern District of New York.
16. The Ecuadorian state soon changed its mind about participating in the lawsuit as co-plaintiff.
17. Letter from Samuel Bellettini (President of National Congress), Rodrigo Gambon (President of Commission on the Environment), Juan Jose Castello (President of Commission on Education and Culture), Maria Eugenia Lima (President of Commission for Political Oversight and Control), and Nepoleon Ycaza (President of Commission for Mines and Petroleum) to President of the Republic of Ecuador, Sixto Duran Ballen, dated 17 January 1994.
18. Resolution, National Congress, The Plenary of the Permanent Legislative Commission, 12 June 1996.
19. "2005 Shareholder Resolution to ChevronTexaco" submitted by Trillium Asset Management and co-filed by The New York State Common Retirement Fund, Amnesty International, Sisters of Mercy of Burlingame, and the Dominican Sisters of San Rafael, California.
20. Conversation with Cristobal Bonifaz, 26 October 2003.
21. Ruling of United States Court of Appeals, Second Circuit, 16 August 2002. Judge Vincent J. Broderick was the judge to whom the US federal court sent the case when it was first filed in November 1993. Judge Broderick died in April 1995, and the case was sent to a new judge.

References

Acción Ecológica. 2003. *Ecuador ni es ni sera ya paiz amazónico: Inventario de impactos petroleros*. Quito: Acción Ecológica.

ACOINCO and CEDIME. 1991. *Los cofanes: Neustra historia—vida y tradiciones*. Quito: CEDIME.

Appadurai, Arjun. 1995. *Modernity at Large: Cultural Dimensions of Modernity*. Minneapolis: University of Minnesota Press.

Bustamante, Teodoro, ed. 1995. *Marea negra en la Amazonia: Conflictos socioambientales vinculados a la actividad petrolera en el Ecuador*. Quito: Abya Yala.

Castells, Manuel. 1996. *The Rise of the Network Society*. Oxford: Blackwell.

_____. 2000. *End of Millennium*. Oxford: Blackwell.

Ferguson, James. 1999. *Expectations of Modernity: Myths and Meanings of Urban Life on the Zambian Copperbelt*. Berkeley: University of California Press.

_____. 2006. *Global Shadows: Africa in the Neoliberal World Order*. Durham, NC: Duke University Press.

Giddens, Anthony. 1990. *The Consequences of Modernity*. Cambridge: Polity Press.

Gomez, Nelson, Segundo Moreno, Orlando Lopez, and Antonio Narvaez. 1992. *Tempestad en la Amazonia Ecuatoriana*. Quito: CIESA.

Gupta, Akhil. 1995. "Blurred Boundaries: The Discourse of Corruption, the Culture of Politics, and the Imagined State." *American Ethnologist* 22, no. 2: 375–402.

Gupta, Akhil, and Aradhana Sharma. 2006. *The Anthropology of the State: A Reader*. Oxford: Blackwell.

Hall, Stuart. 1991. "Old and New Identities: Old and New Ethnicities." Pp. 41–68 in *Culture, Globalization, and the World-System: Contemporary Conditions for the Representation of Identity*, ed. Anthony D. King. Binghamton: State University of New York Press.

_____. 1996. "Gramsci's Relevance for the Study of Race and Ethnicity." Pp. 411–440 in *Critical Dialogues in Culture Studies*, ed. David Morley and Kuan-Hsing Chen. London: Routledge.

Hansen, Thomas Blom, and Finn Stepputat, eds. 2001. *States of Imagination: Ethnographic Explorations of the Postcolonial State*. Durham, NC: Duke University Press.

Hardt, Michael. 1995. "The Withering of Civil Society." *Social Text* 45: 27–44.

Hardt, Michael, and Antonio Negri. 2000. *Empire*. Cambridge, MA: Harvard University Press.

_____. 2004. *Multitude: War and Democracy in the Age of Empire*. New York: Penguin.

Harvey, David. 1989. *The Condition of Postmodernity*. Oxford: Blackwell.

_____. 2006. *Spaces of Global Capitalism: A Theory of Uneven Geographical Development*. New York: Verso.

Held, David, Anthony G. McGrew, David Goldblatt, and Jonathan Perraton. 1999. *Global Transformations: Politics, Economics and Culture*. Stanford, CA: Stanford University Press.

Hiroako, Mario, and Shozo Yamamoto. 1980. "Agricultural Development in the Upper Amazon of Ecuador." *Geographical Review* 70, no. 4: 423–445.

Hurtig, Anna-Karin, and Miguel San Sebastián. 2002. "Geographical Differences in Cancer Incidence in the Amazon Basin of Ecuador in Relation to Residence Near Oil Fields." *International Journal of Epidemiology* 31: 1021–1027.

_____. 2004. "Incidence of Childhood Leukaemia and Oil Exploitation in the Amazon Basin of Ecuador." *International Journal of Occupational and Environmental Health* 10, no. 3: 245–250.

Laclau, Ernesto. 2004. "Can Immanence Explain Social Struggles." Pp. 21–30 in Passavant and Dean 2004.

_____. 2007. *On Populist Reason*. London: Verso.

Laclau, Ernesto, and Chantal Mouffe. 2001. *Hegemony and Socialist Strategy: Towards a Radical Democratic Politics*. 2nd ed. London: Verso.

Mitchell, Timothy. 1991. "The Limits of the State: Beyond Statist Approaches and Their Critics." *American Political Science Review* 85: 77–96.

Nelson, Diane. 1999. *A Finger in the Wound: Body Politics in Quincentennial Guatemala*. Berkeley: University of California Press.

Ong, Aihwa. 1998. *Flexible Citizenship: The Cultural Logics of Transnationality*. Durham, NC: Duke University Press.

_____. 2006. *Neoliberalism as Exception: Mutations in Citizenship and Sovereignty*. Durham, NC: Duke University Press.

Passavant, Paul. 2004. "Introduction: Postmodern Republicanism." Pp. 1–20 in Passavant and Dean 2004.

Passavant, Paul, and Jodi Dean, eds. 2004. *Empire's New Clothes: Reading Hardt and Negri*. New York: Routledge.

Pichón, Francisco. 1993. "Colonozación y deforestación en la frontera agrícola de la región amazónica ecuatoriana." In *Amazonía: Escenarios y Conflictos*, ed. Lucy Ruiz. Quito: CEDIME.

Putnam, Robert D. 2000. *Bowling Alone: The Collapse and Revival of American Community*. New York: Simon & Schuster.

Rosenau, James N. 2003. *Distant Proximities: Dynamics beyond Globalization*. Princeton, NJ: Princeton University Press.

San Sebastián, M., M. Armstrong, J. A. Cordoba, and C. Stephens. 2001. "Exposures and Cancer Incidence Near Oil Fields in the Amazon Basin of Ecuador." *Occupational and Environmental Medicine* 58: 517–522.

Sassen, Saskia. 1996. *Losing Control?* New York: Columbia University Press.

Sawyer, Suzana. 2001. "Fictions of Sovereignty: Prosthetic Petro-Capitalism, Neoliberal States, and Phantom-Like Citizens in Ecuador." *Journal of Latin American Anthropology* 6, no. 1: 156–197.

_____. 2002. "Bobbittizing Texaco: Dis-membering Corporate Capital and Re-membering the Nation in Ecuador." *Cultural Anthropology* 17, no. 2: 150–180.

_____. 2004. *Crude Chronicles: Indigenous Politics, Multinational Oil, and Neoliberalism in Ecuador.* Durham, NC: Duke University Press.

_____. 2006. "Corporate Sovereignty in a Transnational Lawsuit." *Political and Legal Anthropology Review* 29, no. 1: 23–43.

Schmink, Marianne, and Charles H. Wood, eds. 1984. *Frontier Expansion in Amazonia.* Gainesville: University of Florida Press.

Trujillo, Jorge. 1981. *Los obscuros disignios de Dios y del imperio: El Instituto Linguistico de Verano en el Ecuador.* Quito: Publicaciones CIESE.

_____. 1992. "La colonización y el desplazamiento de los grupos indígenas." Pp. 119–148 in *Amazonía Presente y ...?* ed. F. Larrea. Quito: Abya-Yala/Tierra Viva/ILDIS.

Tsing, Anna. 2004. *Friction: An Ethnography of Global Connection.* Princeton, NJ: Princeton University Press.

Uquillas, Jorge. 1984. "Colonization and Spontaneous Settlement in the Ecuadorian Amazon." Pp. 261–284 in Schmink and Wood 1984.

_____. 1989. "Social Impacts of Modernization and Public Policy, and Prospects for Indigenous Development in Ecuador's Amazon." Pp. 407–431 in *The Human Ecology of Tropical Land Settlement in Latin America,* ed. Debra A. Schumann and William L. Partridge. Boulder, CO: Westview Press.

Vickers, William. 1984. "Indian Policy in the Amazonian Ecuador." Pp. 8–32 in Schmink and Wood 1984.

Zevallos, José Vicente L. 1989. "Agrarian Reform and Structural Change: Ecuador Since 1964." Pp. 42–69 in *Searching for Agrarian Reform in Latin America,* ed. William C. Thiesenhusen. Madison: University of Wisconsin Press.

Chapter 4

THE POWER OF ECUADOR'S INDIGENOUS COMMUNITIES IN AN ERA OF CULTURAL PLURALISM

Rudi Colloredo-Mansfeld

Ecuador's indigenous movement spent the 1980s creating a national organization, the 1990s achieving popular legitimacy, and the early 2000s undermining much of what they had gained. To be sure, the general strikes, marches, and political campaigns of the 1990s always fell short of aspirations. Even so, they each added to the capacity of the movement: the power to renegotiate legislation during protests against the 1994 land development law, the formation of a new electoral movement called Pachakutik in 1996 to help indigenous candidates, and the achievement of constitutional reforms in 1998. In the 2000s, however, participation in a coup, backroom deals made by indigenous leaders, and the disconnect between Quito-based politicians and the local

Notes for this chapter begin on page 104.

communities made the movement resemble the old-fashioned politics that indigenous people had hoped to replace.

The provinces remained a bright spot. Rosters of indigenous officeholders grew despite setbacks at the national level. In Imbabura, for example, in the cities of Otavalo and Cotacachi not only did indigenous men win offices, but each faced re-election and won. Meanwhile, the Provincial Council had its first elected indigenous member in its 179-year history. Even here, though, gains no longer seem to be building in the movement. In 2006, Mario Conejo, the mayor of Otavalo, a town with the highest concentration of indigenous-owned industry and capital in Ecuador, resigned from the Pachakutik movement, provoking charges of opportunism and feelings of betrayal.

Such problems were inevitable. The skills and strategies necessary to hold public office and build parliamentary coalitions did not correspond to the community networking and street protests that launched the movement. And if the different constituencies of the movement—Andean peasants, Amazonian nations, pluricultural mestizos—were able to set aside differences in order to win office, conflicts reignited once offices were gained. Even so, the lack of direction and unity has become grave. Commenting on the fallout from Conejo's actions, an indigenous Otavaleña business woman and party supporter told me: "It looks like we are disintegrating."

The premise of this chapter is that, culturally and economically, the disintegration began decades ago and that, politically, it energized indigenous communities. Since the 1970s, community institutions have been forced to coordinate widening differences in wealth, values, knowledge, and interests. What community residents have achieved is not a single, shared way of being indigenous, but rather a means to cope with cultural pluralism at the local level that underpins the fight for pluriculturalism at the national level. Put another way, rather than proving the stability of a native way of being, agreement in street protests or rural uprisings testifies to the power of indigenous communities to solidify relations in circumstances in which a narrow political goal becomes central.[1]

Since the 1970s, Ecuadorian indigenous peoples have created these circumstances through a kind of vernacular statecraft. They have elaborated the apparatus of local government without top-down authority, maximizing functions such as list making, council formation, boundary drawing, and interregional organization. The peasant *comuna* and formal economic associations, two state-sponsored organizational forms, stand at the heart of this effort. Yet embracing state ideals of rural organization has not meant accepting the hegemonic institutionalization of state power, but something more complex. Internally within communities, cultural differences, economic inequalities, and minimal fiscal resources mean enduring rivalry, debate, and frequent failures to unify behind a shared agenda. When consensus is achieved, however, it is often in opposition to state policy, not in step with its implementation. Furthermore, uniform organizational forms and practices borrowed from national models of administration allow opposition to scale up quickly into national protests against the state.

Characterizing this use of state form as 'vernacular', I am thinking more architecturally than linguistically. In vernacular architecture, builders imitate and appropriate standard elements of widely used design, adapting them to local conditions and eschewing detailed blueprints. Additionally, as the *Oxford English Dictionary* puts it, vernacular architecture is "ordinary and domestic rather than monumental." Translated into political terms, vernacular statecraft combines replicable form, local action, and an absence of 'overarching' governmental structure.

I build the case for vernacular statecraft, or a civil society built of state-designed institutions without the hegemonic control of the state, through a set of related tasks. First, ironically, I must go back and write against the standard scholarly narratives of the indigenous movement that tout rural community organizing. Only in this way can I recover the importance of urban careers, money, and know-how and underscore the new plurality of indigenous society as the impetus of community life. Second, I revisit the 1990 uprising and review how it set up the indigenous community as the focus of ongoing indigenous politics. Third, I go on to detail the workings of community self-administration to illustrate how goals are achieved without either forcing unanimity of values or imposing state authority. To begin with, though, I situate the peculiar position of Ecuadorian indigenous communities in terms of recent debates about civil society.

Identity, the State, and Civil Society in Ecuador's Andes

Indigenous movements such Ecuador's are most often analyzed in terms of identity. Indeed, if identity politics refers to "actions that come from a particular location within society, in direct defiance of universal categories" (Hale 1997: 568), indigenous movements could be described as emblematic of this new oppositional approach. In Ecuador and elsewhere, indigenous activists gained attention by breaking publicly with national peasant movements and seeking to protect those values and histories distinctive to their peoples (Hale 1994; Pallares 2002). It is not just that cultural-based claims motivate indigenous politics (Warren 1998). It is the way that identity becomes a means of politics. As Sonia Alvarez, Evelina Dagnino, and Arturo Escobar write (1998: 6): "[N]ew social movements were those for which identity was important, those that engaged in 'new forms of doing politics,' and those that contributed to new forms of sociability. Indigenous, ethnic, ecological, women's gay and human rights movements were the candidates of choice." Participating in the movement becomes a new way of being indigenous, while self-conscious, overt displays of indigenous culture become a new way of being political (Selverston 1994; Selverston-Scher 2001).

While appealing, this linking of the indigenous movement and identity politics is flawed. First, if it is true that identity has become politically central in the discourse of the indigenous movement, it is also widely recognized that there is no shared way of being indigenous (Warren and Jackson 2002). In fact, in Ecuador, the indigenous movement itself publicly marks the beginning of the era in which past polarities that once defined the Indian/white boundary—rural vs. urban, Kichwa vs. Spanish, illiterate vs. educated, peasant vs. professional—become acknowledged internal differences of communities. Put another way, for indigenous peoples, a shared cultural identity is a thin political resource, offering few transcendent values that can be used to mobilize people.[2]

Second, in the list of movements offered by Alvarez, Dagnino and Escobar above—indigenous, ethnic, ecological, women's gay and human rights—an indigenous movement has the clearest roots in something *besides* identity. In both colonial and post-colonial times, those rural communities marked as indigenous were liable for different taxes, received latitude to prosecute aspects of customary law, and were recognized as owning certain types of communal property. That is, they enjoyed a different relationship with the state, and their institutions of local governance occupied a unique space in national civil society. To the extent that indigenous politics still focuses on these differences, the terms of debate shift from the question of identity to the specifics of that civil society.

Still, 'civil society' does not offer much more analytical purchase than 'identity'. In introducing a volume on civil society in Africa, John and Jean Comaroff seem to delight in the incoherence of the term, observing that "in the face of more exacting efforts to pin down its habitations, civil society often melts into air" (Comaroff and Comaroff 1999b: 7). At a minimum, the notion refers to the collection of voluntary groupings that, taken together, is "a part of society which has a life of its own, which is distinctly different from the state which is largely in autonomy from it. Civil society lies beyond the boundaries of the family and the clan and beyond the locality; it lies short of the state" (Shils 2003: 292). Yet this formulation raises immediate questions for the Comaroffs (1999b: 7): "Does civil society exist as the antithesis of the state, in struggle with it, or as a condition of its possibility?"

Nonetheless, if ambiguities exist, the terms of the debate are relatively clear. The need for clarity in matters of civil society grows in epochs when waxing state power and economic modernization crowd out the influence of non-politicians in public life. Historically, an overreaching state has propelled the debate (Robson 2000). So here enters a problem in the Latin American case. In stride with neo-liberal promotion of the market, state-backed initiatives, civil administration, and even reliable control of law and order have in fact declined. Thus, both state and non-state sectors in Latin America need some definition to be reconciled with common conceptions of civil society.

Post-colonial Latin American states have cycled through weakness and strength. In Venezuela and Colombia, anthropologists have detailed the 'magical' appearance of the state in its strong guise, projecting itself as a unifying force "by producing fantasies of collective integration into centralized institutions" (Coronil 1997: 4; see also Taussig 1996). In Venezuela's case, oil revenues inflate the state's 'god-like appearance'. Flushed with petroleum wealth in the 1970s, the Ecuadorian state also intervened widely in rural politics. Designating the terms for registering as peasant communities, cooperatives, and associations, the state both advanced the agenda of land reform and often co-opted its grass-roots leaders (Striffler 2002). The collapse of oil prices and subsequent government fiscal crises, however, terminated agrarian programs before they achieved much. Such lurching from strong activism to minimal participation resulted not so much in a weak state as an 'absent-present' one (cf. Reddy 2001). The state has continued to be present in the organizational forms of rural peoples, the expectations raised, and occasional support for development schemes. Yet its absence is felt in its inability to carry projects to fruition and the leadership that it has ceded to competing NGOs. This combination has proved a fertile ground for the growth of community institutions.

This historic link to the state means that the resultant Andean communities, in fact, fail to fit the common definitions of civil society—voluntary civic and social associations that exist outside of official state administration. Mikael Karlstrom (1999), however, has argued that the strict emphasis on separation from the state ignores the autonomy of many state-initiated communities. He has observed, for example, that local councils in Uganda are not seen by constituents as part of the government. In fact, they may cease to exist when local support wanes and strengthen when seen as vehicles of opposition to the state. Indeed, such amalgamations of state-sponsored forms and local initiative, backed more (if meagerly) by local resources than state funds, may have a more radical, oppositional potential than non-state institutions alone.

I turn now to the arrival of Ecuadorian indigenous communities on the national political stage in 1990.

The Emergence of the Indigenous Movement

Marchers who confronted soldiers during the indigenous uprising of 1990 shouted: "This is not a workers' strike. This is not a teachers' strike. This is not a students' strike. THIS IS AN INDIAN UPRISING." The protest began when indigenous leaders from CONAIE (the Confederation of Indigenous Nationalities of Ecuador) and other activists occupied the Santo Domingo church in Quito at the end of May to protest the failure of the legal system to process land claims. CONAIE had come into existence in the 1980s as a vehicle to unite highland and lowland indigenous organizations in order to pursue structural change on a national level. CONAIE's leaders also saw a general strike for land not merely as a material demand but as a rebuff of values underlying Ecuador's mestizo-dominated political system. The strike widened beyond their direct coordination to include large marches in provincial capitals and the invasion of a hacienda in the central highlands. Coming up on the 500th anniversary of Columbus's first voyage to the Americas, Miguel Lluco of CONAIE said: "We were rejecting the celebration of the 500 years. We said, 'We will at least make it to the 500th anniversary in possession of our land'" (León 1993: 137).

In explaining the appearance of a mass indigenous movement at the end of the twentieth century, a certain conventional wisdom has emerged among scholars and activists alike. First, the case for ethnic politics starts with the premise that land reform efforts in the 1960s and 1970s failed Indians: "The communities lost the game in terms of access to economic resources" (Korovkin 1997: 32; Selverston-Scher 2001). Without having received sufficient land, Ecuador's highland indigenous people could no longer farm full-time. Indeed, the few peasant communities that stayed intact primarily through farming were far more likely to be mestizo—ethnically non-indigenous and allied with the urban Spanish-speaking national culture—than indigenous (Zamosc 1994: 43). Kichwa speakers veered toward careers as semi-proletarian migrants.

Most scholars agree, too, that the urban experience was largely fruitless. Amalia Pallares observes that, destined to circulate endlessly from their communities to cities, Indians suffered continual mistreatment or *maltrato*—the abuse and contempt of civil authorities, fraudulent practices of mestizos merchants, and the scorn of town residents. Work itself was grim. "Towns and cities institutionalized a labor partitioning system that assigned Indians the most menial and underpaid tasks" as maids, porters, and bricklayers (Pallares 2002: 43, 64). When the bottom fell out of the Ecuadorian economy after the 1982 drop in oil prices, this tedious work became even more inadequate. Put simply, conventional wisdom on land reform, racism, and recession holds that Kichwa careers turned into one long losing streak.

And with the material failure of land reform noted and new hardships of urban employment lamented, political analysts switched from economics to community organization. New leadership councils and formal associations that reached across parish boundaries promised hope in the absence of an economic future. "Reform initiated a dramatic growth in indigenous organizing" (Selverston-Scher 2001: 36) and in some places a "provincewide community movement" (Korovkin 1997: 32). Politics, moreover, fed off of a new awareness of culture. The children of the 1950s estate workers were committed to maintain community life and "to promote cultural revitalization and political organization" (Pallares 2002: 43). Only the economics of land ownership remained as a material preoccupation. It surged "as a constant theme and certainly one of the most contemporary and historical problems of the struggle" (Macas 2001: xiv).

I find this story of the peasant-Indian political transition a little too rehearsed. The narrative arc, woven alike into activist accounts and researchers' analyses, colors recent history with messianic tones. Indeed, it is positively Christian: the crucifixion (the bleeding away of subsistence resources), the death (failed peasant farming and descent to temporary urban wage work), and the resurrection (the rebirth of indigenous society through community organizing). The nadir—urban life, a netherworld of laboring bodies and lost indigenous souls—rebounds to a new zenith of assertive, culturally aware collectivities, which grow and connect. Finally, pushed too far by government indifference, they rise up to make their own history.

I want to question two assumptions underlying this scenario in order to present a more realistic account of the way communities work—and for whom. First, although mistreatment and racism have been equated with a generalized failure of the indigenous urban experience, the reality was that the years following land reform saw mobility that was mostly geographic but also social.

The careers of political activists (León 1993), of middle-class Otavalo business-men and -women (de la Torre 1999; Meisch 2002), of artists from Tigua (Colvin 2005), and of former hacienda laborers (Lyons 2006) point to the diverse, post–land reform worlds of indigenous people: peasant, capitalist, vendor, community organizer, and lawyer.

Even if Otavalos are set apart, as Pallares does, her own descriptions of indigenous mistreatment can be read against the grain as accounts of social mobility. She observes (2002: 64) "a substantial increase in the numbers of educated and professional Indians" and records the experiences of a few of them, including an indigenous medical assistant in Chimborazo and an engineer from Cotacachi. The sheer numbers of Indians seeking professional careers helped change a basic tenet of national culture. Education no longer had to be equated with assimilation. Undeniably, racism did rob careers of their real potential. Yet through their own efforts, indigenous people had the know-how gained beyond rural places to defend themselves within them, as will be detailed below.

Second, writers repeatedly see rural organizing as an independent realm built of long-standing indigenous values and practices. Zamosc (1994: 54), for example, writes: "Among the peasants who had to organize in order to fight for the land, a sense of collective purpose emerged based on appeals to primordial loyalties. In reactivating the ties of extended kinship and reciprocity, this pro-cess reinforced (and in many cases even regenerated) the old Indian community as the natural organizational framework." The words "primordial," "kinship," "reciprocity," and "natural" imply that an indigenous destiny is at work. Indige-nous community organizing, however, especially in the decade leading up to the uprising, had less to do with ancient values than with 1980s ambition, change, and urban careers, which produced a new economic elite within communities.

This is shown by Zamosc's (1995) own data, which he later compiled to estimate the size of Ecuador's Indian population. Using a language census from the 1950s, he identified which parts of the sierra were predominantly mes-tizo and which parts predominantly indigenous. He then charted population growth rates, organizational trends, and other demographic indices. Among these, he recorded changes in the registration of *comunas* (peasant communi-ties that hold some resources in common), cooperatives (narrower collectives of peasants using shared land for agricultural enterprises), and associations (groups dedicated to shared economic activity or community development). Numerically, associations had actually become the preferred method of indig-enous organizing (see fig. 1). Encouraged by new legislation in the 1970s, indigenous groups coalesced around trades, specific development projects, or marketplaces. Forming associations did not require fixed rural holdings and afforded more flexibility. In the run up to the 1990 uprising, associations solidi-fied links outside of the framework of the peasant community.

In re-evaluating urban careers and tracing their connection with community organizing, I want to shift away from the crucifixion story of suffering, death, and resurrection to a plot that moves from frustrated growth to internal differ-ence to dialogue to action. Admittedly, 'frustration' is a puny word to portray

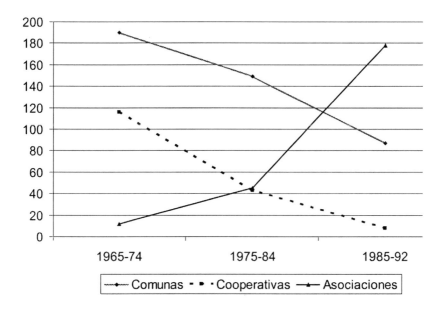

FIGURE 1 Decade to Decade Changes in the Number of Registrations of New *Comunas*, Cooperatives, and Associations in Predominantly Indigenous Areas (Zamosc 1995)

the racism that truncated the potential of many of these careers. However, it suggests that discrimination did not so much cripple aspirations as block and redirect them. Community groups, whether peasant *comunas*, cooperatives, or associations, ultimately benefited from this detour as they became vehicles of ambition. As has been well documented in Zamosc, Pallares, and other accounts of the movement, this new dynamism led to the stacking up of local, provincial, and regional groups into a new national form ultimately led by CONAIE. In the process of the 1990 uprising, Indians had risen to become legitimate interlocutors with the central government, not just with local landowners or sympathetic clergymen.

Consequently, after June 1990 it was no longer just anthropologists asking whether Ecuador was one nation or many. And if many, then whose values, culture, and laws should prevail? The answers in Ecuador after the uprising often came down to a core issue: what it means and what it takes to be an Indian community. Communities came to matter so much for several reasons. First, organizationally, CONAIE's power sprang from the relations it opened with and among local communities. The uprising succeeded because of the scale of unity among notoriously independent peasant *comunas*. Second, the community was not only a means but the ends. Greater autonomy for separate communities lay at the heart of the alternative political model offered by CONAIE. As CONAIE (1994: 55) later put it in their political program, autonomy is "the capacity of indigenous communities and nations to decide and control, in our own territories, the social, cultural, and economic order with the existence and recognition of our own authorities in coordination with central authorities."

Third, despite the challenges and limitations of indigenous identity as a political resource, Ecuador's indigenous movement draws on identity claims to unify peoples, and such claims frequently circle back to community. To be sure, leaders of the 1990 uprising saw identity in terms of history, captured in a shorthand way by the idea of 500 years of resistance. The distinctive manner of their living, though, lay in being part of a community. When asked to comment on the role of women in the 1990 uprising, for example, Blanca Chancozo chose to emphasize less women's leadership than their membership in the community: "[T]here was a woman killed. It was not that one could say she was the primary one or a leader, just one more member of the community and was, in that, the equal of all" (quoted in León 1993: 135).

The importance of community for the movement, however, begs a question. In light of migration, semi-proletarianization, new access to education, growing commercialization, and other changes, how do communities work as reliable building blocks of political action? Understanding the unity and effectiveness of communities under these circumstances requires moving to practices of community management and administration. Here I turn to three ethnographic examples of the business of community: how the exercise of community justice not only challenges state authority but forces a council to legitimize its jurisdiction against rival councils and over a collection of residents; how collective workdays are managed to mobilize internal resources of a community; and how trade association participation can counter state authority without subscribing to the formal rules of membership set down by the state. Contentious and time-consuming, this politics produces local economic infrastructure and holds together the indigenous civil society at the heart of the wider movement.

Ariasucu, Imbabura: Councils and Community Justice

In 1993, three thieves were captured, questioned, found guilty, and whipped in Ariasucu, a densely settled peasant sector near the market town of Otavalo in Ecuador's northern Andes. Only the week before, a neighboring community, La Compañia, had done the same. Both were emboldened by the national movement's defense of indigenous justice as a core element of indigenous autonomy. Each act, in turn, was seen by townspeople—both indigenous and mestizo—as evidence of a radicalizing indigenous politics (Colloredo-Mansfeld 2002; Whitten, Whitten, and Chango 1997). The power on display in Ariasucu, however, was tenuous. The council members could not be confident of their authority even among their own constituents. Class differences in Ariasucu revealed the contours of a potential community split, and rival peasant communities asserted their own authority over the neighborhood. In other words, the future of the council and its political boundaries had been put into play.

In fact, the very presence of Ariasucu's council had more to do with the ambitions of some local returning migrants than with a long-standing tradition of self-government or the incorporation of state-sanctioned communities. Indeed, the council operated for two decades (1982–2002) without formal recognition from the state. In 1982, several unofficially elected representatives successfully solicited an electricity development project. The men who campaigned for the spots and managed the project were all recent returnees, some coming back after years of working in construction in Quito, others from selling in Colombia or elsewhere in Ecuador. Several were building new homes, introducing cement block architecture among the adobe houses, and wanted electricity to further modernize their homes. After the wires were strung, the political entrepreneurship of these and other men only increased. They approached both governmental and non-governmental organization (NGO) agencies about projects ranging from potable water to a child-care center. Competing with the larger neighboring communities of Agato and La Compañia, they appealed to at least 10 different external organizations, all of which promised patronage for development projects (Lema et al. 2000).

The captured thieves were, in fact, an unwanted test for the council. In the past, they would have turned the criminals over to the *teniente politico*, the provincial official in charge of such matters. However, La Compañia's punishment of thieves just the week before was reported on throughout the province. Failing to follow its neighbor's example would have signaled the weakness of their community and induced La Compañia to reclaim its authority over much of Ariasucu's territory. Thus, Ariasucu's council determined to make a show of its power and unity. In the course of the punishment, the council's three men and one woman mimicked each other's moves. Leading the first robber to the middle of the court, the council had him take off his sweater and kneel down before the president, who held a short whip. Before he delivered the first of his two blows, the president made a speech on the theme of "knowing work." He then cracked the whip once against the man's back, continuing the speech and repeating that "not working was not valid." After hitting the man one more time, the president turned the whip over to the vice president, who continued the routine: speech, a single blow, speech, and another blow. The third council member mumbled something inaudible and gave two tentative blows. The fourth council member was much bolder. She took the whip and hit the thief hard across the buttocks, scolded him, then struck again. The other two robbers received the same treatment.

In improvising their procedure, the council fused familial and state forms of power. The emphasis on moral lecturing, for example, reflected a key practice of rural Andean authority and the expectation that elders, parents, and other responsible figures must offer strong guidance to their charges, to advise or 'to give words' (*dar palabras*) that reinforce rightful behavior.[3] At the same time, by rotating the whip among the president, vice president, treasurer, and secretary, the council tapped into the bureaucratic ideals of community leadership. Here all the officers of the community had to step up, even if one had a surer hand with the whip, another had no stomach for it, a third could lecture well, and a fourth just hectored. The involvement of those who occupied state-defined roles depersonalized the actions. In the past, the overt formality of such titles contributed to a council's tenuousness. Seen either as agents of state power or as those seeking a means for personal enrichment, presidents, vice presidents, and other officials received little support outside their efforts to coordinate clearly needed development projects (Becker 1999; Casagrande and Piper 1969; Villavicencio Rivadeneira 1973). However, charged in recent years with everything from redressing the imbalances of past community development projects to carrying out community justice, councils have gained a new backing (cf. Findji 1992).

Despite their careful orchestration, the council members did not win over everyone in Ariasucu. Certainly, they had their support. In the aftermath, my host in the community led me back to his house and showed me a poster above his looms with the Inca greeting, "Ama quilla, ama llulla, ama shua" (Don't be lazy, don't lie, don't steal). He said: "This is the way it was with the Incas. They punished thieves hard, sometimes pushing them into deep gullies." From this man's point of view, the council had done well. It had dealt with the threat posed by robbers and legitimized his own community as an upholder of ancient Andean customs.

Yet others in Ariasucu were dismayed. Forced to lie on their stomachs on the cement volleyball court in their thin T-shirts and frayed soccer shorts, the thieves laid bare the poverty of too many indigenous people. Their shame could not be shrugged off by those who told me that these men were "of our flesh." Furthermore, rather than a triumph of timeless Andean justice, the flogging struck some as flaunting traditional wisdom, which counseled careful deliberations. The division between those who celebrated the punishment and those who identified with the thieves had a rough geography, with council supporters living down on the lower slopes, and dissidents up high, in a neighborhood, not coincidently, largely unserved by the community's power lines. Ultimately, when pushed, almost all residents accepted the council's point of view: the thieves got what was coming to them for robbing when others work hard for their livelihood. Nonetheless, the events revealed that Ariasucu had ironically reproduced within its territory the divides in basic services that had induced them to secede from La Compañia and Agato. The breaking up into two smaller communities with separate councils was conceivable, if unlikely.

Since the 1980s, this division into council-led, bounded territories has altered the Otavaleños' long-standing economic inequality and social diversity. In the 1940s, the area's peasant settlements varied according to craft specialty, income, and cultural skills, with the town nearest to Otavalo already getting ahead in mestizo-dominated institutions (Buitrón 1947; Buitrón and Buitrón 1945). Diffuse domains in local political authority overlay these gradations of wealth and knowledge, raising up different leaders on different occasions.[4] By the 1990s, though, this complexity began simplifying into a type of segmentary pluralism. In place of interwoven settlements with blurred social and physical boundaries, multiple enclaves appeared, each with its own set of institutions. Often, the move to such divisions came with social stratification. Sectors formed with an internal political and economic elite—usually men who had greater contact with cities—ready to direct local priorities. This enclave formation represents a new turn in the region's organizational capacity, making possible broad alliances of similarly sized and composed groups—or an infinite number of rivalries.

Quiloa, Cotopaxi: Community Work Parties and Lists

Of all the tasks charged to community councils, the *minga* (community work party) is the most common. *Mingas*, in fact are so emblematic of community cooperation, development, and self-management that indigenous politicians brandish the word in election campaigns and street protests to rally constituents. The distinctive power of *mingas*, however, comes less from a spirit of volunteerism than from the harnessing of human labor through cash fines and community rosters. In the course of my fieldwork in the early 1990s, I witnessed approximately 20 community *mingas*, mostly to create a water system in Imbabura, but also to build infrastructure, including a communal house, a mill, and a bridge, in the province of Cotopaxi. The bridge *minga* in Quiloa-Tigua, Cotopaxi, was notable because community members provided not only labor but also some of the key materials.

In July 1992, I had moved with my wife to the sector of Quiloa-Tigua for a research project on the indigenous art traditions and tourist painting trade of the residents. We had arrived in time to see several *mingas* happen, almost in parallel. An Ecuadorian NGO named FUNHABIT was running a project to build 40 new houses with small studios for the benefit of the painters. The need to participate in house-building work parties had brought people back to the community. During our third day there, residents took advantage of the returned migrants and organized a work crew to rebuild the narrow footbridge that spanned the gully splitting the sector.

On the morning of the *minga*, the council secretary, a man named Segundo, stood outside in the community plaza, wincing against blasts of wind and dust and writing participants' names in his notebook. A group of men lost patience with the record keeping and headed off to destroy the old footbridge. Meanwhile, wildcat parties of community members armed with axes fanned out across Quiloa, looking for suitable trees that could be claimed for the bridge. One group swarmed across the patio of our hosts, Maria Juana Cuyo and Manuel Cuyo, heading for an unusually thick pine tree. Maria Juana shouted to the axmen that her family needed the wood to carve masks to sell to tourists. The community workers left the tree alone and set off to bring down other trees, felling five large eucalyptuses by the end of the morning. The secretary explained they needed so much wood because their plan was not simply to replace the footbridge but to build a new bridge that could handle cars. The residents wanted to make it possible for tourists to drive in and buy paintings, despite the lack of a serviceable road.

People were forced to cooperate in order to heave the large trees into the gully. At this point, the premature destruction of the bridge became evident. Had it been in place, the new logs could have been ferried across and easily positioned. Not having a bridge meant transporting the trunks down and out of the gully on paths etched by sheep hooves. The course proved too steep, and a large eucalyptus trunk got stuck in the gully. In the afternoon, residents hauled four other trunks to the bridge site. With ropes and timbers, they managed to get two of the lighter logs across. People then called it a day, leaving two other logs on the side of the gully and the large one sticking up out of it. Finally, the secretary got out his notebook and recorded the participation of 42 families. Within a week, community members had mixed and poured the concrete, set the logs, and nailed planks across the top.

Mingas such as this testify to a shared material life that emerges amid Tiguans' individual careers and private landholdings. Indeed, among various mutual labors of Andean community life—planting, harvesting, house building, fiesta sponsoring—community *mingas* have a specific role. They create, maintain, or upgrade physical networks of potable water pipes, electric lines, and paths. Put another way, a *minga* is shared labor that increases circulation, whether it be water, electricity, news, entertainment, or people. This shared 'base' is a kind of human-made commons that underwrites the vitality of private holdings largely by interconnecting them (cf. Gudeman 2001).

A shared base, however, does not translate into shared interests. The seeming inefficiency of Quiloa's bridge *minga* spoke of the varied interests of men and women, of urban laborers and peasant farmers, of project beneficiaries and those who were excluded. For example, if 40 families receiving new houses with painting studios benefited by having access to a tourist-ready road, most full-time residents, who had little to do with the painting trade, would not. No one would visit them, and their meager market purchases would never warrant a truck to deliver them back home. While a new bridge would certainly be useful, a big one that consumed the largest trees in the community's windbreaks did not match many people's priorities.

In any event, no single value related to land or community could be appealed to in order to unite the people. The ability to coordinate residents rested on the few lean resources that the council has: the authority bestowed through democratic election, the capacity to levy fines, the incentive of some external resources, the personal charisma of its leaders, and the recording of lists of participants. In fact, the last of these may be the most useful technology. To be sure, a list is a pretty thin mechanism to engineer feelings of belonging.[5] As James Scott writes, statecraft, not community solidarity, features elaborate list making—tax and tithe rolls, property rolls, conscription lists, and censuses. To accomplish these tasks, the state had to find a way to systematize identities and "create legible people," primarily through the use of patronyms (Scott 1998: 65). Yet in managing modern peasant community politics, lists have a hidden power to create a special currency, *minga* points, and a distinct sphere of exchange, the self-managed peasant *comuna* where such currency can convert individual resources into shared development. Lists achieve this power, not so much for the way that they specify people, as Scott would have it, but for three ways that they generalize individuals into community members.

First, in an Andean community, the use of first and last names that supposedly makes people knowable to outsiders often renders them anonymous to insiders, as the names are too redundant for everyday use. A Quiloan ledger, for instance, offers an unceasing array of Cuyo Cuyos, Vega Cuyos, and Cuyo Vegas. Only officials and anthropologists use these names. Real people use nicknames. Second, if lists seem to rob people of their personal history as encapsulated in their nickname, these records also disarticulate social relationships. Historically, belonging to place meant identifying in terms of *ayllus*, or "named, landholding collectivities" (Salomon and Urioste 1991). Such affiliation locates people in the flow of time and in cycles of growth. Appearing on a list, in contrast, cuts it all down to a single moment of community development. Third, lists also reduce people in a way that makes them strangely convertible. One woman might be a 54-year-old grandmother, an experienced farmer, and a leader in past confrontations with a hacienda (large private estate). Another might be 16, unmarried, and living with her parents. Both, however, are alike on the rolls. Households frequently make use of this reductionism to adapt whatever human resources or underemployed members they have available to get on the list.[6]

In brief, lists are a device to render people anonymous, disarticulated, and convertible. They strip away individual uniqueness to create a generalized resident made exchangeable through labor value. List making is far more about creating a new commodity—the *minga* point—than about legibility. Indeed, people frequently talk about "paying the *minga*" in their home community. This commoditization, however, is precisely where communities can gain power from their rosters and ledgers to defend their territory. *Minga* lists tackle the problem of conflicting interests by creating a special domain of value. Belonging to Quiloa does not mean having to subscribe to a single unifying idea of the 'Quiloan'. Rather, it entails pledging time and effort to accumulate the narrow currency needed to improve one's life within the sector. Different resources can be used to acquire these points; different interests can be served by them. Yet Quiloans themselves are the arbiters of the value. Neither rival sectors nor the state itself can divert the currency of participation.

Otavalo, Imbabura: Associations and Membership

Having concentrated on two aspects of rural community life, I now turn to artisan trades, an activity that many indigenous communities would count among their economic base, along with their fields and homesteads. Producing and selling paintings for tourists, sweaters for export, or belts and sandals for urban indigenous markets link indigenous people in commodity chains that span rural and urban spaces. The sharp rise in recognized trade associations throughout the 1980s testifies that such commerce has a shared, bounded, and political side. Yet where peasant communities have a clear territorial identity and an ongoing investment in community infrastructure that concentrate members' attention, associations have few fixed assets. Their work, in fact, is often event-driven or, better said, crisis-driven. One of Ecuador's largest indigenous associations, UNAIMCO (Union of Indigenous Artisans of the Centenario Market of Otavalo), found itself attracting members as it coped with unpredictable jumps in wool prices in 2000, only to stall for years afterwards in its organizational efforts. It rebounded remarkably in early 2006. The vagaries of its membership illustrate a common issue: the defense of indigenous grass-roots institutions stands apart from coherent participation within them.

Founded in March 1988, UNAIMCO represents the interests of the artisans who work in the Plaza Centenario or Plaza de Ponchos in Otavalo. Beginning with less than 100 members, the group originally focused on improving conditions in the weekly market. However, by organizing the annual festival of Inti Raimi (the celebration of the summer solstice) since the mid-1990s, by backing Mario Conejo in his successful run for mayor in 2000, and by building a substantial new center for artisan training in 2001, UNAIMCO has become one of the most important voices for the Otavaleño artisan. It claims to represent rich and poor—everyone from old-fashioned weavers, who arrive in the plazas on Saturdays to sell their weavings, to the major intermediaries, who batch 30,000 to 40,000 sweaters at a time for sales to London and Tokyo.

In June 2000, a portion of UNAIMCO's constituents, the wool distributors, initiated a boycott of woolen yarn produced in factories near Ambato in order to restore pricing sanity in a badly shaken market. Throughout the first six months of 2000, prices rose sharply and unpredictably. Small-time sweater makers suffered acutely. In March and April, they were arriving in Otavalo on Saturday mornings, selling their wares, buying wool for their next sweaters, and then departing without being able to buy food. After two weeks, the boycotting Otavaleño buyers were able to get the factory owners to agree to come to Otavalo to negotiate. The wool distributors asked the UNAIMCO, as a larger umbrella organization that could draw in other trade groups, to step in and lead the discussions. To all parties involved, the negotiations were clearly more than an economic matter. For the Otavaleños, the meeting mobilized a wide cross-section of the community in a cooperative effort to defend an artisan way of life. For factory owners long used to one-on-one transactions with individual merchants, the boycott signaled an uncomfortable political turn in relations with Otavaleños. It conjured the specter of other large-scale indigenous uprisings of recent times. In fact, the owners insisted that negotiations occur at a neutral site 20 kilometers outside of Otavalo in a restaurant on the Pan-American Highway. Even so, the indigenous organizers of the boycott arranged for buses to bring in 300 knitters, wool distributors, wholesalers, and vendors.

The meeting achieved mixed results. At its culmination, the assembled artisans voted to reject the factory owners' offer of a limited price freeze. As clandestine purchasing began to undermine the boycott two weeks later, though, a temporary freeze and moderated price increases during the rest of 2000 were all that the meeting accomplished. Even so, the boycott represented further maturation of the artisan leadership and a previously unseen capacity for joint action.

UNAIMCO, however, could not build on its gains. Aside from continual diagnostic studies of the plight of artisans and a few training programs aimed at improving dyeing techniques and fashion knowledge, the leadership accomplished little, and fervor seemed to give way to apathy among plaza vendors. Mario Conejo, Otavalo's mayor, publicly spurned the organization in spite of the decisive support it gave him. Saying, "I am not the mayor from UNAIMCO, but the mayor of all Otavaleños," he has given no direct support to any of their recent initiatives. In 2004, when the officers of the organization wanted to step down, no new names came forward, leaving them in lame-duck status. Even the members' participation in the fiesta of Inti Raimi dwindled. The capacity for direct action seems to have evaporated.

Then in January 2006, Mayor Conejo replaced the indigenous commissioner of markets, whom he had originally appointed, with a mestizo politician named Wilson Sanchez. Citing a high degree of absenteeism among the paid-up, registered users of the sales posts in Plaza de Ponchos, Sanchez sent out his policemen to do a census of who was actually selling in the posts. Rumors circulated that the survey was a prelude to the eviction of current owners and the redistribution of the posts to friends of Conejo's administration. On Friday, 29 January, delegates from the plaza came to speak with the president, vice president, and other officers of UNAIMCO. They resolved to suspend market operations the following Monday and call a meeting in the afternoon. By 3:00 PM, nearly 350 artisans and vendors arrived in the grade school assembly hall to listen to Sanchez's explanation of the survey. Put on the defensive, he sought to assure people that he was merely trying to find out the reality of the market and that there was no secret plan in place.

The audience remained deeply skeptical. When Sanchez stopped speaking, a man stood up and explained the unspoken position of many:

> You [in the market commission] are only beginning to work, but we have worked here since years ago, in the rain and in the sun. You really must work with UNAIMCO ... The posts in the market belong to older people, and now their sons and daughters are working them, but this does not mean they are abandoned. Others have traveled, but they have trusted their posts with family members. But on their return, where will they work? Once again in their posts [loud, sustained applause]. Me, for my part, I am not a member of UNAIMCO. I am an artisan, but I am ready to collaborate [with UNAIMCO]. In the case that you commissioners want to clear up problems with the posts, you have to coordinate always with an organization that has many years of experience. We are going to respect UNAIMCO [applause].

Among the five suggestions offered to and largely accepted by the municipality at the end of the meeting were "One must coordinate with the 'mother organization'" (meaning UNAIMCO), and "The users of the Plaza de Ponchos belong to an important ethnic group."[7] From apathy and drift, the organization resurrected itself in a weekend to put the brakes on an initiative that would have defined Mario Conejo's second term in office.

UNAIMCO's trajectory from confrontation to idleness to confrontation illustrates the organizational tendencies of other trade groups. First, even formally recognized associations, such as UNAIMCO, with offices, directors, and staff members, are situational. Power lies more at the periodic, urgent intersections of Otavaleños' diverse interests than in a fixed membership, permanent leadership, and a bedrock of shared world views. UNAIMCO has gotten where it is by finding formulas that focus diverse segments on a single problem and secure their attention long enough to find a solution. Second, institutional clarity occurs at the boundary of confrontation rather than in internal regulation. It was not surprising that the most eloquent advocate of UNAIMCO's authority over the plazas was someone who identified himself as a non-member. Frequently, people will fight hard to ensure that someone from their own organization defends their interests, but they leave open their personal commitments to that group. Resistance to outsiders is emphasized over coherence among insiders.

Conclusion: The Power of Community

Involved for two decades in activism at the national level, Ecuadorian indigenous communities have endured as icons of their country's indigenous culture and as core elements of its politics. When a politician says "in the communities," it is the same as saying "among indigenous people." These communities, however, are not merely peasant communities newly awakened with an indigenous consciousness (*pace* Guerrero Cazar and Ospina Peralta 2003). Encompassing the stressed resources and multi-threaded careers of the post–land reform generation, they span long distances and grow in knowledge and social networks, yet they are declining in shared work routines. Indeed, their political ascendance has come at a moment of great cultural dissonance.

In my analysis of indigenous politics, the goal of putting communities first has meant losing sight of the coordination offered by national organizations such as CONAIE. This leadership has been essential for the movement, but the politics of the national movement and the political power of the indigenous base are distinct. If they were mutually reinforcing in the 1980s, the missteps of the early 2000s have shown how the national groups' fortunes can strengthen or fall independently of the communities. A clearer understanding of indigenous civil society is not merely an effort to understand how communities serve as a base of CONAIE, but also how communities can become organized to operate in parallel or even at odds with the national movement.

An emphasis on community also displaces the importance of identity. Certainly for those who participate in community politics, just as for those who rally around CONAIE, identity is a central concern. Motivated by their sense of identity, many community members become activists to rediscover the value of indigenous history and celebrate ancient commitments to land and family. Just as assuredly, others who are equally inspired by their indigenousness become activists to break with the past and finally modernize their communities. That is, rather than offering bedrock values to unify people, identity claims can bring people into conflict.

Warren and Jackson (2002: 12) describe the political problem posed by such internal difference in terms of representation, pointing out that the politics of indigenous self-representation is double-sided. It entails both "who represents whom" and "which social lives, languages and knowledge should be represented to selves and to others." But why stop at representation? Members of indigenous communities must work out problems beyond discourse, identity, and communication. They pursue conflicting interests, make and unmake relationships, and reproduce shared bases of economic life. The project of self-representation offers one means to work through these issues. However, the importance of indigenous community practice is that it offers other mechanisms to coordinate effort and sustain shared projects.

Peasant *comunas*, commercial associations, cooperatives, and other collectivities have maintained the power of communities locally and escalated their authority nationally through what I conceive as vernacular statecraft. Scott (1998) has argued that state power operates along a set of axes marked as legible/interchangeable/durable. Community power, in contrast, is often contextual/particular/ephemeral—strong on the practical knowledge that Scott refers to as *metis*. As Coronil (2001: 126) observes: "Since Scott restricts his attention to state designs, his pair of binary oppositions between state/society and abstract knowledge/*metis* unfolds as a compound opposition between state-abstract knowledge/society-*metis*." Critics have consequently taken Scott to task for underplaying the mix of abstract and practical knowledge intrinsic to state activity (Coronil 2001; Herzfeld 2005). To build on, yet reverse, the concern, I argue that a civil society, too, blends abstract schemes and *metis*. Further, these mixes, although limited in application, can yield power on a wide scale.

On the one hand, appropriated from below, the state-authorized administrative organization of indigenous communities has lost its 'legibility'. It lacks an easy, systematic order that would enable manipulation from above. Councils operate without being registered with the state. The lists that council members create often track contributions that cannot be exploited beyond the community boundary, with formal names that are used minimally within it. In trade associations, participation may have little to do with official membership. Such disorder reflects a lack of funds, an institutional history of responding to crises and opportunities, and the accommodation of internal rivalries. Ensuring the importance of local knowledge, this lack of compliance preserves a gap between society and state.

On the other hand, working within the organizational map laid down by the state, indigenous community politics becomes scalable. As these institutions and practices replicate across the Andean countryside, indigenous people have gained the means to connect and pursue projects across communities. Thus, the two great accomplishments of indigenous communities in the post–land reform era have been, first, to maintain relations amid the diversity of contemporary indigenous careers while managing circumstances to allow shared projects to move forward, and, second, to mobilize people and resources along with other communities to sustain a national politics. Yet despite the replication of form, consent to collective protests and politics is not spontaneous. After 20 years of national activism, the community itself remains the institution where consensus is hammered out and then acted upon.

Acknowledgements

I am grateful to the University of Iowa, which has supported my recent fieldwork ventures with both a Career Development Award and a Faculty Scholar Award. Generous support has also been provided by a Fulbright Research and Lecturing Award. Finally, I thank Ted Fischer for creating this opportunity for a regional scholarly exchange.

Rudi Colloredo-Mansfeld is Associate Professor of Anthropology at the University of Iowa and a Visiting Professor at the Facultad Latinoamericano de Ciencias Sociales-Ecuador. Since 1991, he has researched and written about the changing social world of native peoples in the Ecuadorian Andes. His first book, The *Native Leisure Class: Consumption and Cultural Creativity in the Andes* (1999), examined the economic and cultural impact of the transnational textile economy centered in Otavalo and its surrounding weaving communities. He is currently at work on a book that explores community politics not only in Otavalo but in Tigua (Cotopaxi province) and in Quito among indigenous migrants.

Notes

1. This description of community borrows Stanley Fish's (1980) discussion of interpretive communities.
2. Hale (2005) goes further to argue that the promotion of unified cultural identities, especially those linked to bounded territorial units, conforms to neo-liberal multiculturalism instead of setting up true oppositional politics. Rather than identity-based movements, he places his hope for change in Central America in politico-territorial units, known as *bloques*, that are multi-communal and multi-racial.
3. For instance, a *madrina de boda* (godmother) who sponsors a young couple's wedding will take time during the second day of the wedding to wash the groom's face, hands, and feet with flowers while lecturing him about staying sober, helping his wife, and working hard. Indeed, one of the precedents cited for the flogging was an occasion when 12 men in La Compañia each delivered three lashes to a man who had beaten his wife—a problem that godparents are traditionally expected to deal with.
4. The senior kinship position usually prevailed in local settlements, while the prestige linked to sponsorship of saint's days of the Catholic Church singled out leaders who spanned neighborhoods.
5. The Andes, though, offer an intriguing example of a list form that bears poetic, ritual, and social potentialities—the *khipu. Khipus* are bunches of dyed knotted strings, most famously associated with Inca record keeping.

6. In some cases, families can bypass the human contribution altogether and pay the *minga* fines, buying credit on the lists.

7. From UNAIMCO's minutes for the Asemblea General Extraordinaria, 30 January 2006.

References

Alvarez, Sonia E., Evelina Dagnino, and Arturo Escobar, eds. 1998a. *Cultures of Politics/Politics of Cultures: Re-visioning Latin American Social Movements*. Boulder, CO: Westview.

———. 1998b. "Introduction: The Cultural and the Political in Latin American Social Movements." Pp. 1–29 in Alvarez, Dagnino, and Escobar 1998a.

Becker, Marc. 1999. "Comunas and Indigenous Protest in Cayambe, Ecuador." *The Americas* 55, no. 4: 531–559.

Buitrón, Aníbal. 1947. "Situación económica y social del indio Otavaleño." *America Indígena* 7: 45–67.

Buitrón, Aníbal, and Barbara Buitrón. 1945. "Indios, blancos, y mestizos en Otavalo, Ecuador." *Acta Americana* 3: 190–216.

Casagrande, Joseph B., and Arthur R. Piper. 1969. "La transformación estructural de una parroquia rural en las tierras altas del Ecuador." *America Indígena* 29: 1039–1064.

Colloredo-Mansfeld, Rudi. 2002. "'Don't Be Lazy, Don't Lie, Don't Steal': Community Justice in the Neoliberal Andes." *American Ethnologist* 29, no. 3: 637–662.

Colvin, Jean. 2005. *Arte de Tigua: Una reflexión de la cultura indígena en Ecuador*. Quito: Abya-Yala.

Comaroff, John L, and Jean Comaroff, eds. 1999a. *Civil Society and the Political Imagination in Africa: Critical Perspectives*. Chicago, IL: Chicago University Press.

———. 1999b. "Introduction." Pp. 1–43 in Comaroff and Comaroff 1999a.

CONAIE (Confederation of Indigenous Nationalities of Ecuador). 1994. *Proyecto politico de la CONAIE*. Quito: Consejo de Gobierno de la CONAIE.

Coronil, Fernando. 1997. *The Magical State: Nature, Money and Modernity in Venezuela*. Chicago, IL: Chicago University Press.

———. 2001. "Smelling Like a Market." *The American Historical Review* 106, no. 1: 119–129.

de la Torre, Carlos. 1999. "Everyday Forms of Racism in Contemporary Ecuador: The Experiences of Middle-Class Indians." *Ethnic and Racial Studies* 22, no. 1: 92–112.

Findji, Maria Teresa. 1992. "From Resistance to Social Movement: The Indigenous Authorities Movement in Colombia." Pp. 112–133 in *The Making of Social Movements in Latin America*, ed. Arturo Escobar and Sonia E. Alvarez. Boulder, CO: Westview.

Fish, Stanley. 1980. *Is There a Text in This Class? The Authority of Interpretive Communities*. Cambridge, MA: Harvard University Press.

Gudeman, Stephen. 2001. *The Anthropology of Economy*. Malden, MA: Blackwell.

Guerrero Cazar, Fernando, and Pablo Ospina Peralta. 2003. *El poder de la comunidad: Ajuste estructural y movimiento indígena en los Andes ecuatorianos*. Buenos Aires: Consejo Latinamericano de Ciencias Sociales (CLACSO).

Hale, Charles R. 1994. "Between Che Guevara and the Pachamama: Mestizos, Indians, and Identity Politics in the Anti-quincentenary Campaign." *Critique of Anthropology* 14, no. 1: 9–39.

———. 1997. "Cultural Politics of Identity in Latin America." *Annual Review of Anthropology* 26: 567–590.

———. 2005. "Neoliberal Multiculturalism: The Remaking of Cultural Rights and Racial Dominance in Central America." *PoLAR: Political and Legal Anthropology Review* 28, no. 1: 10–19.

Herzfeld, Michael. 2005. "Political Optics and the Occlusion of Intimate Knowledge." *American Anthropologist* 107, no. 3: 369–376.

Karlstrom, Mikael. 1999. "Civil Society and Its Presuppositions: Lessons from Uganda." Pp. 104–123 in Comaroff and Comaroff 1999a.

Korovkin, Tanya. 1997. "Indigenous Peasant Struggles and the Capitalist Modernization of Agriculture: Chimborazo, 1964–1991." *Latin American Perspectives* 24, no. 3: 25–49.

Lema, Mercedes, Vanessa Saltos, Jose Barrionuevo, Enrique Chimbo, and Fernando Garcfa. 2000. *Proyecto de investigación, formas indígenas de administración de justicia: Tres casos de estudio de la nacionalidad quichua de la sierra y amazonía ecuatoriana.* Quito: Facultad Latinoamericano de Ciencias Sociales.

León, Jorge. 1993. "Versiones de los protagonistas: Los hechos históricos y el valor de los testimonios disidentes." Pp. 113–144 in *Sismo etnico en el Ecuador: Varias perspectivas,* ed. CEDIME. Quito: Ediciones Abya-Yala-CEDIME (Centro de Investigaciones de los Movimientos Sociales del Ecuador).

Lyons, Barry J. 2006. *Remembering the Hacienda: Religion, Authority and Social Change in Highland Ecuador.* Austin: University of Texas Press.

Macas, Luis. 2001. "Foreword." Pp. xi–xix in Selverston-Scher 2001.

Meisch, Lynn. 2002. *Andean Entrepreneurs: Otavalo Merchants and Musicians in the Global Arena.* Austin: University of Texas Press.

Pallares, Amalia. 2002. *From Peasant Struggles to Indian Resistance: The Ecuadorian Andes in the Late Twentieth Century.* Norman: University of Oklahoma Press.

Reddy, Movindri. 2001. "Ethnic Conflict and Violence: South Africa, Punjab and Sri Lanka." Pp. 295–326 in *Ethnicity and Governance in the Third World,* ed. John Mukum Mbaku, Mwangi S. Kimenyi, Pita Ogaba Agbese, and John Mukum Mbasku. Burlington, VT: Ashgate.

Robson, Terry. 2000. *The State and Community Action.* London: Pluto Press.

Salomon, Frank, and George L. Urioste. 1991. *The Huarochiri Manuscript: A Testament of Ancient and Colonial Andean Religion.* Austin: University of Texas Press.

Scott, James C. 1998. *Seeing Like a State.* New Haven, CT: Yale University Press.

Selverston, Melina. 1994. "The Politics of Culture: Indigenous Peoples and the State in Ecuador." Pp. 131–152 in *Indigenous Peoples and Democracy in Latin America,* ed. Donna Lee Van Cott. New York: St. Martin's Press.

Selverston-Scher, Melina. 2001. *Ethnopolitics in Ecuador: Indigenous Rights and the Strengthening of Democracy.* Miami, FL: North-South Center Press.

Shils, Edward. 2003. "The Virtue of Civil Society." Pp. 292–305 in *The Civil Society,* ed. Virginia A. Hodgkinson and Michael W. Foley. Hanover, NH: Tufts University and University Press of New England.

Striffler, Steve. 2002. *In the Shadows of State and Capital: The United Fruit Company, Popular Struggle, and Agrarian Restructuring in Ecuador, 1900–1995.* Durham, NC: Duke University Press.

Taussig, Michael. 1996. *The Magic of the State.* New York: Routledge.

Villavicencio Rivadeneira, Gladys. 1973. *Relaciones interétnicas en Otavalo: Una nacionalidad india en formación?* Mexico City: Instituto Indigenista Interamericano.

Warren, Kay B. 1998. "Indigenous Movements as a Challenge to the Unified Social Movement Paradigm for Guatemala." Pp. 155–195 in Sonia Alvarez, Dagnino, and Escobar 1998a.

Warren, Kay B., and Jean E. Jackson. 2002. "Introduction: Studying Indigenous Activism in Latin America." Pp. 1–46 in *Indigenous Movements, Self-Representation, and the State in Latin America,* eds. Kay B. Warren and Jean E. Jackson. Austin: University of Texas Press.

Whitten, Norman, Dorothea Scott Whitten, and Alfonso Chango. 1997. "Return of the Yumbo: The Indigenous Caminata from Amazonia to Andean Quito." *American Ethnologist* 24, no. 2: 355–391.

Zamosc, Leon. 1994. "Agrarian Protest and the Indian Movement in the Ecuadorian Highlands." *Latin American Research Review* 29, no. 3: 37–68.

———. 1995. *Estadistica de las areas de predominio étnico de la sierra ecuatoriana.* Quito: Abya-Yala.

Chapter 5

CIVIL SOCIETY AND THE INDIGENOUS MOVEMENT IN COLOMBIA
The Consejo Regional Indígena del Cauca

Joanne Rappaport

A few years ago, I was invited to review a series of presentations on civil society in Colombia. The roster included papers on the movement in the capital city of Bogotá spearheaded by its elected mayors to introduce a new civic consciousness; studies of the Catholic Church, non-governmental organizations (NGOs), and universities; an evaluation of the work of professionals involved in giving psychological assistance to victims of conflict; and, of course, analyses of negotiations with armed actors, such as the guerrilla and para-military organizations. Surprisingly absent was any mention of the popular movements that have had a significant impact on Colombian political and social life over the decades. In particular, the now mature and highly influential indigenous movement, the burgeoning organizations of Afro-descendants, and the historically

Notes for this chapter begin on page 120.

significant union movement were left out of the picture, as though membership in the middle or upper classes or articulation with middle-class institutions was what defined actors as members of civil society.[1]

Contrary to the message given by the organizers of that seminar, the indigenous movement has played a crucial role in redefining what it means to be Colombian. The absence of any mention of indigenous organizing is all the more surprising given the participation of indigenous representatives in the Constituent Assembly that framed the 1991 Colombian constitution, which achieved what had until then been thought to be an unattainable goal: to rethink the Colombian nation as pluri-ethnic and multicultural, instead of homogeneous (Arocha 2004; Van Cott 2000). Since then, indigenous leaders have participated in local, regional, and national institutions as elected officials, most prominent being the Guambiano leader Taita Floro Alberto Tunubalá, who was elected governor of the department of Cauca at the turn of the millennium. Taita Floro instituted a series of grass-roots meetings that he called *mingas*, after the traditional Andean form of labor exchange, in which local people engaged in policy making on the regional level, thus expanding in practice what could be considered civil society (Rappaport 2005). More recently, a groundswell of indigenous opposition to the free trade agreements that Colombian president Alvaro Uribe planned to sign with the United States led to a popular referendum that was held first in native communities and only afterward spread to other members of the Colombian public (although the Uribe administration paid no heed to these recommendations).[2] The indigenous movement has developed its own response to the armed conflict, proposing new forms of negotiation to promote peace in the countryside (ONIC 2002). Indeed, the indigenous movement has constituted what Marcia Stephenson (2002) has called a "counterpublic sphere" (cf. Fraser 1977), a combative and critical component of Colombian civil society that has consistently questioned the state and the armed organizations arrayed against it.

However, indigenous notions of the role of ethnic movements in the construction of civil society have varied widely over time, ranging from armed opposition to an openness to negotiate with the state, suggesting that if we are to comprehend the participation of native organizations alongside the middle-class institutions and organizations commonly identified as constituting civil society, we must trace changing indigenous discourses over time. Using the example of the Consejo Regional Indígena del Cauca (CRIC, Regional Indigenous Council of Cauca), Colombia's oldest indigenous organization, which is based in the southwestern department of Cauca, I will trace the ways in which the indigenous movement has realigned itself with a range of social sectors over the past three decades.[3]

A Brief History of CRIC

The Consejo Regional Indígena del Cauca was formed in 1971 at a massive congress in the northern Caucan town of Toribío. Its goal was to promote an end to the marginalization of Cauca's indigenous population.[4] *Resguardos*, the communal native landholding corporations established by royal title in the colonial period, had been overrun by large landowners, and their residents had been reduced to the status of sharecroppers. Agrarian reform, a hope in the early 1960s, had largely failed to return lands to the land-poor. *Resguardo* councils, or *cabildos*, had fallen into the hands of local power-holders from the dominant Conservative and Liberal Parties. Shamans, who had once played a crucial role in the everyday life of communities, had been forced underground by the Catholic Church, and few native people were aware of their communities' history; most were embarrassed to be indigenous. Dispossessed of their lands, their political autonomy, and their cultural memory, indigenous people were among the poorest of Cauca's citizens.

Throughout the nineteenth century (Sanders 2004) and into the early twentieth century (Castillo-Cárdenas 1987; Rappaport 1998; Vega Cantor 2002), Caucan indigenous leaders had attempted—through participation in national and leftist political parties, community organizing, and armed rebellion—to pull native communities out of their marginalization and create viable physical, political, and cultural space by focusing on the repossession of lands that had been usurped from them under Spanish colonialism and the Colombian republic. With the advent of agrarian reform and the creation of a national peasant association (Zamosc 1986), they attempted to reclaim usurped lands in conjunction with peasants, planting the seeds of the indigenous movement at the heart of the Asociación Nacional de Usuarios Campesinos (ANUC, National Association of Peasant Users) and seeking out the collaboration of local peasant leaders and politically progressive employees in INCORA, the national institute for agrarian reform.[5]

The 1971 founding of CRIC as an autonomous indigenous organization that aimed to unify the *cabildos* of Cauca revived the demands of Manuel Quintín Lame ([1939] 2004), an early-twentieth-century Nasa leader who had mobilized the native communities of Cauca and of neighboring Tolima. CRIC's seven-point program drew upon Lame's earlier demands: (1) the repossession of *resguardo* lands; (2) the expansion of the *resguardos*; (3) the strengthening of *cabildos*; (4) an end to sharecropping; (5) the promotion of the knowledge of indigenous legislation and the demand that it be applied; (6) the defense of the history, language, and customs of native communities; and (7) the training and employment of indigenous teachers (CRIC 2002).

With its people suffering repression at the hands of landlords, the church, and the military, the organization reconstituted *cabildos* that had disappeared over the course of the early twentieth century, established a legal program that sought out *resguardo* titles in local archives, and collaborated with state institutions in the collection of data for an indigenous census that would both contribute to the training of leaders and provide crucial information on the state of native Cauca (Findji 1978). Two years after founding the organization, indigenous people began to occupy and repossess usurped lands and created cooperatives in indigenous communities. By the mid-1970s, land occupations had extended to 12 municipalities, and numerous *cabildos* had been revived as the rank and file of the organization. An education program was founded with the goal of establishing community-run schools as local organizing tools and as spaces in which native cultures could be promoted (Bolaños et al. 2004).

By the late 1970s, CRIC had embarked on a collaborative relationship with the Quintín Lame Armed Movement (MAQL), a largely indigenous guerrilla organization dedicated to the defense of native communities (Espinosa 1996; Peñaranda 1998), with CRIC providing political training for fighters (Rappaport 2005: chap. 2). As a result, the organization became subject to the generalized repression against the Left spearheaded by the Turbay Ayala government, and most of its executive committee were imprisoned. But the CRIC programs providing social services to indigenous communities—legal services, education, and health care—continued to function, lending a growing legitimacy to the organization in the public arena. In the 1980s, CRIC, along with other regional indigenous organizations that had arisen in the course of the 1970s (Jimeno 1996), founded ONIC, the National Indigenous Organization of Colombia, an umbrella organization. As CRIC gained ascendancy at the regional and national levels, it proposed to negotiate with the state to demilitarize indigenous zones. In conjunction with the by then demobilized MAQL, CRIC participated in the Constituent Assembly that drafted the 1991 constitution and saw its militants elected to national, regional, and local offices.

In recent years, CRIC has functioned simultaneously as a movement dedicated to mobilizing Cauca's indigenous communities through alliances with other popular sectors and as an organization providing vital social services to native communities. The 1994 earthquake and landslides that devastated Tierradentro, the heartland of Nasa settlement in eastern Cauca, brought CRIC to the negotiating table with the state organization dedicated to relief services and to purchasing new lands for the displaced (Rappaport and Gow 1997). Along with other Caucan peasant and labor organizations, CRIC established a center for training and dialogue in La María, a Guambiano *resguardo* near the Caucan capital of Popayán that had been the site of multiple blockages of the Pan American Highway with demands of basic social services for indigenous and other marginal populations (Gow forthcoming).

CRIC came to advocate regional-level negotiations with Colombia's armed movements and played a central role in the creation of organizations dedicated to promoting peace, solidifying its role as a national actor. It was also instrumental in fostering national educational legislation promoting ethno-education in indigenous and Afro-descended communities. Over the three decades of its existence, CRIC's militants ensured that the bulk of the indigenous lands usurped in past centuries were reinstated as *resguardos*, leaving them the space to participate in other political and social activities. However, with the consolidation of agribusiness in the portion of Cauca abutting the Cauca Valley, a zone of sugar production and cattle ranching, along with the transferral of large properties into the hands of drug cartel members, territory has once again become a pressing issue for the indigenous movement, spurring new land occupations since the turn of the millennium.

Generic Indianness and Political Militancy

The CRIC of the 1970s and 1980s was a relatively small organization, one that had not yet grouped together the *resguardos* of Cauca, as it has today. In the early days, CRIC was an organization in which there was little differentiation between *cabildo* members and movement leaders, since most of the activities took place on the local level.[6] It thought of itself as an *organización gremial*, something akin to a trade union (which is one sense of how the Colombian usage of *gremio* translates into English, as an occupationally based organization), in the sense that it saw itself as functioning within a matrix of class-based organizations. CRIC affiliates were understood as members of a generic 'indigenous' group that had access to certain fundamental tools—such as indigenous legislation to protect the integrity of the *resguardo*—not enjoyed by other worker and peasant sectors. They were seen as fighting for certain demands specific to indigenous people, such as the expansion of *cabildo* authority and the revaluing of native cultures.

Myriam Jimeno (1996: 70) describes CRIC's identity in the following terms: "Local demands were integrated into an ethnic discourse where the 'Indian,' as a generic category, was seen as subsuming the peculiarities of each ethnic group; the nation and the state were constituted as interlocutors, also generic in nature." Indeed, the organization was structured according to geographic zones—northern Cauca, central Cauca, Tierradentro, and the southern Colombian Massif—not ethnic groups. It was thus perceived by militants as a unified set of grass-roots communities with demands that ran parallel to those of other popular organizations. CRIC's fundamental demand for land was shared with other rural movements, and they saw themselves as allies of these sectors. In fact, even after the founding of CRIC in 1971, an indigenous secretariat operated within ANUC, the national peasant organization, and the indigenous tactic of land occupations had already been employed in the peasant movement (Zamosc 1986).

Many of CRIC's leaders were seasoned leftist militants, highly familiar with class-based discourses, or had participated in the left wing of the Liberal Party before joining ANUC, as Myriam Jimeno (1996: 63–64) so indicates in her biography of Juan Gregorio Palechor, CRIC's first secretary and a member of the *resguardo* of Guachicono in the Colombian Massif:[7]

> In sum, Palechor's education in the confined and isolated life of the *resguardo* was molded by the influence of processes in the national arena and by personal experiences with non-indigenous society. The participation of his ancestors in the civil war at the turn of the century left him with a heroic memory and a party affiliation.[8] Schooling and [obligatory] military service, in addition to [the acquisition of] literacy, left him with a knowledge of national society and its conflicts. These awakened in him a sensitivity to discrimination and social inequality, and an interest in national politics. This interest led Palechor to admire [Liberal populist leader] Jorge Eliecer Gaitán, an eloquent spokesperson for popular causes.[9] Then, in an unfruitful search for social reform, he supported the Revolutionary Liberal Movement, another dissident group in the Liberal Party. Finally, the peasant movements of the 1970s led him to support the creation of new indigenous organizations. The intersection of apprenticeships

in the "larger customs" and national society led him to champion the nascent indigenous movements in Colombia.

This was the discourse that CRIC's leaders knew from long-time experience and out of which they would have to construct a specifically indigenous discourse.

An autodidact, Palechor learned what he knew of indigenous legislation while working as a laborer. He subsequently became a *tinterillo*, a self-educated rural lawyer, who drew up legal documents for a fee for his neighbors and later applied this knowledge in the indigenous organization—at least, until schooled attorneys came on board as non-indigenous collaborators (Jimeno 1996: 64–67). Like others, he was an organic intellectual (Gramsci 1971) of the emerging indigenous movement, dedicated, above all, to reclaiming indigenous lands. Many of his comrades were also unschooled in a formal sense, yet they were astute analysts of national and regional politics.[10] Some of them were quite eloquent writers, as Quintín Lame had been. These were not young men, most of them already into their thirties and with a wealth of political experience under their belts. They lived from hand to mouth in the organization, frequently supported by spouses who worked the land (there were relatively few women in CRIC's early leadership). Most notably, they maintained an entirely contestatory posture in the face of government repression, preferring direct action to negotiation with the state. However, once the organization reclaimed lands, it tapped state institutions, such as the national agrarian reform agency (INCORA), for support in the formation of cooperatives in these territories. As I will demonstrate, this profile of an indigenous leader was abandoned by the organization in later years.

The nature and discourse of an *organización gremial* can be readily perceived in Palechor's own words: "It was felt [in 1971] that the seven-point program [of CRIC] should begin with the repossession of lands; the *compañeros* began the work of repossession. Then the government surrounded the *cabildos* of San Francisco, Toribío, and Tacueyó [in northern Cauca] ... They put them in prison ... Well, in continuation, inside the organization CRIC—I was a witness—we were after the defense of a race, the defense of a class. An organization that sought to reclaim what had been lost, such as the repossession of lands, the refusal [of sharecroppers] to pay rent" (Jimeno 1996: 62). Note Palechor's identification of indigenous people as a "race," harking back to Quintín Lame, and his assignation of CRIC's objectives as "the defense of a class" that "sought to reclaim what had been lost." There is no reference to ethnic specificity or to the myriad cultural meanings of territory in this statement, which is generic and class-based. CRIC's (and Palechor's) focus on land and the control of the means of production converged with the class-based strategies of the peasant movement from which CRIC was born.

Negotiating the Politics of Peoplehood

By the early 1990s, CRIC had gained legitimacy as a regional and national actor, both through its service programs and through its successful land claims strategy, which had done away with sharecropping and considerably expanded the indigenous land base.[11] Along with other indigenous organizations, the Caucan movement was therefore empowered to enter into dialogue with the state at a critical moment in Colombian history when, confronted with the weakness of state institutions, a Constituent Assembly was convoked to rewrite the constitution, rework major state institutions, and decentralize the activities of the national government (Van Cott 2000). The result was a new constitution (República de Colombia 1991) that recognized a certain degree of autonomy for *resguardos* in the administrative, educational, and judicial spheres. The constitution even posed the possibility of a radical restructuring of the national map to include Indigenous Territorial Entities that would administer native territories (Rappaport 1996), although these were never legislated into existence.[12] *Cabildos* would now act as judges of criminal offenses and arbiters of civil cases (Sánchez 2001). They would be responsible for drawing up their own development plans and for spending public monies (Gow 1997, forthcoming). They became formal interlocutors of the state, negotiating such varied issues as the provision of health care and the administration of indigenous schools. The post-constitution era thus marked a shift in which the indigenous organization assumed state-like functions. Some analysts have seen this as a process of co-optation of the indigenous movement (Padilla 1996), while the movement has taken this as a necessary strategy in a neo-liberal environment and as a direct outgrowth of its participation in the writing of the constitution.

At the local level, the face of *cabildos* began to change radically. While previously indigenous governors had moved slowly up the rungs of the *cabildo* administration, achieving the highest office only after many years of political experience, in the 1990s *cabildos* became much younger, with governors sometimes barely into their twenties. Many of them had high school degrees, some of them were schoolteachers, and others had experience in a range of CRIC-sponsored institutions. All were literate and conversant with the language of the national society, although their political experience was more shallow than that of their predecessors. There was now a different feel to the *cabildo*: local authorities were entirely fluent in Spanish, they dressed in stylish blue jeans, some of them were women, most of them had reached adulthood after the disappearance of sharecropping and lived in *resguardos* that had already reclaimed usurped lands. These new authorities, it was felt, would be better able to interact with the state on its own terms and to protect the interests of the local community in the areas of justice, health care, education, and the disbursement of public funds than were their more rustic—and combative—forebears.

Similar transformations were also taking place in the regional organization, whose objectives had shifted away from land claims and toward the provision of basic services to indigenous constituents. Instead of land occupations, CRIC now advocated mass mobilizations blocking the Pan American Highway and marches to major cities to demand these services. In other words, the organization remained contestatory, although its leadership was also open to negotiation with the state, having once established a positive balance of forces through direct action. Thus, each time the indigenous movement and its allies blocked the highway at La

María, a delegation of its leaders met with government ministers to resolve the conflict. As a result, the organization won the right to administer health and educational services on the regional level, marking them as a kind of para-statal presence in Cauca. The organization, in conjunction with the Fundación Sol y Tierra, the NGO established by the demobilized Quintín Lame guerrillas, founded an indigenous political party, the Social Indigenous Alliance (ASI), which won seats in the national and regional legislatures, numerous municipal mayoralities, and the governorship of Cauca. While the first indigenous leader to occupy a seat in the national senate, Taita Lorenzo Muelas, was an unschooled former sharecropper, whose political skills had been honed in the land claims movement as a former *cabildo* governor (Muelas Hurtado 2005), subsequent indigenous candidates were of the new generation of schooled leaders. However, given Taita Lorenzo's vast experience in Guambía, in the Senate, and in the Constituent Assembly, I would be hard pressed to argue that the new candidates and elected officials are more cosmopolitan than he. Thus, despite its continuing combativeness, to some degree the indigenous movement merged with the state, a paradox that I will highlight in the last section of this chapter. The generational changes that had taken place in the leadership of local *cabildos* occurred in the CRIC executive as well, with younger and more highly educated militants occupying CRIC's highest positions.

While these transformations in Caucan indigenous politics occurred in a Colombian political context of government decentralization and responses to armed conflict, the effects of international developments in indigenous organizing and the restructuring of political blocs on a global level were also felt in the region. With the fall of the Berlin Wall, the realignments of the superpowers, and the demise of traditional leftist political parties, a space was opened for the appearance of new social movements (Alvarez, Dagnino, and Escobar 1998). This trend was represented in Latin America by the rise of indigenous organizations as major national and international interlocutors, whose prominence as critics of neo-liberal reform policies is undisputed. Indigenous movements—some of them relatively recent and others, like CRIC, already well established—began to embrace a politics of difference through which they could advance claims to citizenship as ethnic actors (Brysk 2000; Jackson and Warren 2005; Yashar 2005). However, unlike ethnic militants in other parts of the world, Latin American indigenous organizations embraced inclusiveness, membership in the nation. They were not separatist, as the Zapatista movement eloquently demonstrated in its effort to have an impact upon the Mexican national imaginary (Harvey 1998). However, they began to constitute themselves as peoples—*pueblos*—in dialogue with the national society (Jackson and Warren 2005: 553–556).[13]

CRIC was not immune to these discursive shifts. Abandoning its generic discourse of indigeneity in favor of a politics of peoplehood, the various ethnic components of the organization began to assert their cultural distinctiveness. The communities of the Colombian Massif, where Juan Gregorio Palechor was born and where until the late twentieth century people identified themselves by their local communities, adopted the more inclusive ethnonym 'Yanacona' (Zambrano 1992). The Páez, the largest ethnic group in Cauca, chose to identify themselves as 'Nasa', rejecting the Spanish misreading of the name of a conquest-era hereditary chief in favor of an appellation used in their own language. Efforts were begun by communities such as Totoró and Quizgó to revive the Guambiano language. Cosmovision—a modern conceptual category that incorporates secular and spiritual behavior, mythic charters, and historical experience into a politically effective discourse—and history became key elements, not only in educational planning, but also in political rhetoric (Rappaport 2005). Such discourses came to the fore particularly in disputes over the legitimacy and scope of customary law, which political leaders sought to harness in local, regional, and national disputes (Rappaport 2005: chap. 6; República de Colombia 1997; Sánchez 2001). Paradoxically, however, it was the younger militants now at the helm of CRIC and its constituent *cabildos*, many of whom had scant experience in community cultural life, who were to become the standard-bearers of this new discourse of peoplehood.

CRIC and Civil Society

Clearly, whether in the image of a combative land-occupier or of a more conciliatory would-be ethnic citizen, the indigenous movement's insertion into Colombian civil society is not entirely consistent with the character of the middle-class institutions that are normally identified as such. CRIC sees its place in civil society as an organization in militant struggle, making it distinct from the less combative sectors that are generally identified as part of civil society. Their projection of ethnic difference, while currently in vogue in Colombia, also threatens the hegemony of those institutions—such as the Catholic Church—that have played the role of a conciliatory counterpart to the state. In a sense, things have not changed: militant combativeness and ethnic difference have always been part of CRIC's discourse and of its imaginary as part of a contestatory counterpublic sphere that envisions civil society as largely comprised of marginalized popular sectors and their allies. However, as I have tried to show in the previous sections, what constitutes combativeness and what is meant by ethnic difference have varied over time, leading to differing degrees of acceptance of the indigenous movement by the state and by middle-class civil society.

I close this chapter by focusing on three key junctures at which CRIC's own image of its place in civil society has come under dispute, both within the organization and with regard to external forces. These moments constitute the spaces in which the indigenous vision of civil society has been forged over time: (1) an early moment at which the Guambianos break from a *gremialista* CRIC to form an organization focused on a discourse of peoplehood; (2) the turn of the millennium, when the CRIC leadership constituted itself as a 'traditional authority', akin to a *cabildo*, as a way of emphasizing ethnic difference; and (3) the current moment, marked by an emerging dispute between CRIC's aging founders and its youthful leadership, in which the terms of difference and militancy are once again being redefined, but by unlikely actors.

The rupture between CRIC and the Guambianos in the late 1970s constitutes a first step toward a discourse of peoplehood for the indigenous movement in Colombia. Dissatisfied by CRIC's *gremialista* stance and its support of converting repossessed lands into cooperatives instead of incorporating them into the *resguardo* structure, the Guambianos founded an organization that would ultimately be called the Indigenous Authorities of Colombia, AICO.[14] Rejecting the centralization that concentrated CRIC's leadership in its executive committee, AICO's leaders came directly from the *cabildos* that composed the organization, *cabildos* with distinct ethnic identifications—Guambiano, Nasa (then still called Páez), and Pasto—who demanded that President Belisario Betancur meet them on reclaimed lands, 'authority to authority', thus underlining their primordial legitimacy in the face of the state. Although AICO was as militant as CRIC, both engaging in land occupations, its political discourse was accompanied by a distinct verbal, visual, and ritual language of peoplehood, in which its component *cabildos* displayed flags and coats of arms whose constituent elements originated in oral tradition, costume, and *cabildo* ceremony of specific ethnic communities (Rappaport 1992; 1994: chap. 4; 1998: chap. 6). At the time, CRIC continued to promote a more generic indigenous identity through a *gremialista* discourse, fostering a distinct notion of what militant Indianness meant in Colombia.

The lack of distance—indeed, the commonality—between AICO's leadership and that of its constituent *cabildos*, in contrast to CRIC's centralized executive council elected by the *cabildos*, came to denote in the Colombian popular imagination one of the major fault lines in the indigenous movement. For national authorities, even for those who in some way supported indigenous demands, the fact that many ethnic organizations were distanced from their grass roots made them in some way 'inauthentic' native representatives. The Guambianos and AICO gained a certain degree of legitimacy when they demanded that President Betancur meet them 'authority to authority'. But in 1996, when the national indigenous organization ONIC (whose central committee is selected by its constituent regional organizations) attempted to mediate a takeover by the Wayúu of a series of government and church offices, the Division of Indigenous Affairs refused to open dialogue with any indigenous representative other than elected *cabildo* members, underlining what they saw as the 'inauthenticity' of supra-local indigenous organizations (Jackson 2002).

CRIC attempted to resolve the authenticity issue in 1999 when, during a blockage of the Pan American Highway at La María, one of their principal demands was that the state recognize their executive council as a 'traditional authority'. This was the most sensitive negotiating point with the government and the last to be resolved through formal state recognition. Clearly, the conversion of the organizational leadership into something akin to a *cabildo* would afford them a degree of legitimacy that the state was reluctant to permit: they would become a kind of 'indigenous civil society' that the state would be forced to respect. Since then, CRIC's leadership has carried staffs of office, much as do *cabildos*, although I doubt that government authorities recognize them as such. Even internally, it is difficult to envision the CRIC executives as a kind of *cabildo*, given their lack of *cabildo* experience and, in many cases, their relatively brief participation in the bitter struggles that have characterized the organization's relationship with the state. Moreover, they move across a vast provincial territory and are not bound to specific *resguardo* lands legitimized by colonial title or official decree. The executive committee's appeal to authenticity through a politics of peoplehood is, to some degree, still elusive.

The final moment I would like to reflect on also revolves around recent transformations in CRIC's leadership, pointing to the internal ambivalences in the organization's current vision of indigenous civil society. At the 2005 CRIC congress, a Consejo de Mayores (Council of Elders) was established, composed primarily of the surviving founders of the organization. Although initially the purpose of the group was to provide relief to retired militants who had limited means of supporting themselves after decades of unpaid labor in the movement, its objectives swiftly shifted toward exerting a new grass-roots influence on the executive: they demanded that they be recognized as advisers to the CRIC leadership, with the goal of restoring a measure of combativeness to the organization. Among the various junctures at which the executive and the *mayores* clashed was in the spring of 2005, when the youths of northern Cauca organized a land occupation after decades of inactivity. The *mayores* supported them, against the wishes of the executive council, which, in the end, was forced to acquiesce to the youths' demands.[15] In this instance, it was not toward an external audience that the organization was attempting to project its image of what constituted an indigenous counter-public sphere, but toward the very leadership of the movement. In doing so, it lay bare the paradox of a combative leadership that simultaneously had taken on the character of a government apparatus.

Conclusion

In an astute appreciation of the nature of political process in non-Western countries, Partha Chatterjee (2000: 42) argues that we might best understand civil society as a relatively limited sector of society, confined to "those characteristic institutions of modern associational life originating in Western societies that are based on equality, autonomy, freedom of entry and exit, contract, deliberative procedures of decision making, recognized rights and duties of members, and other such principles." Outside of the confines of civil society are what he calls "populations" that lie within the jurisdiction of the state, which attempts to control them through the intervention of government agencies and NGOs. These sectors enter into a political relationship with the state (Chatterjee 2004: 38), although not within the idealized parameters imagined by the bourgeois members of civil society. Consequently, they must engage in a politics that Chatterjee (ibid.: 39) sees as different from that of the elite. This vast swath of the national population, which he refers to as "political society," is necessarily involved in seeking recognition from the government, frequently by means deemed illegal by civil society (ibid.: chap. 3). In other words, in order to reclaim their rights as citizens, members of political society must transgress the limits set by governments in an effort to expand democracy to include them: "If we have to give a name to the major form of mobilization by which political society (parties, movements, non-party political formations) tries to channel and order popular demands on the developmental state, we should call it democracy ... Just as there is a continuing attempt to order these institutions in the prescribed forms of liberal civil society, there is probably an even stronger tendency to strive for what are perceived to be democratic rights and entitlements by violating those institutional norms" (Chatterjee 2000: 46–47). It is their very exclusion from civil society that forces organizations within political society to mobilize.

The articulation of indigenous organizations with civil society is an incomplete project in most of Latin America, for the reasons that Chatterjee provides. Ecuador and Guatemala, where the indigenous populations are considerably larger than in Colombia and where native leaders have participated in national governments at the cabinet level, are good cases in point. Here, state-sponsored multicultural reform has led to some recognition of the rights of ethnic citizens and of indigenous collectivities but not to long-term changes in the articulation of ethnic minorities within the structures of the dominant society (Hale 2002; Jackson and Warren 2005: 551–553). Instead, neo-liberal reform has passed on responsibilities that were formerly required of the state to private individuals and groups, including indigenous communities (Postero 2007: 15–18). While in theory this move appears to admit such groups under the inclusive 'civil society umbrella', it does not allow indigenous communities to achieve a greater impact upon the broader society because their minority status within an electoral democracy continues to dilute their power (Mouffe 1995). Bolivia is the exception to the rule. Aymara activist Evo Morales's election to the presidency in this majority-indigenous country suggests that in Bolivia notions of citizenship have been transformed to such an extent that 'indigenous' and 'citizen' are now coterminous. At the same time, the nature of indigenous organizing in Bolivia has transcended a purely ethnic focus to comprise a broad range of political activities associated with the struggle for citizenship rights by marginal populations (Postero 2007).

Colombia presents an extreme case that mirrors much of Latin America. With only 2 percent of the population claiming indigenous identity, the impact of ethnic organizations is muted in comparison to countries such as Bolivia, Ecuador, and Guatemala. As a result of continuing conflict—bolstered by US support for counter-insurgency warfare and the eradication of illicit crops, both of which have an unequal impact upon indigenous populations, given the fact that native territories are battlegrounds in the wider conflict and sites of coca and poppy cultivation—and a national government policy that labels many popular organizations as subversive, the space of action for indigenous organizations has been narrowed. While on an internal level CRIC's membership has battled to define and redefine what it means to constitute an indigenous component of civil society, the organization's identity as a member of the panoply of social forces operating parallel to the state is still under debate and under attack.

Since the 1991 constitutional mandate reserving seats in the Senate for indigenous representatives, native legislators have been elected largely by urban intellectuals, not by the indigenous sector, whose votes are divided among indigenous candidates and those from the traditional political parties.

Some movement leaders—Lorenzo Muelas being one of them—have become respected national personalities. But under the current political climate, with a national administration bent upon curbing insurgency even to the point of sacrificing the rights of its own citizens, at worst, the indigenous movement is seen as a dangerous ally of the guerrillas and, at best, as an insignificant representative of a minuscule sector of the national population. In the last congressional elections, indigenous candidates vying for native-held Senate seats were listed on a separate ballot from other candidates, and voters were allowed to fill in only one of the two ballots. Predictably, the indigenous ballot garnered too few votes to constitute a viable election, and the matter of which indigenous leaders would fill the two available Senate seats had to be negotiated. Despite its 30 years of struggle and the fact that the indigenous movement is, at present, the most vocal and powerful popular movement in Colombia, it has still not been able to constitute itself in the eyes of the nation as a legitimate member of civil society.

Acknowledgments

This chapter is based on research conducted in collaboration with the Consejo Regional Indígena del Cauca from 1999 to 2002, under an international collaborative grant from the Wenner-Gren Foundation for Anthropological Research. This grant supported the development of an international and inter-ethnic collaborative research team made up of indigenous researchers, Colombian scholars, and international scholars, which engaged in a far-ranging dialogue on ethnic politics in Cauca since the 1991 constitution. Team members included indigenous activists Adonías Perdomo and Susana Piñacué, both members of the Bilingual and Intercultural Education Program (PEBI) of CRIC, Colombian researchers Myriam Amparo Espinosa and Tulio Rojas Curieux of the Universidad del Cauca, and international scholars David Gow of George Washington University and myself. My own ongoing collaborations with Graciela Bolaños and Abelardo Ramos Pacho of PEBI, during and beyond the grant period, have also contributed to my analysis of CRIC as a component of civil society.

Joanne Rappaport teaches Latin American cultural studies and anthropology at Georgetown University. Her major interests include intellectuals and indigenous movements, native literacy in the colonial and modern periods, and race and *mestizaje*. She conducts most of her research in Colombia, frequently in collaboration with indigenous organizations. Her books include *Cumbe Reborn* (1994), *The Politics of Memory* (1998 and 1990), *¿Qué pasaría si la escuela ...?* (2004), *Intercultural Utopias* (2005), and *Retornando la Mirada* (2005).

Notes

1. A similar narrow view of civil society can be found in the social science literature on the Colombian conflict (Hoskin and Murillo-Castaño 1999).
2. Information on indigenous responses to free trade can be found at http://www.nasaacin .net, the Web site of ACIN, the Association of Indigenous Councils of Northern Cauca.
3. According to ONIC (National Indigenous Organization of Colombia), in Colombia there are approximately 800,000 people—or 2 percent of the national population—who identify themselves as indigenous, belonging to 85 ethnic groups, with approximately 110,000 living in the department of Cauca (see http://www.onic.org.co/nuevo/historia.shtml). At the national level, there are a number of competing organizations, the largest being ONIC and AICO (Indigenous Authorities of Colombia), which represent different ethnic groups. Most indigenous communities are represented by a major organization, with the majority affiliated with regional organizations belonging to ONIC. CRIC, an affiliate of ONIC (and one of its founding organizations), represents most of the indigenous communities of Cauca, with the exception of the approximately 15,000 Guambianos, who are affiliated with AICO. Cauca's indigenous population comprises 30 percent of the total population of the department. Although there are competing indigenous organizations at the national and regional levels, they come together at times of mobilization.
4. This history of CRIC was assisted by a CD-ROM of the conclusions of CRIC's congresses prepared by the organization (CRIC 2002). Early on, CRIC's leadership promoted the organization internationally through the publication of articles outlining its demands (Avirama and Márquez 1995; Morales 1979). There has not, however, been a comprehensive history of CRIC published by activists or academics, although a few publications (Gros 1991, 2000; Hernández Delgado 2004) provide useful information and analysis for a history of the organization.
5. In Colombia, unlike in other Andean nations where native people are commonly labeled as 'peasants', indigenous people are distinguished as an ethnic group from non-indigenous peasants, the latter including both mestizos and Afro-descendants, whose ethnicity goes unmarked in the peasant sphere. Moreover, peasant organizing is seen as class-based, while indigenous organizing is ethnic in nature. In the past decade, the notion of ethnicity has also come to define Afro-Colombians, although some peasants of African descent continue to participate as peasants in political movements, while others have created burgeoning ethnic organizations (Ng'weno 2007).
6. CRIC began with only 11 affiliated *cabildos*. Today, almost all of the Nasa *resguardos* are associated with CRIC, as are the Yanacona *resguardos* of southern Cauca and the Guambiano-Kokonuko *resguardos* around Popayán. Eperara communities on the Pacific Coast are also integrated into the organization. Guambía, a very large *resguardo* of Guambiano speakers who held leadership positions in CRIC in its early years, broke off from the organization in the late 1970s to form a parallel organization, the Indigenous Authorities of Colombia (AICO). The Guambianos (and, at the time, some Nasa communities that have since regrouped with CRIC) criticized CRIC for what they saw as its burgeoning bureaucracy and because in the early period, many of the repossessed lands were not incorporated into the *resguardo* structure but were instead converted into cooperatives (Findji 1992). They also distrusted the non-indigenous collaborators who worked in the organization, preferring to erect a non-native solidarity group operating parallel to AICO (Caviedes 2000; Vasco Uribe 2002). In recent years, however, CRIC and AICO have entered into coalitions to support major mobilizations and the candidacy of Taita Floro Alberto Tunubalá—a Guambiano and AICO member—and many of their strategies and organizing tactics have come to resemble one another.
7. Palechor's life history was recently published as a volume (Jimeno 2006).
8. The War of the Thousand Days, fought between Liberals and Conservatives in the last years of the nineteenth century and the beginning of the twentieth century (Safford and Palacios 2001), was participated in by many indigenous leaders, including Manuel

Quintín Lame (Rappaport 1998: chaps. 3–4). Unlike Lame, however, who was a Conservative, Palechor inherited from his ancestors an affiliation with the Liberal Party.

9. Gaitán was a populist leader in the Liberal Party who was assassinated during the presidential campaign of 1948. His death provoked a popular uprising in Bogotá and led to the mid-century civil war called 'La Violencia' (Safford and Palacios 2001).

10. One of the few exceptions to this rule was Marcos Avirama, from the *resguardo* of Coconuco, who was president of CRIC in the late 1970s when its executive committee was imprisoned. Avirama had a high school degree and had briefly been a student at the National University in Bogotá before being expelled for political activities.

11. Nevertheless, the current administration of Alvaro Uribe Vélez has at various points in his presidency accused the indigenous movement of being subversive, sending troops against a 2006 indigenous summit in La María that had proposed negotiations with his government.

12. Two indigenous representatives, Lorenzo Muelas (Guambiano) and Francisco Rojas Birry (Embera), were elected to the Constituent Assembly. After the successful negotiations of the MAQL with the Colombian government, one of its commanders, Alfonso Peña, also joined the Assembly. These men established alliances with other progressive forces in the Assembly, most notably, with the 19th of April Movement (the M-19), a demobilized guerrilla organization-turned-political party with whom the MAQL had collaborated in its years of clandestinity. It was in the interests of the national government to have indigenous organizations participating in the Assembly and aligning themselves with the state, given that native communities were located in many of the major zones of guerrilla conflict, thus constituting a buffer between the insurgency and the state.

13. With the exception of Bolivia, where the indigenous majority has succeeded in taking the reigns of the national government, the minority status of Latin American native populations has precluded the possibility of separatist strategies. This is particularly true in Colombia, where only 2 percent of the population is identified as indigenous.

14. The new organization was initially called the Indigenous Authorities of the Southwest (AISO), becoming AICO when it incorporated ethnic groups from other parts of Colombia (Findji 1992).

15. This is an example of the solidarity of alternating generations that I had studied as an undergraduate but never expected to observe during my research of indigenous politics.

References

Alvarez, Sonia, Evelina Dagnino, and Arturo Escobar, eds. 1998. *Cultures of Politics/Politics of Cultures: Re-visioning Latin American Social Movements.* Boulder, CO: Westview.

Arocha, Jaime, ed. 2004. *Utopía para los Excluidos: El multiculturalismo en África y América Latina.* Bogotá: Facultad de Ciencias Humanas UN, Colección CES.

Avirama, Jesús, and Rayda Márquez. 1995. "The Indigenous Movement in Colombia." Pp. 83–105 in *Indigenous Peoples and Democracy in Latin America*, ed. Donna Lee Van Cott. New York: St. Martin's Press.

Bolaños, Graciela, Abelardo Ramos, Joanne Rappaport, and Carlos Miñana. 2004. *¿Qué pasaría si la escuela ...? Treinta años de construcción educativa.* Popayán: Programa de Educación Bilingüe e Intercultural, Consejo Regional Indígena del Cauca.

Brysk, Alison. 2000. *From Tribal Village to Global Village: Indian Rights and International Relations in Latin America.* Stanford, CA: Stanford University Press.

Castillo-Cárdenas, Gonzalo. 1987. *Liberation Theology from Below: The Life and Thought of Manuel Quintín Lame.* Maryknoll, NY: Orbis.

Caviedes, Mauricio. 2000. "Antropología y movimiento indígena." PhD diss., Universidad Nacional de Colombia, Bogotá.

Chatterjee, Partha. 2000. "Two Poets and Death: On Civil and Political Society in the Non-Christian World." Pp. 35–48 in *Questions of Modernity*, ed. Timothy Mitchell. Minneapolis: University of Minnesota Press.

_____. 2004. *The Politics of the Governed: Reflections on Popular Politics in Most of the World*. New York: Columbia University Press.

CRIC (Consejo Regional Indígena del Cauca). 2002. *Memoria colectiva, historia para reinterpretar hoy: Congresos CRIC, febrero de 1.971 a marzo de 2.001*. Popayán: Consejo Regional Indígena del Cauca (CD-ROM).

Espinosa, Myriam Amparo. 1996. *Surgimiento y andar territorial del Quintín Lame*. Quito: Editorial Abya-Yala.

Findji, María Teresa. 1978. *Elementos para el estudio de los resguardos indígenas del Cauca: Censo indígena del Cauca, 1972*. Bogotá: Departamento Administrativo Nacional de Estadística.

_____. 1992. "From Resistance to Social Movement: The Indigenous Authorities Movement in Colombia." Pp. 112–133 in *The Making of Social Movements in Latin America: Identity, Strategy, and Democracy*, ed. Arturo Escobar and Sonia E. Alvarez. Boulder, CO: Westview.

Fraser, Nancy. 1977. *Justice Interruptus: Critical Reflections on the "Postsocialist" Condition*. New York: Routledge.

Gow, David D. 1997. "Can the Subaltern Plan? Ethnicity and Development in Cauca, Colombia." *Urban Anthropology* 26, no. 3–4: 243–292.

_____. Forthcoming. *Countering Development: Indigenous Modernity and the Moral Imagination*. Durham, NC: Duke University Press.

Gramsci, Antonio. 1971. *Selections from the Prison Notebooks*. New York: International.

Gros, Christian. 1991. *Colombia indígena: Identidad cultural y cambio social*. Bogotá: CEREC.

_____. 2000. *Políticas de la etnicidad: Identidad, estado y modernidad*. Bogotá: Instituto Colombiano de Antropología e Historia.

Hale, Charles R. 2002. "Does Multiculturalism Menace? Governance, Cultural Rights and the Politics of Identity in Guatemala." *Journal of Latin American Studies* 34: 485–524.

Harvey, Neil. 1998. *The Chiapas Rebellion: The Struggle for Land and Democracy*. Durham, NC: Duke University Press.

Hernández Delgado, Esperanza. 2004. *Resistencia civil artesana de paz: Experiencias indígenas, afrodescendientes y campesinas*. Bogotá: Editorial Pontificia Universidad Javeriana.

Hoskin, Gary, and Gabriel Murillo-Castaño. 1999. "Can Colombia Cope?" *Journal of Democracy* 10, no. 1: 36–50.

Jackson, Jean E. 2002. "Contested Discourses of Authority in Colombian National Indigenous Politics: The 1996 Summer Takeovers." Pp. 81–122 in *Indigenous Movements, Self-Representation, and the State in Latin America*, ed. Kay B. Warren and Jean E. Jackson. Austin: University of Texas Press.

Jackson, Jean E., and Kay B. Warren. 2005. "Indigenous Movements in Latin America, 1992–2004: Controversies, Ironies, New Directions." *Annual Review of Anthropology* 35: 549–573.

Jimeno, Myriam. 1996. "Juan Gregorio Palechor: Tierra, identidad y recreación etnica." *Journal of Latin American Anthropology* 1, no. 2: 46–77.

_____. 2006. *Juan Gregorio Palechor: Historia de mi vida*. Bogotá: Universidad Nacional de Colombia, Facultad de Ciencias Humanas/Instituto Colombiano de Antropología e Historia and Popayán: Universidad del Cauca/Consejo Regional Indígena del Cauca.

Lame, Manuel Quintín. [1939] 2004. *Los pensamientos del indio que se educó dentro de las selvas colombianas*. Cali and Popayán: Editorial Universidad del Valle/Editoral Universidad del Cauca.

Morales, Trino. 1979. "El movimiento indígena en Colombia." Pp. 41–54 in *Indianidad y descolonización en América Latina: Documentos de la Segunda Reunión de Barbados*. Mexico City: Nueva Imagen.

Mouffe, Chantal. 1995. "Democratic Politics and the Question of Identity." Pp. 33–45 in *The Identity in Question*, ed. John Rajchman. London: Routledge.

Muelas Hurtado, Lorenzo, with the collaboration of Martha L. Urdaneta Franco. 2005. *La fuerza de la gente: Juntando recuerdos sobre la terrajería en Guambía-Colombia*. Bogotá: Instituto Colombiano de Antropología e Historia.

Ng'weno, Bettina. 2007. *Turf Wars: Citizenship and Territory in the Contemporary State*. Stanford, CA: Stanford University Press.

ONIC (Organización Nacional Indígena de Colombia). 2002. *Los indígenas y la paz: Pronunciamientos, resoluciones, declaraciones y otros documentos de los pueblos y organizaciones indígenas sobre la violencia armada en sus territorios, la búsqueda de la paz, la autonomía y la resistencia.* Bogotá: Ediciones Turdakke.

Padilla, Guillermo. 1996. "La ley y los pueblos indígenas en Colombia." *Journal of Latin American Anthropology* 1, no. 2: 78–97.

Peñaranda, Ricardo. 1998. "Historia del movimiento armado Quintín Lame." MA diss., Universidad Nacional de Colombia, Bogotá.

Postero, Nancy Grey. 2007. *Now We Are Citizens: Indigenous Politics in Postmulticultural Bolivia.* Stanford, CA: Stanford University Press.

Rappaport, Joanne. 1992. "Reinvented Traditions: The Heraldry of Ethnic Militancy in the Colombian Andes." Pp. 202–228 in *Andean Cosmologies Through Time: Persistence and Emergence,* ed. Robert Dover, Katharine Seibold, and John McDowell. Bloomington: Indiana University Press.

———. 1994. *Cumbe Reborn: An Andean Ethnography of History.* Chicago, IL: University of Chicago Press.

———, ed. 1996. *Ethnicity Reconfigured: Indigenous Legislators and the Colombian Constitution of 1991.* Special issue of *Journal of Latin American Anthropology* 1, no. 2.

———. 1998. *The Politics of Memory: Native Historical Interpretation in the Colombian Andes.* Durham, NC: Duke University Press.

———. 2005. *Intercultural Utopias: Public Intellectuals, Cultural Experimentation, and Ethnic Dialogue in Colombia.* Durham, NC: Duke University Press.

Rappaport, Joanne, and David D. Gow. 1997. "Cambio dirigido, movimiento indígena y estereotipos del indio: El estado colombiano y la reubicación de los Nasa." Pp. 361–399 in *Antropología en la modernidad,* ed. María Victoria Uribe and Eduardo Restrepo. Bogotá: Instituto Colombiano de Antropología.

República de Colombia. 1991. *Nueva Constitución Política de Colombia.* Pasto: Minilibrería Jurídica Moral.

———. 1997. *"Del olvido surgimos para traer nuevas esperanzas": La jurisdicción especial indígena.* Bogotá: Ministerio de Justicia y del Derecho/Ministerio del Interior, Dirección General de Asuntos Indígenas.

Safford, Frank, and Marco Palacios. 2001. *Colombia: Fragmented Land, Divided Society.* Oxford: Oxford University Press.

Sánchez, Beatriz Eugenia. 2001. "El reto del multiculturalismo jurídico: La justicia de la sociedad mayor y la justicia indígena." Pp. 5–142 in *El caleidoscopio de las justicias en Colombia,* vol. 2, ed. Boaventura de Sousa Santos and Mauricio García Villegas. Bogotá: Siglo de Hombre Editores.

Sanders, James E. 2004. *Contentious Republicans: Popular Politics, Race, and Class in Nineteenth-Century Colombia.* Durham, NC: Duke University Press.

Stephenson, Marcia. 2002. "Forging an Indigenous Counterpublic Sphere: The Taller de Historia Oral Andina in Bolivia." *Latin American Research Review* 37, no. 2: 99–118.

Van Cott, Donna Lee. 2000. *The Friendly Liquidation of the Past: The Politics of Diversity in Latin America.* Pittsburgh, PA: University of Pittsburgh Press.

Vasco Uribe, Luis Guillermo. 2002. *Entre selva y páramo: Viviendo y pensando la lucha india.* Bogotá: Instituto Colombiano de Antropología e Historia.

Vega Cantor, Renán. 2002. *Gente muy rebelde.* Vol. 2: *Indígenas, campesinos y protestas agrarias.* Bogotá: Ediciones Pensamiento Crítico.

Yashar, Deborah J. 2005. *Contesting Citizenship in Latin America: The Rise of Indigenous Movements and the Postliberal Challenge.* Cambridge: Cambridge University Press.

Zambrano, Carlos Vladimir, ed. 1992. *Hombres de páramo y montaña.* Bogotá: Instituto Colombiano de Antropología/Plan Nacional de Rehabilitación.

Zamosc, Leon. 1986. *The Agrarian Question and the Peasant Movement in Colombia: Struggles of the National Peasant Association, 1967–1981.* Cambridge: Cambridge University Press.

Chapter 6

INDIGENOUS NATIONS IN GUATEMALAN DEMOCRACY AND THE STATE
A Tentative Assessment

Demetrio Cojtí Cuxil

In Guatemala, ethnic and 'racial' differences are not enjoyed; they are rejected and suffered. With the exception of a brief democratic period from 1944 to 1954, Guatemalan history has been marked by authoritarian and conservative governments in which dictatorships were common and toward which people generally turned a blind eye. Only since 1985 has the country entered a period of transition to democracy. Sadly, this political transformation has not led to a genuine progression from mono-ethnicity to multi-nationality, or from colonialism to the liberation of indigenous groups. As such, the state, as well as the democratic system, remains structurally colonialist and racist.

The majority of Guatemala's population is indigenous (representing 60 percent of the total population), a fact that becomes particularly important when the

References for this chapter begin on page 146.

principle of proportional representation is applied to categories of state employees. Three distinct indigenous nations exist within Guatemala: the Maya, the Xinka, and the Garífuna. The Maya are the largest of these three ethnic groups, and the Maya nation consists of 23 linguistic communities or nationalities. In their political discourse, non-indigenous politicians proclaim that Guatemala is multi-ethnic, pluri-cultural, and multi-lingual. Although these statements may be viewed as positive in that they define national identity in a way that includes the Maya, Xinka, and Garífuna nations,[1] it would be more productive to translate rhetoric into action.

From 1821 to 1944, ladino (non-Indian) and mestizo officials made promises to improve the situation of the indigenous nations by granting citizenship to indigenous individuals and enacting policies of ethnic assimilation. In practice, segregation was maintained in order to supply the cheap, unskilled labor force needed by landowners (Taracena 2002: 35–39). Beyond symbolic, judicial, and cosmetic measures, no substantial steps have been taken since 1944 to combat the colonialism and racism directed toward Maya, Xinka, and Garífuna. Any measures that were taken in favor of these indigenous groups were contradicted by others that worked against them. Likewise, during the 2003 electoral campaign, the current (2004–2008) government leaders signed a declaration (the Declaration of Iximché) to support indigenous nations. Today, indigenous peoples recognize that the presidential and vice-presidential signatures on this declaration are useless, as very little to none of its promises have been implemented. Considering present and past governments, none of Guatemala's rulers have moved beyond discourse to action, which indicates the lack of importance of indigenous groups to the state, its democratic government, the political class, and the non-indigenous ruling class. When indigenous reforms are authorized, they generally take the form of limited symbolic and peripheral measures.

The government has not translated the constitutional and political recognition of the country as multi-ethnic, multi-lingual, and pluri-cultural into action. Instead of developing national policies to promote multi-ethnicity, the majority of government officials wait for civil society to become multi-ethnic or multi-lingual without such transformations in the government or state. Perhaps a public as well as private transition from mono-nationality to multi-nationality is necessary. Although societal and individual transitions could occur simultaneously, this transformation would be more efficient and consistent if the state and its officials led by example, engaging civil society.

This chapter offers an empirical analysis of how the Guatemalan state and its officials perpetuate colonialist and racist stances against indigenous nations.

The Legal Framework of Creole-Ladino Racism

The world view of the inhabitants of Guatemala is rooted in a racist paradigm that the state cultivates and reproduces. In biological terms, racism implies the supremacy of the white race (the creole) and of the 'mixed race' (the mestizo, the ladino) over the Maya, Xinka, and Garífuna. Racism has taken the form of cultural assimilation (validated by discourse, the army, and the education system) and segregation (validated in practice), both of which reject the ethnic diversity represented by indigenous nations. Despite changes in governments, political systems, and the restructuring and modernization of the state, there has been no change in the colonialism and racism leveraged against indigenous peoples. As a result of the social application and reproduction of this 500-year-old ethnic-racist paradigm, the Guatemalan state remains mono-ethnic or ethnically creole-ladino in all of its dimensions. Ladino-centrism in the Guatemalan state and the democratic system can be seen in the following various realms.

Political-Administrative Divisions of Guatemala

The political-administrative divisions of the country and its organization into departments do not correspond to the distribution of the Maya, Xinka, and Garífuna nations and linguistic communities. While the country's administrative divisions have been reorganized several times, these changes have been carried out according to each ruler's political needs, thus precluding lasting administrative and cultural recognition of the indigenous nations.

Legislation

A predominance of laws uphold the existence of a mono-ethnic state. The Law of Executive Organization makes no reference to the representation that the indigenous nations should have in this branch. Because of the prevalence of the racist paradigm, when legislation regarding indigenous nations is not made explicit, it is taken as proof that they do not exist. Consequently, the law favors ladinos and creoles, is directed toward their culture, and is applied only in Spanish. Indigenous peoples are usually mentioned only in negative legal contexts, such as the Law of Obligatory Military Service. Legislation that recognizes indigenous groups positively is rare, tends to be forgotten, or is not applied, as in the case of the 1996 Peace Accords that were designed to favor indigenous peoples.

Ethnic Composition

There are no linguistic or ethnic criteria for obtaining political office. As a result, the delivery of public services is not carried out with consideration of the ethnic or linguistic population to which they are directed, and the number of indigenous public functionaries is minimal or incidental. For example, the Law of Civil Service does not take into account ethnic and linguistic requirements for state employees working in indigenous areas. Although the Law of National Languages does include ethnic and linguistic criteria, actual appointments do not comply with these requirements. None of the legislation that forms the infrastructure of the democratic system considers the participation and representation of indigenous groups to be necessary in public organizations or branches of the central government. The demand for representation of indigenous groups has been denied by ladino public officials based on the self-serving pretext that "we are all Guatemalans."

Institutional Culture

The everyday identity and culture of public institutions is creole or ladino. This includes protocol, the paraphernalia associated with public acts and events, and the institutional environment. There are many naive ladino functionaries who believe that administrative spaces have no relation with the culture(s) of the country. In a multi-ethnic country, all of the common public spaces should be multicultural, yet with the exception of a few peripheral adornments and painted murals, the institutional culture of the Guatemalan state remains creole and ladino.

Programmatic Structure

The policies and projects implemented by each government have rarely taken the multi-ethnic nature of the country into account. As a result, the Maya, Xinka, and Garífuna nations have been treated as if they were ladinos, with the pretext that they have not been discriminated against. The indigenous demand for development programs that speak to their distinct identities has not been heard by the leaders of the country. This situation is illustrated by social policies that do not include respective ethnic policies. It is easier for the state to categorize and accept the indigenous as 'poor and excluded' rather than as nations or 'ethnic groups'. Nevertheless, the government has not even supported these groups as 'poor'. There is a serious lack of development policies to combat poverty and discrimination against indigenous peoples. In the view of the state, poverty and racism are not suffered by the same people.

Budgetary Structure

The design and structure of the budget elaborated by the Ministry of Finance and approved by Congress reflects that of a mono-ethnic and mono-lingual country. The various sections of the budget are not even organized according to the current colonial administrative division. Consequently, the budget hides social, ethnic, and gender discrimination leveraged by the state in investments and operation. For example, the Guatemala City metropolitan region receives the major part of the country's budget. The 1996 Peace Accords describe four types of discrimination (ethnic, gender, social, and geographic) that are to be remediated, but the manner in which the budget is designed and presented does not allow indigenous nations to observe or monitor these forms of bias in terms of the investment of state monies.

Mindset of Functionaries

Ladino-centrism minimizes, hides, and disqualifies the presence, needs, and actions of indigenous nations. The majority of ladino officials believe that they represent only ladinos and so are obligated to serve only ladino needs. They feel that acting on behalf of indigenous persons would disparage and betray the country. Ladinos have been educated to avoid and distance themselves from Indians and to treat them with violence in order to maintain their status as sub-citizens. The Indian who seeks equality is punished, and the 'equal' Indian is hated. In a best-case scenario, the indigenous are treated as second- and third-class citizens. The mentality of the non-indigenous is molded in such a manner that they can conceptualize only creole and ladino men composing the first tier of citizenship, with indigenous individuals and women making up the second and third tiers. This ingrained view shapes the administrative conduct, social dealings, and public decisions of non-indigenous officials. Thus, when a public functionary shouts, "Long live Guatemala," he is not saying, "Long live the Maya and Garífuna" but only "Long live the creoles and ladinos," for only they are Guatemalans.

In summary, the branches of the state—judicial, legislative, executive—and their diverse offices and programs segregate and discriminate against indigenous peoples on a daily basis. The majority of public offices discriminate against the Maya, Xinka, and Garífuna only when they approach the state, but some branches of the government are directed toward the elimination and subjugation of the indigenous nations within Guatemala's territory. In effect, some state entities, such as the national army, the Ministry of Education, the Ministry of Government, and the Tribunals of Justice, have been used as instruments of ethnocide and genocide against indigenous nations. These organizations have their greatest presence in indigenous communities and exercise policies of negation, rejection, and aggression against indigenous persons. The media and organized religions also engage in acts of discrimination and thus reinforce the anti-indigenous character of the state.

At specific moments in history, the national army has carried out genocide and ethnocide against indigenous nations. Since 1871, it was considered to be a 'good agent of civilization' of the indigenous, and because of this it violently undermined the languages and cultures of indigenous recruits and soldiers. In all of its institutional history, the army has regarded indigenous peoples as 'internal enemies' and has executed three genocides against them: in 1871, 1954, and 1975–1985. This last genocide occurred during the civil war from which Guatemala recently emerged (CEH 2002: 64).

Initiating the Transition to a Multi-national State

Despite the dominance of creole- and ladino-centrism in these various government bodies, steps toward the transition to a multi-national state have been taken through legislative and administrative reforms. First, the Political Constitution of 1985 instituted a new paradigm in which ethnic equality and pluralism were emphasized. The Constitution recognizes that the country is composed of various ethnic groups, including those of Maya ancestry, who have a right to their cultural identity. Similarly, and for the first time in 184 years of the country's independence, the state's obligation to recognize, respect, and promote cultural symbols and characteristics of the indigenous nations was acknowledged.

The second important step was the signing and ratification in 1996 of the International Labour Organization (ILO) Convention 169 Concerning Indigenous and Tribal Peoples in Independent Countries. Guatemala's Constitutional Court has declared ILO 169 to be constitutional. Similarly, the signing of the 1996 Agreement on Identity and Rights of Indigenous Peoples (part of the Peace Accords) elaborated upon and complemented many of the indigenous rights recognized in the 1985 Constitution and in ILO 169. The United Nations Verification Mission in Guatemala (MINUGUA) called this Agreement a watershed, as the state had never so openly and completely recognized the extent of racial, cultural, and linguistic divisions of the country, nor had it so clearly promised to rise above these differences (MINUGUA 2001: 11). The National Languages Law (Decree 19-2003) of 2003 is the most recent law that supports indigenous cultural rights and is the most progressive. It establishes precisely the ways in which public entities should act toward the indigenous linguistic communities or nations.

Despite these resolutions, little or no progress has been made toward realizing indigenous legislation within the state or toward establishing indigenous civil society. A number of individuals and institutions have pointed out the general lack of compliance with the 1996 Agreement on Identity and Rights of Indigenous Peoples (hereafter, the Indigenous Accords) and current legislation that supports indigenous rights. Supporting evidence is provided by reports from MINUGUA (2001), the Office of the High Commissioner for Human Rights (OACDH 2003: 35–37), and the Presidential Commission against Discrimination and Racism against Indigenous Nations (CODISRA 2004: 31). These reports suggest that there has been little to no progress toward recognizing and respecting indigenous identity in establishing a multi-national state, with the result that (1) the ethnic diversity of the country is still not recognized as one of its greatest riches, (2) the state model of exclusion and mono-culturalism continues to exist, and (3) the continued existence of racism(s) indicates the absence of a national project and the lack of a national agenda that includes the Maya, Xinka, and Garífuna nations.

These institutional reports also agree that there is no political will to transform the state (Flores Alvarado 2003), including the following observations: (1) there are no state policies directed toward reporting the indigenous presence or the situation of the Maya, Xinka, and Garífuna nations in government data; (2) there are significant limitations regarding the initiation of changes that would break the mono-cultural structure and racial discrimination; (3) there is an absence of political will to implement changes put forth in the Peace Accords; (4) there are no disaggregated statistical data for ethnic nations or communities; and (5) public officials do not assume serious responsibility for the integral development of ethnic groups and individuals, as the Constitution mandates.

The ninth and last report by MINUGUA (2004: 10–12) indicates that after eight years of implementation of the Indigenous Accords, more progress has been made in terms of legal structure than in action that directly affects indigenous people at the local level. Although the report describes the judicial and institutional reforms within the state as progressive, it notes that the debate on racism and discrimination is incipient. But it also recognizes that the daily life of the indigenous population, in general, has changed very little. In its own report, CODISRA (2004: 31) concludes that the lack of coordination between the three branches of the Guatemalan state in the formulation and implementation of public policy has led to a stagnation of the country's development.

Although the legal advances discussed here show that the transition to a multinational state has begun, it has not been carried out in a way that is programmatic, institutional, budgetary, structural, or territorial/administrative. In the end, state leaders continue to think and act in a creole-centric and ladino-centric manner. Despite the fact that the recognition of indigenous groups as a constitutive part of the nation is law, the documents have no force, and thus the transition to a multi-ethnic state has advanced mainly in discourse, not in policies.

It would seem that the transition from military authoritarianism to democracy is easier than the transition from a mono-ethnic state to a multi-ethnic state. This is due to the world view and interests of the majority of the ruling ladino and creole class, which, in accordance with the racist paradigm, needs to continue to reproduce the stigmas and general prejudices against indigenous people. For those in power, the positive recognition of ethnic diversity is the enemy of democracy, of development, of unity, of peace, of human rights, and of territorial integrity.

Minor State Concessions to Indigenous Nations

Common belief and standard practice hold that the state and the government belong to the creoles and the ladinos, and because of this, the indigenous, as individuals and as nations with specific cultures, do not enter into and do not have a place in the state or government. Whatever space or recognition is accorded to the indigenous by and within the state is regarded as dangerous, abnormal, and invasive in the context of an almost religious belief in the paradigm of ethnic racism. The Guatemalan state is not indigenous, and it continues being non-indigenous despite making some concessions to indigenous peoples. The government tolerates the indigenous presence to an extent, allowing some policy implementation yet maintaining its decision-making power and responsibility.

Traditional and Symbolic Concessions

Not all of the state's concessions to indigenous peoples actually represent real openings—some are instrumental, others superficial and false, and others only temporary. Before and during the current democratic transition, the state has included indigenous nations in the following ways.

INDIGENOUS PEOPLES AS 'WETBACKS' IN THE STATE. The only form for indigenous persons to enter the state has been and continues to be as 'wetbacks', which is to say, laborers who will do the work that no ladino or creole wants to do because of the conditions (distance, low pay, manual and dirty labor). Just as Guatemalan immigrants (ladino and indigenous) who go to the United States do the work that North Americans no longer want to do, the indigenous are 'wetbacks' in the Guatemalan state. Thus, the majority of indigenous individuals with state jobs work as drivers, messengers, domestic personnel, cleaning persons, porters, guards, and so on. This also applies to positions that are well-paid but located in inhospitable and remote regions of the country, such as teachers, nurses, and community developers working in Ixcán, Petén, or Huehuetenango. In addition, ladino employees may be punished by being sent to work in indigenous areas.

These 'wetback' indigenous employees are expected to be dependable, put in long hours, and perform high-quality work. But they are not credited for their work, as they must enter, work, and leave by the back door. All are aware of the unwritten rule that an indigenous government employee is expected to carry out twice the amount of work at a level of perfection that is not demanded of a non-indigenous laborer in the same position. In addition, the lower a position's salary, the greater the possibility that an indigenous person will occupy it, while the higher a post's salary, the greater the possibility that a ladino or creole will occupy it.

THE INDIGENOUS AS DECORATION. Indigenous peoples have a presence in many public offices as a kind of ornamentation—just like paintings and textiles, tablecloths, and wall hangings. Rarely, programs or projects in some public office are named for the indigenous people. While this could be positive, it is actually often contradictory because the same public offices that use indigenous names and decorations discriminate against the living Maya, Xinka, and Garífuna.

Responding to both internal and external pressures, some non-indigenous officials have self-servingly allowed indigenous individuals to enter the government in order to defend themselves against criticisms that the state discriminates against the indigenous. The objective here is not to transform the state; rather, it is to present a non-discriminatory front or to authenticate the tourist industry through group dances, folkloric ballet, and the exoticization and folklorization of the elements of indigenous cultures.

Few ladino officials who allow the Maya access to the state do so based on duty and the conviction that the state must be multi-ethnic and multicultural. When indigenous people have been appointed, they have principally been given mid-level posts. Granted, there continue to be exceptions: secretaries, accountants, general managers, protocol managers, and technical personnel, among others. Thus, there are some sectors of the government that comply with current indigenous legislation and that have allowed indigenous people to participate in the state based on human rights policies.

CONSECRATED NATIVES AS SYMBOLS OF THE NATION AND NATIONAL IDENTITY. The Guatemalan state has tolerated symbolic recognitions of indigenous peoples, yet these acknowledgments maintain the racist paradigm rather than undermine it.

For example, Tecún Umán has been declared a national hero, Days of Indigenous Peoples have been recognized, and 12 October has been declared the Day of Interculturality. Other representations include indigenous cultural symbols and adornments (e.g., photos of Maya pyramids, components of Maya dress) that are used in Guatemalan embassies to demonstrate the originality and authenticity of Guatemalan 'national identity' for foreigners.

INDIGENOUS CULTURES EXPLOITED BY THE TOURISM INDUSTRY. The tourism industry has always exploited indigenous cultural differences to attract foreign travelers and has done so with state support. Some of these representations of indigenous people suggest that they are savages who belong to nature or that they are naive or ignorant. Certain indigenous dances have been folklorized and distorted by dance teams directed by public tourism offices, and then these dances are presented to tourists as authentically indigenous. Although such appropriation of the indigenous is the norm, there are some exceptions: the achievements of UNESCO, which declared certain practices of the indigenous culture as cultural patrimony of humanity, and the efforts made by a few in the anthropological and historical branches of the Ministry of Culture.

ABSURD RECOGNITIONS BY THE NATIONAL ARMY. The way that the national army recognizes and appropriates indigenous culture is both contradictory and farcical. The army names some special combat units and specific military operations with the names of indigenous heroes in order to use them against the Maya. The report by the Commission of Historical Clarification on the last genocide against the indigenous population reveals this type of 'acknowledgment'.

None of these 'concessions' helps to change the state's traditional colonialist and racist treatment of the indigenous nations and cultures. They are symbolic, inconstant, temporary, and circumstantial recognitions of indigenous peoples, some of which verge on the point of absurdity.

New Democratic Concessions

With the advent of a new ethnically equalizing and pluralistic paradigm, government leaders have made some internal concessions, yet have done so without fully implementing their previous symbolic and contradictory concessions.

RARE DESIGNATIONS OF INDIGENOUS INDIVIDUALS AS PUBLIC FUNCTIONARIES. The most recent governments, in line with multicultural and intercultural policies, have tolerated and 'permitted' indigenous individuals to work as high-level functionaries in the legislative, executive, and judicial branches. The title 'functionary' indicates that the person belongs to the ruling party.

The Law of the Executive Branch (Decree 114-97) recognizes the following high-level posts: 1 president, 1 vice president, 6 secretaries, 12 ministers, and 22 department governors and directors of social funding. Each minister generally has two vice ministers but is allowed to have three (ONSEC 1999: 38–65). Most indigenous functionaries have been appointed to posts in the executive branch, and the majority have been appointed since the presidency of Ramiro De León Carpio (1993–1996). But such appointments are not institutionalized, and because of this they have been haphazard and serendipitous.

As table 1 shows, there is no consistency in the number or kind of positions filled by indigenous persons in the four governmental terms analyzed here, which confirms the lack of institutionalization and the lack of proportional representation. Indigenous individuals have occupied posts as ministers, vice-ministers, secretaries, and commissioners; however, they are few in number, and there is no constancy in appointment of indigenous individuals to any post. The same is the case in other lower-ranking positions, such as departmental governors, general directors, assessors, etc. Although some of these posts may be high in the administrative hierarchy, they do not carry much political power because the 'invited' indigenous officials do not always belong to the governmental party.

TABLE 1 Number of High-Level Indigenous Officials in the Executive Branch

Government Periods	Ministers	Vice-Ministers	Diplomats	Sec. and Directors	Assessors
1993–1996	1	1	0	0	0
1996–2000	0	0	0	0	0
2000–2004	1	4	2 ambassadors 2 state reps.	2 directors of social funding	0
2004–2008	1	1	1 ambassador 2 state reps.	1 secretary 1 director of social funding	4

Source: Cojtí Cuxil (2005: 153).

In the executive branch, indigenous politicians do not directly represent the indigenous nations and organizations. Their appointment is based on personal reasons and merit, yet they are selected because they are indigenous. The civil society indigenous organizations do not usually propose these indigenous functionaries, and as a result, they do not have the right to demand accountability from them or to monitor them. They should have these rights because the indigenous official belongs to the same nation and because he or she belongs to one or another indigenous civil society organization. Because institutionalized mechanisms do not exist for the appointment and representation of indigenous nations and communities, indigenous officials are selected based on their indigeneity.

The indigenous people demand that indigenous appointments to government posts be powerful and strategic, and that indigenous-occupied posts correspond to a plan of internal network creation. They ask that these officials promote the demands of the indigenous rural lower class as well as those of the indigenous urban middle class (Velásquez Nimatuj 2005: 11).

INDIGENOUS CANDIDATES FOR POSTS IN POPULAR ELECTIONS. Since the establishment of democracy in 1985, Guatemala's political parties have given indigenous peoples marginal and haphazard participation in the government. Indigenous candidates compete for posts in popular elections and thus serve as high- and middle-level public officials, such as congressional representatives and mayors. The quantitative advance of elected indigenous candidates for municipal mayors has been progressive but sustainable, explained by the fact that political parties nominate indigenous men and women who have the ability to 'pull votes', since indigenous voters tend to vote for their fellow indigenous candidates. The last three elections indicate a progression of 1 percent, as table 2 indicates. Of the 119 currently elected indigenous mayors, 9 belong to independent civic committees.

TABLE 2 Number of Indigenous Mayors in Guatemala's 331 Municipalities (1996–2008)

Period	Total Number of Mayors	Number of Indigenous Mayors
1996–2000	331	110 (33.23%)
2000–2004	331	113 (34.13%)
2004–2008	331	119 (35.95%)

Source: Cojtí Cuxil (2005).

The number of elected indigenous representatives in the legislative branch has always been minimal. Due to the lack of institutionalization of indigenous participation and representation, to the variation of the total number of delegates that should be designated for a given office, and to the fate of the electoral game, the number of indigenous legislative representatives has been variable and unpredictable (see table 3).

TABLE 3 Number of Delegates Elected to the Republic of Guatemala's Congress

Government Period	Total # of Congressional Delegates	# of Indigenous Delegates	% of Indigenous Delegates
1985–1990	100	8	8.0
1990–1993	116	6	5.2
1996–2000	80	6	7.5
2000–2004	113	13	11.5
2004–2008	158	12	7.6

Source: URL and INGEP (2005: 237).

Although indigenous participation in Congress has never exceeded 12 percent, there are significant differences in the number of indigenous delegates serving in a given term. For example, according to Hugo Cayzac (2001: 233), in the period 2000–2004, there were 14 indigenous delegates, whereas a study by the Universidad Rafael Landívar (URL 2005) indicates that there were 13. These variances are explained by different criteria used to identify indigenous delegates, the source, and the ethnic identification self-ascribed by delegates.

Nonetheless, the difference between elected delegate and functional delegate must also be recognized. Various elected indigenous delegates are not working as such in Congress because they have renounced their post in order for their subordinates to rise, or because they accept posts in the executive branch. For example, Jaime Cupil (2005) found that 17 indigenous delegates were elected to Congress in the 2003 elections but only 12 are actually serving in their congressional posts.

Moreover, the indigenous delegates do not represent ethnic communities or Maya cultural identities in any strict sense. Rather, they represent inferior levels of the political-administrative division of the state (administrative regions and departments), and above all they are based on electoral districts. Because of this, it is possible to say that the delegates have an administrative representation but not an ethnic representation.

Political parties provide the mechanism to access Congress, yet marginalization and discrimination against indigenous people are evident in them, which is revealed by comparing the number of indigenous members of parties to the number of party leaders. Of 20 political parties analyzed in terms of the number of indigenous members relative to their respective executive councils, Cupil (2005) found that only 2 approach the 50 percent composition of their indigenous members: URNG (Guatemalan National Revolutionary Unity), with 7 indigenous officials out of 20 members, and TRANSPARENCIA, with 5 indigenous representatives out of 12 members.

The parties that have the fewest indigenous members are those that give indigenous individuals secondary posts and non-essential roles, such as deputies, special secretaries, adjunct secretaries, sub-secretaries, etc. Following are examples:

- In GANA (Grand National Alliance), the indigenous member with the highest post in the party hierarchy serves as the eighth-ranking voting member.
- The indigenous member with the highest post in PAN (Party of National Advancement) serves as a congressman.
- In MR (Reforming Movement), three indigenous politicians occupy congressional posts.
- In Unionista (The Unionist), the best-situated indigenous member is the ninth-ranking deputy.

These data show the lack of indigenous participation in key political party posts. Clearly, this is only one indicator, as we have not considered the policies that the parties formulate, the politics of intra-party negotiation, and the degree of racism toward indigenous party members by non-indigenous members.

Another point of consideration is the absence of positions that are specifically designated for indigenous persons in the political structure. For example, only four parties have created a Secretary of Indigenous Affairs, which is generally filled by an indigenous member who acts only as a recruiter.

The judiciary is perhaps the most advanced branch of the three state branches with regard to positive recognition of indigenous peoples. An indigenous magistrate is in place for the first time in the judicial branch. He was elected for the period of 2005–2009 as one of the 13 members of the Supreme Court of Justice. Likewise, a Commission of Indigenous Affairs of the Judiciary has been created, and a slow process of recruitment has been initiated in the judiciary for judicial workers who are bilingual Maya-Spanish speakers (see table 4). In addition, the judiciary has been studying the possibility of limited recognition of indigenous rights through sentences that have been commuted by 'indigenous tribunals'.

TABLE 4 Number of Bilingual Maya-Spanish Judicial Employees

Bilingual Posts	Number
Bilingual judges with some certification in indigenous rights	98
Bilingual assistant justices	323
Bilingual interpreters	43
Bilingual administrative personnel	107
Total	**571**

Source: Cojtí Cuxil (2005: 114).

Because there is no institutionalized quota of indigenous public servants, indigenous participation in popular elections is haphazard. The election of an indigenous person in indigenous regions is not guaranteed, and thus indigenous participation in popular elections and the election of indigenous officials is not sustainable. Some think that this participation serves decorative ends rather than the functional and operational purpose that would reflect the ethnic diversity of the population.

CREATION AND APPROVAL OF PRO-INDIGENOUS LEGISLATION. The Guatemalan state has made significant advances in pro-indigenous legislation, principally in regard to culture and language, including Constitutional Articles 58 and 66; international agreements, such as ILO 169; and national legislation, such as the Law of National Languages, the Law of Educational Promotion against Discrimination, and the Reform of the Penal Code to Classify Discrimination as a Crime. Another body of national laws exists in which indigenous concerns are included, but they are inadequately enforced. These laws, including the Law of Urban and Rural Development Councils, the Law of Decentralization, and the new Municipal Code, allude to the indigenous population in their declaration of considerations and principles but not in their substantive and operative parts.

In a democracy, the principal function of the state is to normalize the relations between its citizens and its nations and then to comply with and enforce these norms. In the case of Guatemala, a long path remains toward democracy, since the rights of self-government and of representation of the indigenous nations are not contemplated in any congressional decree. These two fundamental rights guarantee a degree of decision-making power for each ethnic community, the mechanisms to defend their interests, and, finally, the survival and development of their cultures and economics.

In a comparative analysis—undertaken by the Inter-American Development Bank in 22 Latin American countries—on legislation that favors indigenous nations, Guatemala falls in the middle; it is not very advanced nor very far behind. It lacks progress in legislation regarding new areas or fields of indigenous rights, and it lacks compliance with the indigenous legislation currently in place. This middle-road position is a result of the actions of government leaders who have not governed for or with the indigenous nations, but who have instead worked against them.

CREATING SPECIFIC INDIGENOUS PUBLIC OFFICES. In the executive branch, more than 15 public offices, generally of the third and fourth tier, have been created to deal with indigenous matters (see table 5). These offices may be autonomous and decentralized, bipartite (public and private), subordinate or dependent, and located within a ministry or an administrative apparatus. Although some of these entities are at a high administrative level and have some managerial autonomy, the majority are mid-level and as such they have no autonomy in terms of public management.

Of these 16 government institutes, only 3 have any managerial autonomy: FODIGUA, ALMG, and CODISRA. Although the remaining 13 may have indigenous directors, they must answer to non-indigenous authorities. Some of these entities have established a dialogue with civil society indigenous organizations, with whom they consult and conduct joint activities. The creation of these public entities directed toward the indigenous population is important, as it shows the results of lobbying and pressure by the Maya movement on the government as well as the government's interest in resolving some problems faced by the indigenous population. But in the long run, these offices are discriminated against within the state. While these offices certainly suffer from the same limitations as do non-indigenous offices (insufficient funds, few personnel, inadequate technical support, etc.), they are further weakened because they do not have the political support of those in power (even if they have a clear mandate). As a result, they do not have a budget or the operational capacity to serve their population or accomplish their goals. One of the conclusions of the CODISRA report (2004: 31) is that "the existence of institutions and requests that address issues related to indigenous groups but that do not have an adequate budget does not resolve the situation of exclusion, and it replicates other forms of discrimination in the structural and institutional levels."

TABLE 5 Public Entities Created in the Executive Branch to Serve the Indigenous Population and Members of the Indigenous Inter-Institutional Coordinator of the State

Institution	Branch	Reps. to the CIIE
MICUDE Ministry of Culture and Sports	Unit of Ethnic and Gender Equality	Manuel de J. Salazar Saraih Acevedo
MINTRAB Ministry of Labor	Department of Indigenous Nations	Patricia Ajcam
FODIGUA Indigenous Development Fund of Guatemala		David Son Turnil Mario Patal
PDH: Attorney for Indigenous Rights	DIGEBI: General Direction of Bilingual Education	Tomas Ixtamalic Rodrigo Chub
ALMG: The Academy of Mayan Languages of Guatemala		Modesto Baquiax Inocencio N. Aguilar
DEMI: Defense of the Indigenous Woman		Teresa Zapeta
SEPREM: Presidential Secretariat of the Woman	Sub-Management	Delfina Mux Caná
CONALFA: National Literacy Council	Department of Bilingual Literacy	Jaime David Sucuc Nelson Méndez
SEPAZ: Secretariat of the Peace	Office of the Development of Indigenous Nations	Norma Quixtán Carlos Cu Cab
Goodwill Ambassador		Rigoberta Menchú Marciano Sucuqui M.
COPREDEH: Presidential Commission for Human Rights	Sub-Management	Manuela Alvarado Rosendo Ordóñez
CODISRA		Ricardo Cajas Ramiro Lopez
SEGEPLAN: General Secretariat of Planning	Unity of Indigenous Nations/Group	Alma Sacalxot Hugo Us Álvarez
Public Ministry	Fiscal of Indigenous Nations/Groups (in preparation)	Edgar Batres
Ministry of Environment and Natural Resources Environment and Natural Resources	Unity of Maya, Garífuna and Xinka Nations for the	Mario A. Coroxon

Source: Cojtí Cuxil (2005) and CODISRA (2004).

In fact, these offices are institutional inlays, isolated and abandoned to luck. They have little power inside or outside of the ministry or secretary in which they are located, and they are often terminated because they depend on the cooperation of an institution that has only tolerated them. They are 'small windows of indigenous inclusion', fissures tolerated in the compact non-indigenous and anti-indigenous structure of the state.

Ironically, the support that these branch offices receive from international organizations is understood by the rest of the governmental entities as reverse racism, directed toward ladino public institutes that serve the indigenous population as if they were ladinos. As a result, it can be said that the creation and multiplication of this type of office is a false indigenous institutionalism. State funds are not used to help them, nor are they allowed to operate with funds from international organizations, and thus the state maintains these public indigenous offices as ignorant and submissive, propagating its internal racism.

Another example involving indigenous organizations created in the executive branch are concessions of state property to indigenous institutions and organizations (television's Channel 5, the presidential house, land for the Maya university). Yet these concessions are isolated from any technical and financial support from the state and thus are non-functional. State and non-state indigenous institutions are too weak—financially, technically, and politically—to properly operate these concessions, and the state has already appropriated some of them in order to pass them on to non-indigenous entities and individuals.

STATISTICAL RECORDS ON THE HIRING OF INDIGENOUS IN THE STATE. The statistical invisibility of indigenous peoples is one of the classic characteristics of colonialism—to omit them, ignore them, and minimize their existence. Until now, the general discourse has been that there is no need to carry out ethnic registries to avoid discrimination because 'we are all Guatemalans'. Based on this unjustified pretext, statistical discrimination has continued and has hidden actual discrimination. This form of colonial oppression has begun to decrease somewhat due to the initiation of a statistical registry of the number of indigenous laborers in some public offices, including the General Management of Statistics, the Office of Multiculturality in the National Police, the Judicial Branch, the Ministry of Education, and the Ministry of Culture. These offices register data regarding hires, number of years of service, linguistic community to which the worker belongs, the post she or he occupies, and the location of posts.

The documentation of these data is important because it points toward the beginning of a recognition of the multi-ethnic nature of the state. These statistics provide evidence of the pay grade and level of inclusion of indigenous employees in public offices. However, some of this data collection has been discontinued by the current government. These statistical registries on the ethnic identity of public employees are often not exact because, due to the existence of the racist paradigm, indigenous identity is still hidden, whether it is on the part of ladino employees or by the indigenous employees themselves. Any motive is utilized as a pretext for not recognizing the ethnic identity of the indigenous people: (1) not wanting to discriminate against the indigenous, because the person does not know his or her own ethnic identity, (2) the difficulty in identifying who is indigenous or not indigenous, (3) the desire to avoid problems for the organization in question, (4) not knowing how to write the indigenous names, (5) backwardness and lack of prestige, or (6) a lack of space or paper to develop such registries.

MULTICULTURAL TRAINING FOR LADINO PUBLIC FUNCTIONARIES. Various certification programs and postgraduate courses in 'interculturality' and 'multiculturality' have been started by universities and academic centers, financed with both public and private (international) funds. The objective is to make high-level ladino functionaries aware of multicultural issues, but, lamentably, the individuals who participate in these courses are generally third- or fourth-level employees whose absence at work is not critical and who have little to no power to transform the state. In addition, these courses produce few results because they are not mandatory, there is no proof of completion, the courses are not required by the high offices of the government, and they are not put into action in the workplace. In the best-case situation, and when dealing with long-term processes, these courses serve to reduce the intensity of racist and exclusionary attitudes of non-indigenous participants. In the worst case, they provide yet another certificate for the public functionary to add to his or her résumé. These workshops do not change diehard racists because they already have taken a determined position against the indigenous and indigeneity. Thus, we can classify these academic activities as symbolic.

TREATMENT OF MULTICULTURALITY AS A CROSS-CUTTING THEME. The idea of multiculturality is new in Guatemala. It can be said that no one (university administrators, public officials, political leaders, union leaders, indigenous activists) has been trained to understand and implement it, and, as a result, multiculturalization advances slowly and cautiously. In their desire to publicize widely the attention that they have given to indigenous nations (but not indigenous people), some high-level functionaries treat the indigenous theme as a cross-cutting issue, which is comparable to doing more of the same and therefore equivalent to doing nothing. No public entity is concerned with the indigenous if this is not its explicit job, and no one is concerned with the indigenous if it is the work of all.

Others occasionally accept the introduction of ethnic criteria in competitions for prizes to encourage indigenous competitors, bilingualization of official invitations to public events, and explicit approval of the use of Maya dress in public acts and social events. These advances could be significant because they question the Spanish and creole protocol that operates in the state, but they are marginal, incidental, and demonstrative, and in the end only maintain the mono-ethnicity and structural racism of the state.

A brief analysis of steps taken by the state toward multiculturalism leads one to conclude that very little has been done. Incomplete legislation and the creation of inoperable institutions represent bureaucratic exercises that lead nowhere rather than productive reforms. Power in the state is held by the creoles and ladinos of the governing political party and its financiers. If any progress has been made, it is in spite of their indifference and disapproval. Due to the ethnic composition of the state and its rulers, the Maya, Xinka, and Garífuna may make proposals and perhaps pressure the state, but for now ladino rulers have the last word. The national army also has its concepts of patriotism and a mono-ethnic nation and utilizes some of its non-violent capacities to impose these views on the general population.

What is important in quantitative and qualitative terms is that the 'proportional representation' of indigenous peoples in the state does not correspond to their demographic density. Indigenous peoples represent approximately 60 percent of the total population, but their presence in the state is at most symbolic. In 2005, the percentage of indigenous officials in high levels of the state was as follows:

- 7.6 percent of the total number of congressional representatives in the legislature (12 of 158)
- 5.0 percent of the total number of congressional representatives in the Central American parliament (1 of 20)
- 35 percent of the total number of municipal mayors in all of the republic (119 of 331)
- 8.3 percent of the total number of ministers in the executive (1 of 12)
- 7.6 percent of the total number of magistrates in the Supreme Court of Justice (1 of 13)

One of the few studies that has pointed out this under-representation of indigenous peoples is that coordinated by Sáenz de Tejada (URL 2005: 244). The study revealed that of the 22 departments in the country, indigenous mayors were elected in only 3 (Totonicapán, Sololá, and Chimaltenango).

Creole-Ladino Racism and Resistance to Change

Dealing with the indigenous issue is not easy due to the racism that prevails in all levels of society and among high-level officials and public employees. There are subtle variations of racism in the powerful class that blame the victims of racism for its cause. It is said that indigenous peoples are the cause of creole or white racism because of the cultural differences that they represent or are associated with (such as language and dress). If racism against the indigenous population exists, it is the fault of the indigenous people and not of the racist creole. Some members of the country's politically and economically powerful sectors act according to these concepts. Racism is prevalent among public functionaries, yet it is not always perceptible because it is expressed as a form of socially tolerable racism. Unacceptable racism remains hidden from indigenous peoples, to be revealed only in front of other ladinos. It is manifest when racists allow themselves to express their thoughts freely without risk of being criticized, repressed, or disqualified. Examples of this intolerable racism include statements that the Spanish were poor conquistadors because they did not exterminate all of the Indians and criticisms of former dictator Efraín Ríos Montt because he did not eliminate the indigenous during the Civil War. These perspectives cause one to question the criteria of selection of personnel stipulated by the Civil Service Law, which does not prohibit public employees from being racist. Racist functionaries and public employees continue defending archaic and illegal approaches to ethnic diversity. Among the radical solutions to the indigenous problem that they promote are that all indigenous people should be exterminated, that they should be expelled from the country, and that they should continue assimilating, as they are currently doing.

According to proponents, these radical solutions have the virtue of resolving the indigenous problem in a definitive manner. For them, the problem is not the ladino government, nor is it the state; rather, it is the indigenous people who want to meddle in the state and change it. The functionaries who are believers in this savage racism can be mid-level employees or directors of offices. These public servants may also be university professors, as it is common that the professional public employee complements his salary with a post at some university. On the other hand, there is a minority of ladino public employees who do not take such radical positions against indigenous issues, preferring a mediating position in opinions and conduct. Although they have not established a clear model of the multi-ethnic state, they intuitively know what it could be.

Types of Opposition to State Multi-nationalization

Following Albert Memmi's (1980: 29–90) scheme of the colonized and the colonizer, we may classify the types of people who deny or support the incorporation of indigenous issues into the state agenda into the following categories.

THE CONFESSED COLONIALIST AND THE COLONIALIST IN DENIAL. These people deny that they reject indigenous peoples and culture. They say that they would never oppose the indigenous people, but their actions are contradictory. The same is apparent in racism: while no one identifies him- or herself as a racist, there is acceptance that racism exists and that the racists are other people. In contrast, one who confesses to being a colonialist does not agree with any type of multi-ethnicity or interculturality. The confessed colonialist takes a position against all that is considered indigenous (the issue, persons, projects, content, form), against the implementation of the Peace Accords, and against current indigenous legislation. These confessed colonialists block the current transformation of the mono-ethnic state, refusing to accept even symbolic concessions to the indigenous population. They sabotage all that favors the indigenous nations. Among them are people who publicly proclaim their racism against the indigenous and boast of doing so. They know that they may be reproached for their racism but that they will not be punished for it.

THE COLONIALIST WHO LOOKS THE OTHER WAY. These are colonialists who use multiculturality and interculturality as a means to maintain the creole-ladino state and to construct a mono-ethnic nation. They do this by continuing the subjugation and/or assimilation of the Maya, Garífuna, and Xinka nations. They promote change only in discourse, not in institutional practice. In the best case, they believe that the indigenous nations should have some representation, but in a symbolic manner. For example, they may support indigenous individuals who are acquiescent and agreeable figureheads. These colonialists block the transformation of today's mono-ethnic state and accept indigenous people within the state only when they fill a second- or third-level post. They repeat the discourse of inclusive democracy, but their words are not reflected in politics, programs, budgets, or the distribution of public services with linguistic and cultural pertinence. Through the construction of inclusive and intercultural democracy, they intend to maintain the current situation of racism against indigenous nations.

THE ASSIMILATED AND DECLARED COLONIALIST. These colonialists accept bilingualism, multiculturality, and interculturality, but only when they are applied in programs and institutions that are dedicated to indigenous nations, and only so long as indigenous peoples continue to assimilate to the ladino culture and language. They represent a change in discourse, and some even demonstrate a change in ethnic practices. The fashionable concepts of multiculturality and interculturality are used by them to continue the traditional programs of ladinoization. These colonialists do not block the transformation of the mono-ethnic state, but they establish periods of duration, speed bumps or ceilings, rhythms of progress, and limits that the multi-ethnicizers of the country should respect.

This solution has been anticipated in the state's discourse for many years, but it has not been applied because segregation has been more feasible or productive for a certain sector of the country's ruling classes. It is common to hear them say: "We don't have any need to learn indigenous languages because they have no use. Bilingual education is good for the indigenous living in rural areas. There is no need to make bilingual materials for the students, only for the teachers because they transition their students toward Spanish. The Spanish language is what will allow the indigenous to progress." These colonialists are the ones that fall back on arguments about reverse racism, supposedly practiced by the indigenous against the ladinos.

Types of Support for the Multi-ethnicization of the State

There are groups within Guatemala who, to varying degrees, accept the idea of multiculturalism and are in favor of according indigenous peoples recognition and the right to be represented in the government, as the following categories demonstrate.

PERIPHERAL ANTI-COLONIALISTS. These are people who respect the identity of the Maya, Xinka, and Garífuna nations and would give them real participation and representation, but only in regional and local offices. Their efforts to include the indigenous do not change the fact that the central government remains in the hands of ladinos nor that its mono-ethnic and mono-lingual character is based on the assumption that the culture that has a future is the ladino culture, in both the national context and the international sphere.

'LAISSEZ-FAIRE' ANTI-COLONIALISTS. These anti-colonialists accept the establishment of autonomous states similar to those in Spain. They would give indigenous peoples participation and representation in the central government but without institutionalizing it. At this level of the central government, the law of the richest must apply: he who wants political power will have to work for it. The anti-colonialists realize that no political party can win the elections or govern if it does not have the support of big capital and the private media. Therefore, as long as private money is the deciding factor in political parties and governments, there are few probabilities of completely democratizing and multi-nationalizing the state.

INTEGRAL ANTI-COLONIALISTS. These are the anti-colonialists who accept the recognition of indigenous peoples, including the right of self-government at the regional and local level of government, as well as the right of representation in the central government. This means that they support the establishment of the model of autonomous states for regional and local governments and that they agree with the establishment of the model of shared power at the level of central government.

These ladinos or creoles are partisans of equality between the Guatemalan nations and between ladinos and indigenous; as such, they are the constructors of the future multicultural Guatemala. The three branches of the Guatemalan state should have members of the four Guatemalan nations represented in proportion to the population of each of these ethnic groups. The same should apply at all levels of the hierarchy. These anti-colonists include a few ladino functionaries who have sought the implementation of the Peace Accords to the greatest extent possible.

If the opposition to state multiculturalization is considered, about 15 percent of state employees oppose the transformation of the ladino state (in word or practice). Another 15 percent support state multi-nationalization. These percentages are estimates based on observation; this 30 percent is identifiable by their central role in voicing opinions as well as by their attitudes and conduct. Racists do not always express their opinions or act unless they have a position of authority. For example, a racist might be a member of the government in power or a relative of some general in the national army. Similarly, members of a given government can also be central oppositionists to the positive recognition of the indigenous because they are 'well-connected', meaning that they know that they are difficult to dismiss or that the same political party has not taken a position in respect to the issue. The higher the position occupied by these opponents or advocates, the more damage or good they can do in terms of multiculturalization.

Nevertheless, this identifiable group of supporters and enemies of state multi-nationalization is a minority compared to the great majority of state techno-bureaucrats who, in order to keep their jobs, behave obediently and indeliberately, keeping their opinions to themselves. This 70 percent includes honest employees in public administration, yet if they lean one way or another, they tend toward opposition to multiculturalization due to the entrenched nature of racism. Many of them exhibit a passive resistance or turn a blind eye to new government policies. Some implement the policies enthusiastically in the presence of public authorities but with indifference in their absence. Their consolation is knowing that no public policy need last more than four years, at which point a new government will be elected.

Conclusions

In its last report, MINUGUA (2004) agreed that there has been greater progress toward state multi-ethnicization in terms of discourse than in action. Advances include juridical reforms, the creation of indigenous public offices, and some debates about racism and discrimination. But in general, the quotidian reality of the Maya, Xinka, and Garífuna populations has changed little or not at all.

The data presented in this chapter indicate the incongruences, limitations, and obstacles to the progress that has been made regarding indigenous issues in Guatemala. The data indicate that without abandoning colonial forms of treatment of the indigenous peoples, the government has begun to generate and approve measures that recognize indigenous nations, although they are at present inoperative and symbolic. The basic structure of the state remains mono-cultural, mono-lingual, mono-ethnic, and mono-juridical, and the official concessions and acknowledgments made to the indigenous peoples remain superficial. There is a clear under-representation of the indigenous population in the higher echelons of the state (legislative, judicial, and executive). The vertical approach creates institutions specifically dedicated to indigenous issues; however, not only are these institutions discriminated against, they are also dysfunctional. This current approach is insufficient and does not respond to the rights of self-government and representation of the indigenous nations. Likewise, gaps remain in the path to complete state multi-nationalization and to achieving equality between the Guatemalan nations. One of the most significant of these is the lack of an ideal model of the multi-national Guatemalan state.

In the contemporary world, the principle of unity that postulates that the state corresponds to a nation is being substituted by the principle of diversity, which promotes the co-existence of different nations within the same state. It has been shown that subordinate nations have the will to be recognized in their cultural, linguistic, historical, political, and geographic specificity, and as a result there are successful formulas of sovereignty and association (Dieckhoff 2000: 239–246; Kymlicka 1995: 183–207; Lijphart 2001: 33–73).

Only very few public offices are studying racism, raising sensitivity, and working for the principle of ethnic diversity in the state and Guatemalan society. On the contrary, almost all public entities continue to implement and develop the principle of unity in ethnic uniformity, a unity that is formed through subordination of the indigenous nations. The 1996 Peace Accords and specifically the Agreement on Identity and Rights of Indigenous Peoples have not directed the decisions and actions of the government.

Acknowledgments

The present chapter is an expanded extract based on an essay in an earlier publication, *Ri K'ak'a Saqamaq' pa Iximulew* (2005).

Demetrio Cojtí Cuxil teaches at the Instituto de Estudios Interétnicos at the Universidad de San Carlos, Guatemala. He also consults for the Organization of American States. He has previously worked for UNESCO and served as Guatemala's Vice Minister for Education. Among his many publications are *Configuración del pensamiento político del pueblo maya* (1991), *Ri maya' moloj pa Iximulew: El movimiento maya (en guatemala)* (1997), and *Ri K'ak'a Saqamaq' pa Iximulew* (2005).

Note

1. For the author, the concepts of multi-lingualism, pluri-culturality, and multi-nationality are synonymous. There is also a certain synonymity between the concepts of linguistic communities, ethnic groups, and communities with their own language.

References

Cayzac Hugo. 2001. *Guatemala, proyecto inconcluso: La multiculturalidad, un paso hacia la democracia*. Guatemala City: FLACSO.

CEH (Comisión para el Esclarecimiento Histórico). 2002. *Guatemala memoria del silencio*. Guatemala City: USAID-Guatemala.

CODISRA (Comisión Presidencial Contra La Discriminación y el Racismo Contra los Pueblos Indígenas). 2004. *Informe de CODISRA en el marco del contenido de la declaración de Iximché, en los primeros 100 días del gobierno de Oscar Berger*. Guatemala City: CODISRA, Litografía Nawal Wuj.

Cojtí Cuxil, Demetrio. 2005. *Ri K'ak'a' Saqamaq' pa Iximulew (La Difícil Transición al Estado Multinacional: El caso del Estado Monoétnico de Guatemala, 2004)*. Guatemala City: Editorial Cholsamaj.

Cupil, Jaime. 2005. "Que demandan los pueblos indígenas a la política partidaria: El caso de Guatemala." Talk given at the Organization of American States conference, "Democratizando la democracia: Pueblos indígenas y partidos políticos," Guatemala City, 13–14 September.

Dieckhoff, Alain. 2000. *La nation dans tous ses états: Les identités nationales en mouvement*. Paris: Flammarion.

Flores Alvarado, Humberto. 2003. *Los compromisos de paz: Sinopsis de su cumplimiento*. Guatemala City: Secretaría de la Paz (SEPAZ).

Kymlicka, Will. 1995. *Ciudadanía multicultural*. Mexico City: Paidós.

Lijphart, Arend. 2001. *El enfoque del poder compartido para sociedades multiétnicas*. Cuadernos Pedagógicos No. 6. Guatemala City: Ministerio de Educación.

Memmi, Albert. 1980. *Retrato del colonizado precedido por retrato del colonizador*. Buenos Aires: Ediciones de la Flor.

MINUGUA (Misión de Verificación de las Naciones Unidas en Guatemala). 2001. *Los pueblos indígenas de Guatemala: La superación de la discriminación en el marco de los Acuerdos de Paz*. Guatemala City: MINUGUA.

_____. 2004. *Estado de cumplimiento de las recomendaciones de la Comisión para el Esclarecimiento Histórico*. Guatemala City: MINUGUA.

OACDH (Oficina del Alto Comisionado para los Derechos Humanos). 2003. *Informe del Relator Especial sobre la situación de los derechos humanos y las libertades fundamentales de los indígenas*. Guatemala City: OACDH.

ONSEC (Oficina Nacional de Servicio Civil). 1999. *Digesto de la administración de personal del Sector Público*. Guatemala City: ONSEC.

Taracena, Arturo. 2002. *Etnicidad, estado y nación en Guatemala: 1808—1944*. Guatemala City: CIRMA/Litografía Nawal Wuj.

URL (Universidad Rafael Landívar) and INGEP (Instituto de Gerencia Política). 2005. *Elecciones, participación política y pueblo maya en Guatemala*. Ed. Ricardo Sáenz de Tejada. Guatemala City: Editorial Serviprensa.

Velásquez Nimatuj, Irma Alicia. 2005. "Lo indígena como mercancía." *El Periódico*, 22 May.

Chapter 7

REFORMULATING THE GUATEMALAN STATE
The Role of Maya Intellectuals and Civil Society Discourse

Marta Elena Casaús Arzú

The relationship between civil society and the state remains one of the most hotly debated issues in the social sciences, marked by vastly different understandings of the bonds between civil society, political society, and the state. The term 'civil society' was defined by Hegel, and later Marx, as the sphere in which economic relations are established, that is, "the set of economic relationships that constitute the basis on which the legal/political superstructures rest" (Bobbio 1987: 40). Thus, for Hegel as well as Marx, civil society is the sphere that opposes the state. The tug of war between the two is also related to another classical dichotomy—that of public space, which contains the ideological and political superstructure, and private space, which serves as a venue for individual and economic struggle.

Marx tends to lessen the significance of the private sphere by equating civil society to the market, an aspect that is further developed by Marxist theorists (Bobbio 1987; Pérez Díaz 1994). Gramsci, on the other hand, introduces the

Notes for this chapter are located on page 163.

concept of a political society located within the superstructure that sometimes is equated with the state and sometimes occupies an intermediate position between the state and civil society (Portelli 1973: 27). According to Gramsci, civil society is the space for the enactment of ideologies and the struggle for hegemony, which is why he defines intellectuals as participants and prime movers in this sphere of collective action. Intellectuals are the 'living cells' of civil and political societies, the people in charge of constructing ideologies that serve the purposes of their class, of which they are an organic element. The church, the media, the educational system, and, in short, everything that Althusser (1977) subsequently defined as ideological state apparatuses are also located in the civil sphere because of their fundamental role in spreading ideologies in the struggle to maintain a power bloc's cultural hegemony.

Gramsci's concept of political society is more elusive. Sometimes it is considered an element of the state, linked to the state's coercive and repressive functions. However, it can also mediate between civil society and the institutional body, at which point, Gramsci argues, "economic concerns give way to strictly ethical and political ones" (cited in Portelli 1973: 28). This process of cathartic mediation provides the space within which intellectual consensus is negotiated. As Gramsci puts it, public opinion "is the point of contact between the civil and political societies" (cited in ibid.: 74), and it is in this space where the struggle for class hegemony is waged most plainly (Gramsci 1970; Grisoni and Maggiore 1974; Portelli 1973). Even if the civil and political societies both take part in the coercive activities of the superstructure and its struggle to maintain power, Gramsci shows that political parties, parliaments, unions, and public opinion can also mediate between civil and political societies and the state (Gramsci 1974; Grisoni and Maggiore 1974; Portelli 1973).

More importantly, in Gramsci's eyes, civil society fulfills a role that goes beyond the merely economic, playing a crucial part "in the [superstructure's] intellectual struggle for hegemony" (Gramsci 1972: 16; Portelli 1973: 71). He posits that the relationship between the state and civil society is not necessarily contradictory or antagonistic but can also be complementary. Of course, civil society's role in a democratic system, in which pacts and agreements foster a balance of power, is vastly different from its function in a dictatorship, in which the relationship is much less egalitarian. In Gramsci's view, this results in idolatry of the state and the shrinking of civil society under coercion and repression (Gramsci 1972; Portelli 1973: 39).

According to Bobbio (1987: 46), due to their poor understanding of Hegel, Marx and his followers had a limited view of civil society that confined it to the economic sphere, whereas Gramsci's interpretation blurs the limits between civil society and the state and retrieves the meaning of a civil society based on consensus and the search for hegemony. In short, civil society represents the ethical and political impulse through which legitimacy is attained, while the state represents the political force through which power is conserved and exercised (ibid.: 43).

Another key concept developed by Gramsci is the organic role of intellectuals within the historical bloc. In his view, every intellectual belongs to a class and seeks that class's supremacy, which means that every social group constructs its own intellectuals in an attempt to build homogeneity and cultural and political direction. As the 'living cells' of the civil and political societies, intellectuals develop their respective class's ideology, which then feeds civil society and the superstructure (Gramsci 1974; Portelli 1973).[1]

I end this introduction by recalling an image initially used by Hegel and retaken by Víctor Pérez Díaz (1994) in his book *La primacía de la sociedad civil* (The Primacy of Civil Society). To Hegel, the sea represents potential turmoil and constant change, although it can also be calm and is subject to regular phases such as the rise and ebb of tides. In contrast, the coast is solid and stable, and the changes that it undergoes due to the erosion caused by tides progress slowly and oftentimes imperceptibly. While civil society behaves like the sea, impetuously and sometimes violently, the state can be compared to the land, which is subject to the power of the sea but remains much more stable and unyielding to quick change.[2] As in the case of the tides, this relationship follows a pattern: when civil society grows and becomes cohesive, it forces the state to retreat and modify its ways; when the state forcibly takes over civil spaces, civil society shrinks and loses ground. This chapter seeks to explore the role of Guatemala's Maya intellectuals in the changing interactions between the country's civil society and the Guatemalan state, while paying particular attention to the Maya search for ideological and political hegemony.

The Rising Tide: Civil Society's Comeback

One of the most important features of Guatemala's Maya movement is its lack of trust in the Guatemalan state, which is perceived as homogeneous, mono-ethnic, mono-cultural, partisan, and, above all, unwilling or unable to deal with the Maya population's basic needs and the distribution of public resources. This distrust of a creole state that is patently racist and favors the ladino (non-Indian) classes features prominently in the discourse of Maya intellectuals, regardless of their participation in or exclusion from political processes (Cojtí Cuxil 2006; Quemé Chay 2006a, 2006b; Veláquez Nimatuj 2006).

Since the signing of the Peace Accords on 29 December 1996, Guatemalan civil society has become a venue for active social and political participation, especially for Maya and women's groups. This phenomenon has received little attention from either Guatemalan or foreign researchers, despite the fact that it exemplifies some novel trends in Maya political involvement and administrative participation at the local, regional, and national levels. The last 10 years have seen considerable changes in the field of inter-ethnic relations and the perception of the Guatemalan state and its institutions (Bastos and Camus 2004; Brett 2006; Fischer 2001; Warren 1998).

The last decade has been marked by an increase in the creation and use of public spaces with enough outreach to influence social movements, political parties, and even the state itself. These spaces have been termed *rendijas de participación* (participation chinks) and *ventanillas de inclusión* (windows of inclusion). There are concerns that such openings are simply mechanisms of what has been termed the *indio permitido* (sanctioned Indian) (Hale 2006; cf. Cojtí Cuxil 2005). However, these participatory windows constitute a new arena of political participation and public representation in Guatemala and have propelled substantial changes in the civic and political culture of the country, opening up new avenues of interaction between the state and civil society while noticeably contributing to the country's democratization.

Warren (1998), Wilson (1999), and Fischer (2001) were among the first researchers to identify this new type of Maya activism. Warren (1998) focused on public intellectuals and their critics, Fischer and Brown (1999) emphasized the role of culture in the construction of a 'pan-Maya identity', and Fischer (2001) studied the differences between local and national leaders. Hale (2004, 2006) has explored the issue of ladino identity in the face of rising Maya movements and ladinos' response to the ongoing reconstruction and renegotiation of ethnic identities, while Bastos and Camus (1995) have approached these changes from a more classical anthropological perspective.

This research focuses on the relationship between Guatemala's Maya intellectuals and the Guatemalan state. The boom of the Maya movement and the participation of Maya elites in the last three Guatemalan administrations have been conspicuous, as have Maya political contributions to the implementation of the Peace Accords and their theoretical assistance on issues of racism, discrimination, and the public agenda. Guatemala's chance of having a female indigenous president by 2007 is high, and the candidacy of Rigoberta Menchú (regardless of the outcome) is a notable event for the Guatemalan political process.

The last two decades have seen the emergence of a new type of 'indigenous elite' that is focused on the recuperation of ethnic identity and the affirmation of human and ethnic rights in particular and that questions the existing Guatemalan nation-state model. The ultimate goal of these Maya elites, who have risen in response to the crisis undergone by the homogeneous and monocultural Guatemalan state, is the creation of a legitimately plural state and a multicultural nation. They demand the creation of more inclusive and dynamic citizenship models that recognize ethnic differences within an intercultural milieu (Castillo, Villoro, and Kymlicka 2002; Villoro 1998).

In this context, the present study seeks to answer the following questions. First, how do Maya elites perceive the state and how do they define their relationship with it? Second, what kind of state do they propose and what sort of nation do they imagine? Third, can we assert, along Putnam's (1993) lines, that given their historical interactions, Maya elites deeply distrust the state and are searching for a more balanced relationship between civil society and the state? Finally, can we say that a questioning of the homogeneous state is now taking place and that this is leading toward a plural state model?

Methodology

This study takes a multi-disciplinary approach that combines history, anthropology, political science, and an analysis of the discourse employed by Maya and ladino elites. We invited a group of 14 intellectuals—Maya and ladino, male and female, from areas as diverse as politics, business, and literature—to write an essay in response to a prearranged set of questions addressing the issues of racism and discrimination. The participants were also asked to propose public policies that they thought would be most effective in fighting these problems.[3] The essays were then processed by a qualitative analysis program, which picked out the concurrences and correlations between a series of concepts related to the state, civil society, racism, discrimination, and public policies. This processed material was returned to the essayists, and they were asked to select the terms, concepts, or basic definitions that they found most useful in the process of constructing the public policies.[4]

These commissioned essays, as well as press clippings and other written sources, were analyzed to document conceptual interconnections between the state, civil society, and the citizenry, as well as the frequencies that these concepts were used in combination with other key words (see the appendix to this chapter). The results were used to construct dendrograms and other graphic representations that illustrate the relationships between certain key terms/concepts and Maya/ladino discourses regarding the nation-state and its constituency (see fig. 1). Finally, in order to incorporate other voices and complement our analysis, we looked at the work of Maya intellectuals with strong communal agendas. Having put all of this material together, we were able to find the terms and notions that establish a consensus between Maya and ladino elites on the subjects of the state, racism, and discrimination.

Maya Intellectuals' Struggle for Hegemony: Toward a Reformulation of the Guatemalan State and Nation

This section focuses on the four Maya essayists who have most clearly addressed the role of Maya intellectuals in the reformulation of the present Guatemalan nation-state. It also includes additional material by other Maya and ladino

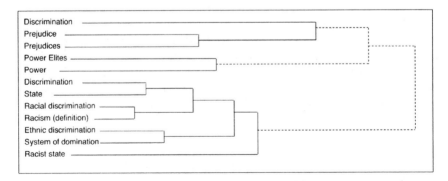

FIGURE 1 State Racism and Discrimination

intellectuals who have analyzed the nature of the role that the state would need to play within multi-ethnic, multi-lingual, and multicultural Guatemalan society. The four featured Maya authors, who have engaged in this debate with the greatest clarity and have confronted the topic of nation and state most profoundly, are Demetrio Cojtí Cuxil, Estuardo Zapeta, Irma Alicia Velásquez Nimatuj, and Rigoberto Quemé Chay. Cojtí received his PhD in social communications from the University of Louvain in Belgium; Zapeta has an MA in anthropology from the State University of New York at Albany; Velásquez Nimatuj got her PhD at the University of Austin, Texas; and Quemé Chay has a PhD in anthropology from the Sorbonne, in addition to having been mayor of Quetzaltenango and the founder of Guatemala's first intercultural political movement, Xeljú. These four are affiliated with different Maya organizations and have diverse perspectives: Cojtí supports the struggle for the autonomy of the Maya people; Zapeta is informed by neo-liberal and postmodern theories; Velásquez Nimatuj's outlook is academic and geared toward political action; Quemé Chay has opted for a civic and political approach with national outreach. It is important to note that all of them have held administrative positions in either the central or municipal governments at one time or another, and their essays reflect on these experiences. Here, their views on the Guatemalan state and nation in light of the Agreement on Identity and Rights of Indigenous Peoples (part of the 1996 Peace Accords) are reviewed, and their most relevant aspects, coincidences, and disagreements are discussed.

Demetrio Cojtí has been an avid proponent of a 'state of autonomies', or a federal entity that allows for an ethnically diverse nation with a multi-national state (Cojtí Cuxil 2005). For him, the Maya people are an intrinsic part of an 'ethnic nation' whose consolidation has been prevented by ongoing colonialism and a culturally repressive ladino-centric state that has historically sought assimilation. According to Cojtí, the Maya people constitute a legal community (*pueblo*) and, in accordance with the Charter of the United Nations, possess certain basic rights including sovereignty. Maya sovereignty can be exercised internally or externally but should always have "the power to determine its political statutes and act freely in order to attain its economic, social, and cultural development" (Cojtí Cuxil 1994: 29). Cojtí is aware that, at this point and pragmatically speaking, the Maya movement must not demand total autonomy or seek to secede from the Guatemalan ladino state, but he does believe that the Maya people have the right and ability to do so.

The way Cojtí sees it, the present character of the Guatemalan state impedes, or at least slows down, the development of a multi-national state. Mono-ethnic in nature, it is based on a centralized political and administrative division that does not address the needs of indigenous groups and does not recognize them as entities with political representation in an ethnically diverse society. The Guatemalan state's institutional policy is 'ladino-creole'. The mono-cultural and ladino-centric nature of its civil servants is reflected in the national censuses and the handling of the national budget, which is designed to hide "the social, ethnic, and gender discrimination exercised by the state when allocating money and determining public spending" (Cojtí Cuxil 2005: 20).

Cojtí Cuxil (2006: 103) defines the Guatemalan state as "creole- and ladino-centric, designed and structured in a mono-ethnic, mono-legal, mono-lingual, and mono-cultural manner." Any analysis of public life will reveal these characteristics, so that it can ultimately be said that the state is also "designed and structured to act against the indigenous peoples" (ibid.). Hence the need for a multi-national state that Cojtí envisions (although he does not clearly define it) as a plural entity that recognizes the diverse ethnic identities of indigenous peoples, enables their autonomy within a Guatemalan framework, and "establishes a shared power structure that guarantees the political influence and the autonomy of the diverse peoples and linguistic communities" (Cojtí Cuxil 2005: 44).

Cojtí suggests that a multicultural state must be accomplished gradually and will require the political willpower of all players. The rights of indigenous peoples must be acknowledged and exercised, and the political costs incurred by ladinos who support change must be measured. Administrative issues, such as increased indigenous representation and participation in the higher political echelons, along with the creation of political seats and administrative positions, must be addressed. In short, "the structure of the state's plural democracy should be ethnically diverse" (Cojtí Cuxil 2005: 48). Cojtí stresses the fact that the present Guatemalan state's failure to incorporate the history and rights of the Maya people is preventing the construction of a new type of nation, stating that its policies "marginalize, exclude and disqualify indigenous peoples inside the Guatemalan nation's territory" (ibid.). Until the state is able to ensure complete equality for all Guatemalan citizens, national integration will not be possible (Cojtí Cuxil 1997, 2005).

Estuardo Zapeta has been strongly influenced by postmodern theory and neo-liberal ideology. His focus is on the concept of the nation rather than the state, and many of his essays lament Guatemala's inability to construct a national entity, a problem to which neither Maya nor ladinos pay enough attention. For Zapeta (1999: 72), the construction of a nation and a national identity should be valued over the transformation of the state and the legislation, since the nation "includes us all, indigenous groups and ladinos, creoles and mestizos." Zapeta (1998: 12) defines the nation from a civic-political perspective rather than an ethnic-cultural one—it is the "multi-ethnic, multi-lingual, multi-cultural and multi-religious reality that, by sharing space, time, and geographical territory, has come to be known as Guatemala."

Zapeta does not refer to exclusive ethnicities or peoples. He focuses on the bonds formed by a common history, shared spaces, territories, and ethnic diversity, along with other differences, and it is clear that his concept refers to a political nation with cultural characteristics. Unlike Cojtí and, as we shall see later, Quemé, Zapeta sees the Peace Accords as a potential threat to the essence of the Guatemalan nation, which, according to him, supersedes ethnic rights, indigenous autonomy, or the official endorsement of diverse languages. A plural, diverse, and unified nation should serve both Maya and ladino interests and, through internal negotiation, create the basis for national legitimacy. Neither the state nor the ruling class, with its myopic understanding of the inevitable changes brought on by history, should be held solely responsible. The common citizenry should be actively involved in the building of the nation. Like Quemé, Zapeta highlights the role of civil society and believes that it should be the source of the national identity-building initiative, placing "the national before the ethnic," the citizenry before the community, and communal rights before differentiated rights. All of these processes evidently require negotiation and the creation of social pacts between the diverse groups and ethnicities, including ladinos: "[W]e must all enclose ourselves within the national framework" (Zapeta 1999: 38).

Zapeta also argues against Mario Roberto Morales's (1998) contention that ladinos fear defining their own identity, since it lacks any essential 'features' not defined in opposition to Maya identity. According to Zapeta (1998), both ladinos and Maya should define themselves in relation to a national concept without either of them becoming representative of the country. He seeks to provide (ibid.: 12) "an organic vision that is inclusive of the ladino and mestizo aspects" and asks that "the construction of a national whole should prevail over strong ethnic bases. Peer commissions could be the first step toward the construction of a Guatemalan nation." Zapeta (2004: 11) has publicly denounced what he calls the "mistake of the [Peace Accords'] Indigenous Agreement," arguing that it resulted in the marginalization of the ladino population in the process of national reformulation: "[T]he Accord should have never been conceived as a limiting or divisive element in the construction of the Guatemalan nation."

Zapeta's nation project coincides with a wider political and national scheme that is centered on the idea of the individual as a transformative agent and the citizen as a historical entity: the individual, rather than the people, becomes the last stronghold of popular sovereignty, the individual subject of the law, and the foremost player in the construction of the nation. This discourse does not contemplate a dichotomy between peoples and/or ethnically defined nations and the state, nor does it require (or desire) the polarization of Maya and ladino identities. 'Ethnic essentialism' gives way to the building of a new nation that is inclusive of all citizens, regardless of specific rights or collective identities.

Zapeta is highly critical of Maya visions of ethnic exclusion, Marxist theory, and international organizations, especially the latest UN Human Development Report regarding Guatemala, which supplied a decontextualized and dichotomist view of inter-ethnic relations that ignored historical and political reality. Faced with these simplistic and ethnicist approaches, derived from cultural anthropological theory of the 1940s, Zapeta was the only Maya intellectual in our sample to offer a forthright critique:

> [A] conscientious debate with the radical ethnicists is impossible; they have little to debate. I am indigenous, and, I insist, this should not comprise the standard under which I am judged ... Those influenced by the thought of former guerrillas, along with the developmental and culture devotees (among which I include many of the protectors of the 'Indians'—or rather, those who 'live off' *indigenista* discourse), are not academically honest people. Their interest in

maintaining the indigenous discourse conforms to their desire for monetary gain and prestige.

... They avoid discussing the clash between ethnicity and class because they sense that, as far as ethnicity is concerned, they lack argumentative bases, and when it comes to 'class', their claims for linguistic multiculturalism cannot sustain themselves. This is why, when someone speaks of ethnicity, they quickly take refuge in 'class', and when you question the homogenization of 'the class', they hastily jump back to ethnicity. Yet when I want to debate both points, they flee the field like cowards. I will forgive their ignorance, but not their cowardice.

Zapeta focuses on two key aspects for the construction of a plural state and a multi-lingual, multi-ethnic and multicultural nation. First, he centers the debate on the concept of citizenship, rather than ethnicity or class, and confers upon the sovereign citizen a series of rights and obligations that prevail over specific rights addressing ethnicity, gender, or class. Second, he maintains that the building of the nation and national identity should be based on the common elements to be found among social and ethnic multiplicity—what Taylor (1996) considers a "shared identity"—and does not seek a mere reformulation of the state based on ethno-cultural distinctions. Responsibility is shared by all citizens, and political will is required of all individuals. The national project no longer is exclusively imposed by the state but rather results from a social pact that includes all Guatemalan inhabitants.

Zapeta does agree with Cojtí about the need for administrative decentralization and a state of autonomies that, in Zapeta's view, does not confer autonomy on the Maya people and does not include ethnic and linguistic segregation but rather is based upon a social pact among citizens. Intercultural relations take on additional importance since, according to Zapeta, Guatemalan citizens share many "unifying elements, while the ones that supposedly separate us are few or non-existent." While this position is not shared by other Maya leaders who emphasize the differences (Zapeta 1999, 2004), Cojtí certainly advocates for a multicultural society.

Irma Alicia Velásquez Nimatuj's (2002) book, *La pequeña burguesía indígena comercial de Guatemala* (Guatemala's Indigenous Commercial Petite Bourgeoisie), and her (2004) essay, "Traje folclorización y racismo en la Guatemala post-conflicto" (Dress, Folklorization and Racism in Post-conflict Guatemala),[5] deal extensively with the role of the state and its interaction with different ethnicities and cultures. According to her essay for this project: "[T]he state's racism is systematic and framed by a structure of power relations that is not always evident. Omi and Winant argue that the exercise of racism is often covert and that institutional racism is not necessarily explicit. In Guatemala's case, although exclusion, segregation, and racial discrimination are not written into law, this is unnecessary, given the way in which they are practiced and socially accepted, just as if they were legal." She also pinpoints the historical character of this state-based racism: "This is why historical and contemporary racism should not be reduced to biological categories or confused with cultural ones, as many intellectuals, academics, and leaders have done ... Racism is intrinsically tied to the perpetuation of a system that grants economic and legal privileges to specific sectors of society. The Maya people have not been the victims of chance, ignorance, or the malice of Guatemalan leaders and the ruling elites. Laws and military force have historically kept the majority of indigenous peoples away from education and political power, forcing them into an enslaved workforce."

Of the four essayists' visions, that of Rigoberto Quemé Chay is probably the most global and multicultural in nature. Quemé served as mayor of Quetzaltenango for two terms, has been a presidential candidate, and is a highly respected intellectual and politician. His political career has prevented his published output from being as vast as that of the other essayists, but his work is no less mature and thoughtful, and it is informed by a profound knowledge of the workings of the state (see Quemé Chay 2006a, 2006b).

Quemé takes a look at the historical role of the state as purveyor and characterizes it as racist, sexist, and authoritarian, insofar as it has excluded indigenous peoples as a whole from the institutions of power and, above all, has impeded their access to the resources and services it provides. His essay clearly exemplifies the dichotomy between the state and civil society: "Legally we are a state with nation-like aspirations; ostensibly homogeneous, built in accordance to the victor's criteria, integrationist, and with a tendency toward the European state model ... However, the fact that two-thirds of the population are related to the Maya nation, its culture and cosmology, and have historically been at odds with the state ... forces us to review the nation-state concept and re-create it in a manner that is representative of the aspirations and interests of the majority of the population in all its diversity and specificity." Quemé associates this racist and exclusive state model with the failures of Latin American democracies and, in the specific case of Guatemala, the reinforcement of a system of domination that impedes universal citizenship. This kind of state is also characterized by a "mono-cultural outlook" that permeates "the law, governmental structures, institutions, procedures, public policies—especially economic ones." The lack of access to "justice, lands, political power, etc., results in an unequal distribution of income that leaves the larger part of the population, which is mostly indigenous, in a state of poverty."

One of Quemé's most interesting observations ties the racist nature of the state to poverty and exclusion, which in turn obstruct economic development and political participation, thus hindering democratic exercise. "Besides poverty, racism, and economic inequality, Guatemalan society also suffers from a poor democratic culture," he argues. This has resulted in "a historically weak political party system that is hardly representative of the Guatemalan population and has mostly conservative and rightist tendencies," as well as "popular distrust of the state and its institutions." It has also led to "popular electoral apathy on the one hand and, on the other, the mono-cultural character of the political and legal system, which frames the majority of Guatemalan social relations and excludes the indigenous population."

Quemé is one of the few authors who link the country's structural problems to popular distrust of the state, an aspect observed by Putnam (1993) in his studies on southern and northern Italy. According to Quemé, Guatemala's political, administrative, geographic, and economic centralism is responsible for the country's exploitative, discriminatory, and marginalizing social aspect. Like other Maya intellectuals, such as Son Turnil, Edgar Ajcip, and Delfina Mux Caná, all of whom hold highly respectable social and administrative positions, Quemé also sees Guatemala's problems of poverty and exclusion as economic and political rather than merely ethnic (Casaús Arzú and Dávila 2006).

Quemé's most novel idea might be his proposed transformation of a homogeneous nation-state into a plural one, a process that should stem "from the political space where the demands, proposals, and actions geared toward the creation of a democratic and plural state originate." Civil society should be in charge of questioning the state, demanding plurality, becoming "more highly organized and [addressing] the general interests of the population, the social classes or social groups." It should also "generate new leaderships that possess plural, inclusive, and modern outlooks informed by social, academic, and political views; have knowledge of contemporary reality and national history; are sensitive to external changes and social, scientific, and technological development; and are open to the traditional values and practices of indigenous peoples, their dreams and viewpoint as Guatemalans."

This proposal is political and national in nature, does not employ the indigenous-ladino dichotomy present in other discourses, and considers issues of ethnicity to be of secondary importance. It does not advocate an ethnically and culturally based nation, an ethnic pact, or a multi-national state. Rather, it seeks the creation of a state that is truly national in character and responds to the needs of all Guatemalan citizens (although special emphasis is placed on indigenous women, whom Quemé considers the most vulnerable sector of the population).

Maya and Ladino Intellectuals' Perception of the Guatemalan State as a Locus for Racism: Toward a Plural State

This section analyzes the textual discourse present in the solicited essays of 12 Maya and ladino intellectuals while remaining focused on the Maya elites' discussion of the state. A recurrent theme in all of these texts is that the state is the source of institutional racism in Guatemala and should be held accountable. There is a certain tendency to demonize the state and portray it as the cause of all the nation's evils. One respondent wrote of a "corrupt and corrupting state incapable of legislating," while another focused on the "arbitrariness and fragility of the state's legal system." Other authors also had their say, writing about a "degenerate state that infects the citizenry with its moral fragility"; a "ladino-centric state designed and structured in a mono-ethnic, mono-legal, mono-lingual and mono-cultural manner"; a "state that exercises discrimination and does not provide all citizens with equal opportunities"; a "racist state that is designed and structured to act against indigenous peoples"; a state that, along with its institutions, is "the main source of racism." In short, "Guatemala's problem is rooted in its state model, which is exclusive, racist, sexist, and authoritarian."

In the frequency index used to track conceptual sequences, the term "the state" appears in third place with a total of 20 occurrences, following "racism" and "discrimination," which were mentioned 23 and 27 times, respectively. A substantial number of essays assert that the exclusionary and racist state model dates back to colonial times and was consolidated during the liberal period. Most of the processed text fragments point out that state-based institutional racism is a legacy of the colonial period. As Otilia Lux de Cotí (2006: 131–132) explained in her essay:

> Guatemalan society, racist and misogynistic as it is, cannot accept that a Mayan individual, least of all a woman, should have a high-ranking government position. She is charged with incompetence and unsatisfactory management of her duties while her image is tarnished in the media, resulting in her political decline.
>
> The Guatemalan state's structure, along with that of its judicial and political institutions, does not correspond to the multi-ethnic, cultural, and lingual character of the Guatemalan population. This plays an important role in the discrimination [experienced by] indigenous peoples.

The Guatemalan state's failure to 'ladinize' all of the country's populace is best exemplified by the fact that the right to common citizenship was not declared until 1944. As Roberto Gutiérrez (2006: 42) states: "[W]e can empirically prove that Guatemala has not had an egalitarian society with a common citizenship where the state provides equal opportunities to all inhabitants. Despite the allegedly universal character of the legal system and our supposed legal equality, prompt and effective access to justice is beyond the means of anyone who does not have the necessary economic, cultural, or political resources."

The divergences between Maya and ladino intellectuals are interesting. Eduardo Mayora Alvarado, a ladino, sees the Guatemalan state as responsible for all of the nation's evils, but not because of its exclusive or racist character; instead, he focuses on its corruption and interventionism. Although he acknowledges the presence of discriminatory features in the Spanish legislation of the colonial period, he also maintains that racism ceased to be an issue in Guatemala after the constitutional incorporation of a model of universal citizenship: "[T]here is no discriminatory practice more odious than the one exemplified by public institutions who do not protect my rights but protect those of another; they will not even do so when I approach them in order to denounce such institutional discrimination" (Mayora Alvarado 2006: 70–71).

Some ladino businessmen agree on the need to transform the state and move toward plural and multicultural models. In the words of Gutiérrez (2006: 47): "The Guatemalan state must recognize and appreciate communal cultures, stimulate a dialogue between them, and strengthen the concept of the individual. All of this will play a vital role in the modeling of the citizenry and facilitate co-existence without discrimination. [We urgently need to] construct a universal Guatemalan citizenry that respects cultural diversity and voluntarily accepts others, their values and traditions. This will be the basis for Guatemalan integration and solidarity, the foundation of a socially cohesive state." Businessman Álvaro Castillo Monge (2006: 155) openly acknowledges the fact that racism and discrimination hinder the development of the country by fueling poverty and arresting national development: "[R]acism and discrimination help deepen economic and social disparity. Discrimination starts with the stereotyping of peoples and populations and leads to a reduction in employment-related or educational opportunities that might have helped reduce the social gap. We must definitely fight these problems and learn to value our multicultural society, regarding it as an asset rather than a problem."

Maya Intellectuals and the New Balance between Civil Society and the Guatemalan State

One surprising result of this study is the high proximity and correlation between concepts of state, racism, and discrimination. There is a tendency to exculpate all social actors and focus on the state as the sole responsible party in charge of defeating these problems. The presence of 'the state' in the discourse of Maya elites is a fairly new yet now common phenomenon. It became increasingly common during the 1990s, with Casaús Arzú (1995, 1998, 2003, 2006), Smith (1990), and Cojtí Cuxil (1994, 2005) introducing the notion of a racist state, an aspect that had not been rigorously addressed in the past. According to our qualitative analysis, the frequency with which "the state" appears alongside mentions of "discrimination" and "racism" is 20/19 and 20/23. Mentions of a "racist state" surpass 12 counts, and the idea that the state and its institutions are the major locus for racism exceeds 24 occurrences. If we add the incidences of "state" and "racist state" that appear in the different texts, the total jumps to 29 occurrences, a rate higher than that of any other term found in the 14 essays that comprised our study (see fig. 2). The notion that racism is expressed through institutions

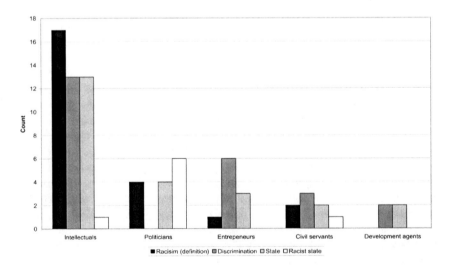

FIGURE 2 Frequency of Discursive Markers by Occupation

exceeds 13 occurrences, and the idea that it is rooted in a historical structure gets 10 counts. Clearly, the perception that Guatemalan racism is expressed through the state, and that this problem also involves ideological tools, repressive elements, and society as a whole, deserves detailed analysis. In the specific case of Maya intellectuals—and regardless of tendencies, ethnic particularities, sensibilities, or identities—there is a clear propensity to portray the state as the main source of racism and the cause of all national evils.

The depiction of the state as an irresponsible demiurge, whose duty is to solve all national problems and exercise its exclusive ability to do so, plainly demonizes institutions. However, it can also serve as a basis for a collaborative search for points of reference and new hypotheses to approach, understand, and alleviate the effects of racism and discrimination. Having analyzed the perception of the state among Guatemalan elites in general, and Maya elites in particular, I suggest a somewhat provocative hypothesis that lends itself to further interdisciplinary research: for the first time in Guatemalan history, Maya intellectuals and institutionally marginalized groups are beginning to take possession of the state and believe that political participation can indeed change the disparate structure of the country. There is a growing awareness that civil society provides a space for negotiating with the state over the allocation of resources and that civil society institutions (representing citizens) can pressure the state to fulfill its responsibility to act as arbitrator with the common interests of the populace in mind. Working through civil society, Maya intellectuals demand reforms and concrete measures. They note that previously excluded actors are now participating in state institutions, seeing them as valid, permeable, accessible, and necessary structures that can be used to make changes that benefit society as a whole.

I suggest that this new relationship between civil society and the state has been brought about by a moderation of the state's exclusivity and repressiveness in the hands of the military and an oligarchy. A gradual transition toward democracy and a plural state (and a reduction in the use of brute force) has changed both the nature of the state and the role of formerly excluded and/or marginalized groups, who may come to feel themselves part of a multicultural society, to trust governmental institutions, and to believe in institutional reform. Such a perspective problematizes the disparaged 'sanctioned Indian', showing a process more complex and relevant than social scientists generally allow.

How has the state come to be seen in political discourses as the solution to Guatemala's many problems, when not long ago there was absolutely no faith in its purpose or effectiveness? This might well be due to the recent presence of Maya intellectuals in the struggle for cultural hegemony and Maya participation in the state. As was mentioned previously, many of the essayists have held or still hold administrative positions; their experience has been positively judged, both by themselves and society in general. According to Putnam (1993), once citizens have come to trust the state and its institutions, horizontal networks based on cooperation, trust, and reciprocity begin to foster a civic culture. Citizens become aware of their role in a civic-political community and, in the name of common interest, begin to demand individual and collective rights and benefits from the state. At this point, citizen participation increases, social capital grows, and horizontal relationships among groups take precedence over former vertical interactions.

Thanks to the recent surge in social movements, social participation, and the political work of Maya leaders on local, regional, and national levels, Guatemala is now producing strategies for political and institutional change, establishing a new type of relationship between indigenous groups and the state, and working on the creation of public policies that address pertinent issues. In this context, anger toward the state can be read as a positive sign of social inclusion and proof that previously excluded sectors are now starting to perceive themselves as full-fledged citizens and actors in the democratic arena. In short, the interactions between land and sea have become more regular and stable, and, as Putnam (1993) would put it, Guatemalans are learning to construct a participative democracy.

The last four policies approved by the Berger administration—the Policy for Agrarian Development, the Policy for Integral Rural Development, the Policy against the Discrimination of Women, and the Public Policy for the Elimination of Racism and Discrimination—constitute a new and hopeful sign. They are evidence of the influence and growing participation of indigenous movements and Maya intellectuals in the creation of a new, plural state.[6] When we consider the amount of work undertaken by indigenous groups for the creation of these policies and their evident willingness and ability to intervene, negotiate, and participate without forgoing their cultural beliefs and patterns of identity, it must be said that marginalizing terms, such as the previously mentioned 'sanctioned Indian' and 'windows of inclusion', do not describe the intricate role of indigenous peoples in the contemporary Guatemalan state.[7]

I want to close this chapter with the words of Delfina Mux Caná (2006: 23), a young Maya woman with ample experience in the field of public administration and currently serving as vice-minister of women's issues.

> Given its nature, our country is best served by a plural state and a nation that respects cultural diversity. This should not be limited to the co-existence of multiple cultures, their traditions, languages, and viewpoints. A plural state and a diverse nation should contain other substantive elements (such as the economic factor) that take into account the various views and perspectives of the different sectors and peoples (peasants, women, indigenous peoples, ladinos, entrepreneurs, etc.) that constitute the Guatemalan nation.
>
> A plural state cannot exist in a context of oppression, discrimination, racism, and social inequality. Honoring diversity implies the destruction of such a system; the deconstruction of stereotypes ascribed to indigenous peoples and women; the deconstruction of internalized oppression and the conditions of extreme poverty under which indigenous groups presently live.
>
> Plurality and tolerance for cultural diversity will have a merely decorative function unless all of these issues are addressed alongside plans for the economic, political, and social development of indigenous peoples. Only then can we build a nation and a state under equal and just conditions.

Acknowledgments

The author wishes to extend thanks to Ted Fischer for the invitation to participate in this project and to the anonymous reviewers for their helpful comments.

Marta Elena Casaús Arzú is Professor of American History at the Universidad Autónoma de Madrid, where she also directs a European Master program in Latin American Studies. In Guatemala, she leads the Masters in Sustainable Development Management. Her work has focused on family and elite power networks in Central America, intellectuals and nation building, and key elements of Latin American modernity. Among her many publications are *Guatemala: Linaje y racismo* (1992), *La metamorfosis del racismo en Guatemala* (1998), *Desarrollo y diversidad cultural en Guatemala* (2000), and *Las redes intelectuales centroamericanas* (2005). Her most recent work is reported in the five-volume series, *El diagnóstico del racismo en Guatemala: Informe para la elaboración de una política pública para la eliminación del racismo y de la discriminación* (2006).

Notes

1. I disagree with Guillermo Padilla's (2006) idea that indigenous intellectuals have ceased to be an intrinsic part of their class because of their ties to international organizations and wider interests.
2. Francisco Tomás y Valiente (1996) explores the relationship between civil society and the state, as well as civil society's need for public spaces and venues.
3. For a detailed account, see the appendix in Casaús Arzú and Dávila (2006).
4. The employed methods allowed us to bring together discourses, life histories, and discriminatory practices. For more details, see the chapter "Metodología cualitativa y participativa: Hacia la construcción colectiva de conceptos" in Casaús Arzú and Dávila (2006).
5. Velásquez Nimatuj was once barred from entering a public establishment because she was wearing a 'traditional dress'. This crass act of racist humiliation led to a backlash against the establishment and a nationwide campaign against racism.
6. Here, the term 'plural state' refers to a state that recognizes cultural diversity within its unitary body. According to Villoro (1998), it results from the free and voluntary union of all pertinent groups. Its main goal is to avoid conflict through active negotiation and communication, and its purpose is to arbitrate rather than subject.
7. It is interesting to note the increase of indigenous participation in several organizations such as CONIC, COCODES, Plataforma Agraria (Agrarian Platform), and Mesa de Diálogo Maya (Roundtable for Maya Dialogue). The Maya presence can be seen in some of the most influential bodies in charge of public policy: CODISRA, MDPDRI, Mesa Intersectorial de Diálogo (Roundtable for Intersectoral Dialogue), SEPREM, and Secretaría Permanente de la Mujer (Permanent Ministry for Women's Issues).

References

Althusser, Louis. 1977. *Ideología y aparatos ideológicos de estado: Freud y Lacan.* Barcelona: Anagrama.

Bastos, Santiago, and Manuela Camus. 1995. *Los mayas de la capital: Un estudio sobre identidad étnica y mundo urbano.* Guatemala City: FLACSO.

———. 2004. "El movimiento maya: Una mirada en perspectiva." *El Periódico,* Nueva Época, Suplemento Diálogo 31.

Bobbio, Norberto. 1987. *Estado, gobierno y sociedad: Contribución a una teoría general de la política.* Barcelona: Plaza y Janés.

Brett, Roddy. 2006. *Movimiento social, etnicidad y democratización en Guatemala, 1985–1996.* Guatemala City: F y G Editores.

Casaús Arzú, Marta Elena. 1995. *Guatemala: Linaje y racismo.* 2nd ed. San José: FLACSO.

———. 1998. "Reflexiones en torno a la legitimidad del estado, la nación y la identidad en el marco de los Acuerdos de Paz en Guatemala." Pp. 116–139 in *Guatemala After the Peace Accords,* ed. Rachel Sieder. London: Institute of Latin American Studies.

———. 2003. *La metamorfosis del racismo en Guatemala.* Guatemala City: Cholsamaj.

———. 2006. "Genealogía de los conceptos de racismo y discriminación en las ciencias sociales guatemaltecas (1950-2006)." Pp. 37–68 in Casaús Arzú and Dávila 2006, vol. 3: *Prácticas discriminatorias y construcción colectiva de conceptos.*

Casaús Arzú, Marta Elena, and Amílcar Dávila, eds. 2006. *Diagnóstico del racismo en Guatemala: Investigación interdisciplinaria y participativa para una política integral por la convivencia y la eliminación del racismo.* 5 vols. Guatemala City: Serviprensa.

Castillo, Rolando, Luis Villoro, and Will Kymlicka, eds. 2002. *Democracia, ciudadanía y diversidad: Un debate político.* Guatemala City: PNUD.

Castillo Monge, Álvaro. 2006. "Definitivamente, entre más racismo, menos desarrollo (entrevista)." Pp. 155–158 in Casaús Arzú and Dávila 2006, vol. 4: *Perspectivas y visiones ciudadanas.*

Cojtí Cuxil, Demetrio. 1994. *Políticas para la reivindicación de los Mayas de hoy.* Guatemala City: Cholsamaj.

———. 1997. *Ri Maya Moloj pa Iximulew: El movimiento maya (en Guatemala).* Guatemala City: Cholsamaj.

———. 2005. *La difícil transición al estado multinacional: El caso del estado Monoétnico de Guatemala: 2004.* Guatemala City: Cholsamaj.

———. 2006. "Insumos y criterios para el diseño y factibilidad de políticas públicas contra el racismo y la discriminación." Pp. 99–118 in Casaús Arzú and Dávila 2006, vol. 4: *Perspectivas y visiones ciudadanas.*

Fischer, Edward. 2001. *Cultural Logics and Global Economies: Maya Identities in Thought and Practice.* Austin: University of Texas Press.

Fischer, Edward, and R. McKenna Brown. 1999. *Rujotayixik ri Maya' b'anob'al: Activismo cultural maya.* Guatemala City: Cholsamaj.

Gramsci Antonio. 1970. *La filosofía de la praxis.* Barcelona: Península.

———. 1972. *Los intelectuales y la organización de la cultura.* Buenos Aires: Nueva Visión.

———. 1974. *Antología.* Prologue and notes by Manuel Sacristán. Mexico City: Siglo XXI.

Grisoni, Dominique, and Robert Maggiore. 1974. *Leer a Gramsci.* Madrid: Editorial Zero.

Gutiérrez, Roberto. 2006. "Racismo y discriminación en Guatemala (ensayo sociológico)." Pp. 39–52 in Casaús Arzú and Dávila 2006, vol. 4: *Perspectivas y visiones ciudadanas.*

Hale, Charles. 2004. "'Racismo cultural': Notas desde Guatemala sobre una paradoja americana." Pp. 211–234 in Heckt and Palma Murga 2004.

———. 2006. *Mas que un indio: Racial Ambivalence and Neoliberal Multiculturalism in Guatemala.* Santa Fe, NM: School of American Research.

Heckt, Meike, and Gustavo Palma Murga, eds. 2004. *Racismo en Guatemala: De lo políticamente correcto a la lucha antirracista.* Guatemala City: Avancso.

Lux de Cotí, Otilia. 2006. "Estudio de factibilidad y diseño de políticas públicas en contra del racismo y la discriminación en Guatemala. Ensayo sobre políticas culturales, educativas y lingüísticas." Pp. 129–141 in Casaús Arzú and Dávila 2006, vol. 4: *Perspectivas y visiones ciudadanas.*

Mayora Alvarado, Eduardo. 2006. "Reflexiones sobre la discriminación y el racismo en Guatemala." Pp. 61–74 in Casaús Arzú and Dávila 2006, vol. 4: *Perspectivas y visiones ciudadanas.*

Morales, Mario Roberto. 1998. *La articulación de las diferencias, o el síndrome de Maximón.* Guatemala City: FLACSO.

Mux Caná, Delfina. 2006. "Visión de nación y del estado guatemalteco." Pp. 21–28 in Casaús Arzú and Dávila 2006, vol. 4: *Perspectivas y visiones ciudadanas.*

Padilla, Guillermo. 2006. "Resistencia local y discurso global: Comentarios en torno a la multiculturalidad y al neoliberalismo." Paper presented at the Fifth Conference of Legal Anthropology, Madrid.

Pérez Díaz, Víctor. 1994. *La primacía de la sociedad civil.* Madrid: Alianza Editorial.

Portelli, Hugues. 1973. *Gramsci y el bloque histórico.* Mexico City: Siglo XXI.

Putnam, Robert. 1993. *Making Democracy Work: Civic Traditions in Modern Italy.* Princeton, NJ: Princeton University Press.

Quemé Chay, Rigoberto. 2006a. "Ensayos sobre el racismo en Guatemala." Pp. 29–36 in Casaús Arzú and Dávila 2006, vol. 4: *Perspectivas y visiones ciudadanas.*

_____. 2006b. *La paz en Guatemala: ¿Una posibilidad histórica o coyuntural?* Quetzaltenango: Departamento de Investigaciones Económicas y Sociales.

Smith, Carol, ed. 1990. *Guatemalan Indians and the State.* Austin: University of Texas Press.

Taylor, Charles. 1996. "The Politics of Recognition." Pp. 25–73 in *Multiculturalism: Examining the Politics of Recognition,* ed. Amy Gutman. Princeton, NJ: Princeton University Press.

Tomás y Valiente, Francisco. 1996. *A orillas del estado.* Madrid: Taurus.

Velásquez Nimatuj, Irma Alicia. 2002. *La pequeña burguesía indígena comercial en Guatemala: Desigualdades de clase, raza y género.* Guatemala City: Avancso.

_____. 2004. "Traje folclorización y racismo en la Guatemala postconflicto." Pp. 235–270 in Heckt and Palma Murga 2004.

_____. 2006. "Racismo y discriminación: Un acercamiento conceptual." Pp. 85–96 in Casaús Arzú and Dávila 2006, vol. 4: *Perspectivas y visiones ciudadanas.*

Villoro, Luis. 1998. *Estado plural y pluralidad de culturas.* Mexico City: UNAM-Paidos.

Warren, Kay B. 1998. *Indigenous Movements and Their Critics: Pan-Maya Activism in Guatemala.* Princeton, NJ: Princeton University Press.

Wilson, Richard. 1999. *Resurgimiento maya en Guatemala (experiencias Q'eqchi'es).* Antigua, Guatemala: CIRMA.

Zapeta, Estuardo. 1998. "Indígenas debaten la nación." *Siglo XXI,* 6 February.

_____. 1999. *Las huellas del Balam.* Guatemala City: Cholsamaj.

_____. 2004. "Los errores del acuerdo indígena." *Siglo XXI,* 2 March.

Appendix: Text Excerpts from Selected Essayists about the Nature of the Guatemalan State

Excerpts	% Words
El Estado de Guatemala tiene un carácter ladinocéntrico. Está diseñado y estructurado para actuar y ser monoétnico, monojurídico, monolingüe y monocultural. Su composición étnica, su estructura administrativa, sus reglas protocolarias, su división política y administrativa, son la prueba de su carácter ladino y criollo. El Estado también está diseñado y estructurado para actuar contra los pueblos indígenas. Hay suficientes datos y estudios que demuestran las medidas anti- indígenas tomadas por los diferentes gobernantes, desde la independencia patria de España. En discurso, la salvación de los indígenas era la asimilación. En la práctica, implementaba la segregación étnica y racial y la marginación social y económica contra ellos.	1.6%
Desde el punto de vista de los intereses de las clases dominantes, el Estado debe tener desorganizado y dividido a los pueblos indígenas. Esto tiene la ventaja de que mantiene "bajo control a la indiada" pero a costa de la destrucción de los elementos culturales propios del país, del desperdicio de la identidad y creatividad de los pueblos indígenas, y de los costos del racismo en el campo del desarrollo. Un gobierno conservador y racista puede tener este tipo de visión y estrategia, pero no un gobierno de democracia liberal.	0.8%
El poder de grupo es, fundamentalmente, una forma de control: el espectro y la naturaleza de las acciones del grupo "minorizado" se ven limitados por la influencia de los del grupo dominante. En otras palabras, el ejercicio del control social limita la libertad de los grupos "minorizados". Como se dijo, la base del poder también se define en términos de estatus y privilegios, así como de ingresos, capacidad de acceso al trabajo, escolarización (sobre todo superior), etc. Ni moral ni legalmente puede justificarse este control y sus consecuencias. Estas son el eje de todas las formas de discriminación social y de racismo.	1.8%
La visión monocultural de nuestro Estado no es mas que la herencia colonial con sus características: dominante y homogeneizante, del criollo-ladino que persiste en nuestros tiempos. Dan cuenta los indicadores de pobreza producto de sus propias políticas de explotación, de exclusión, de desprecio, de asimilación, de discriminación y racismo. Tanto las estructuras de poder como sus esquemas mentales han Estado enraizadas con modelos económicos, políticos culturales y sociales, que han sostenido desigualdades profundas. Esta afirmación, ha hecho difícil realizar en Guatemala cambios substanciales para lograr un verdadero y real desarrollo con identidad y desarrollo humano particularmente para los pueblos indígenas.	1.5%

Chapter 8

EL OTRO LADO
Local Ends and Development in a Q'eqchi' Maya
Community

Avery Dickins

Locals in the Q'eqchi' Maya village of Muqb'ilha' refer to the recently developed tourism complex as *el otro lado* (the other side), contrasting it with the 'lived side' where the community is located. The visitor center and bungalows sit on the bank of the Candelaria River, across from the homes, the corn mill, and the local public school used by the community's 55 families on the opposite side of the river. Yet the reference goes beyond a physical division, as the tourism center provides a window to the globalized world beyond this remote community. In 2004, a two-kilometer gravel road was opened through the rain forest in order to connect the village to the main highway that takes inhabitants to markets, schools, and medical clinics in the larger towns of Raxruhá and Chisec. To access these and other services, residents must pass through the tourism complex and then ascend the footpath that leads to the road.

Muqb'ilha' sits within the Candelaria Cave system, which runs for 12 kilometers in the Chisec region of Guatemala's northern department of Alta Verapaz. The subterranean Candelaria River emerges briefly in the community's lands and then runs back underground into the caves, which is reflected in the name of the community: *muqb'il* means 'hidden or buried' and *ha'* means 'water' in Q'eqchi' Mayan.[1] Several communities in this area have been targeted by non-governmental organizations (NGOs) in the past few years for the development of economic alternatives to subsistence farming, including the introduction of new cash crops and the establishment of community tourism. Like other areas of Latin America, the implementation of neo-liberal policies in Guatemala has led to a reduction in state services and an increased reliance on both national and foreign NGOs to provide skills and livelihoods for residents of impoverished areas (Gwynne and Kay 2000). Much of the development work in the Chisec area is being carried out by US and European NGOs and supported through funding from USAID and the European Union. Development programs here thus entail foreign perspectives on needs, economic strategies, and the execution of projects, which can differ from local perceptions of needs and desires. Nonetheless, residents of Muqb'ilha' have taken advantage of the knowledge and connections brought by NGOs and have applied them toward local initiatives not specifically targeted by development programs.

Residents of Muqb'ilha' receive direct economic benefits as a result of their participation in the tourism enterprise, but they also gain social capital and skills through their interaction with outsiders, who introduce new forms of knowledge through training workshops and who can provide access to alternative life choices. Development agents, many of whom are native Q'eqchi' speakers, offer inspiration for the village's youths, who have few role models due to the limited educational and work opportunities in the village. *El otro lado* appeals to locals as it represents a step toward the world beyond the village, which is associated with learning and possibilities. Although residents invest much of their time in activities associated with *el otro lado,* they are more dedicated to the lived side than they appear to be at first glance. Individual members of the village employ opportunities that have resulted from development programs situated on *el otro lado* toward obtaining funding to support the basic needs of the village. This allows them to direct community development according to their own terms. The interface between indigenous communities and international NGOs examined here highlights ways in which local actors use development projects and conservation measures toward their own ends.

Local History and Regional Development Programs

During the last six years, the lowland Chisec region has seen a boom in the number of development programs, most of which are led by NGOs and are directed toward the improvement of nutrition, access to basic health care, obtaining land titles for the region's Q'eqchi' Maya inhabitants, and introducing alternatives to subsistence agriculture. Over 90 percent of Chisec's population is indigenous (INE 2002), with Q'eqchi' Maya representing the majority group. Inhabitants of the region plant maize and beans for subsistence and cultivate cardamom and allspice as cash crops. Chisec is located in the department of Alta Verapaz, an area that has been historically marginalized due to its distance from the nation's political center in south-central Guatemala, the lack of educational opportunities, a high rate of illiteracy, and a limited state presence since the sixteenth century.

Natives of Alta Verapaz experienced a significantly different form of colonization than populations in the southwestern highland regions of Guatemala, who were brutally dominated by Spanish conquistadors. Alta Verapaz's unique history is partially due to the Spaniards' inability to conquer its inhabitants rapidly in battle, which led them to call the region "Tuzulutlan," meaning "the land of war" (King 1974: 17). In light of these challenges, the temporary governor of Guatemala, Alonso de Maldonado, allowed the Dominican Order to put Fray Bartolomé de las Casas's ideas of peaceful conquest through religious conversion into action in 1537 in what is now Guatemala's Verapaz (True Peace) region. The area was not opened up to settlement until the late nineteenth century, when Rufino Barrios's government encouraged both foreigners and ladinos to purchase the most fertile lands in Alta Verapaz and convert them to coffee *fincas* or plantations (ibid.).

Abigail Adams (2001: 204) points out that scholars have overplayed the historical "exceptionalism" of Alta Verapaz by de-emphasizing the dispossession of land and forced labor policies carried out by the Dominicans against the indigenous population. Although the colonial period was not peaceful for natives of Alta Verapaz, their history differs from that of other indigenous groups living in Guatemala because power was wielded by the Dominicans during the colonial period and later by coffee barons who directed 'development'. Nor did Q'eqchi' communities receive the development aid from foreign governments and NGOs that helped established cooperatives and trade unions in the western highlands of the country in the 1960s (Wilson 1995: 209). Marginalization from the state is especially pronounced in northern lowland areas of Alta Verapaz that remained relatively uncolonized until the mid-twentieth century and that continue to have limited communication services (Foster and Araujo 2004).

Over the last hundred years, as a result of land scarcity and the dissolution of *fincas*, Q'eqchi' native to Alta Verapaz's highland centers of Cobán and Carchá have migrated northeast, settling in lowland areas of Alta Verapaz, Guatemala's departments of the Petén and Izabal, and Belize (Siebers 1999). Settlement in northern Alta Verapaz was promoted in the 1950s by INTA (National Institute of Agrarian Transformation) as part of its larger plan to colonize the Northern Transversal Strip, which stretches from Huehuetenango to the Atlantic Coast (Grandia 2006; Pérez 2005). Although it falls within this belt, Chisec was not heavily settled until the 1970s, in part due to the region's hilly topography and karstic soils. But now the region is experiencing rapid growth. According to census data, the Chisec municipality's population has grown from less than 10,000 to approximately 70,000 over the last three decades (INE 1973, 2002), facilitated by the construction in 1976 of a rough gravel road that connected Chisec to Cobán (Grandia 2006).

Rural families in the Chisec region today have over six children on average, which has led to demographic pressure even in recently settled communities.[2] Men without land work locally as agricultural day laborers or engage in seasonal migrant labor to support their families. In addition to the scarcity of jobs, educational opportunities are limited,[3] reflected by the high percentage of illiteracy (38 percent) in the Chisec municipality. Q'eqchi' residents of northern Guatemala have the least access to telephone and electricity services in the country (Foster and Araujo 2004), and in most small villages, such as Muqb'ilha', the primary school serves as the only government institution. Between 2001 and 2002, the road between Chisec and Cobán was paved, thereby providing a link with the national capital of Guatemala City. The asphalt road has facilitated the entry and establishment of international development organizations, businesses, and tourist services in the town of Chisec, in the process increasing their access to and presence in smaller communities in the municipality as well. Unlike the southwestern highland area of Guatemala, where a strong pan-Maya activism has developed, there is little sense of pan-Maya identity or Q'eqchi' mobilization in Alta Verapaz.[4] Due to the limited presence of the government and the absence of a strong organization around ethnic identity in rural villages, NGOs serve as the most salient civil society players in community development here.

In 2003, six communities in the region (Muqb'ilha', Candelaria Camposanto, Sepalau, El Porvenir I, La Unión, and El Zapote)[5] were targeted by development programs that sought to establish the cultivation of cash crops (including cacao, vanilla, and allspice), to diversify subsistence crops, and to develop community-based tourism. Together, these communities have been designated as the Puerta al Mundo Maya, based on their proximity to the northern department of the Petén, the heart of classic Maya civilization. The NGOs leading these projects include US-based Counterpart International, AGEXPRONT (Gremial Association of Exporters of Guatemala), and SANK (a local Q'eqchi' non-profit organization).[6] They also rely on US Peace Corps volunteers to assist them in carrying out their projects.[7] Although these organizations are led by foreigners or ladinos (non-Indians) and follow top-down approaches, the local development workers who interact most extensively with community residents are Q'eqchi' Maya from highland Alta Verapaz. The groups working with these communities also emphasize sustainable local development, meaning that the Q'eqchi' residents of the communities operate and manage the tourism and agricultural projects. As such, NGO activities primarily consist of training and management workshops, as well as educational seminars directed toward conservation ideals and practices.

Muqb'ilha'

Muqb'ilha' consists of approximately 55 families, all of whom speak Q'eqchi' Mayan, with the exception of one ladino family who are native Spanish speakers. The village's first settlers were *chicleros* (people who collect the sap of the

Manilkara chicle tree, which is used to make chewing gum) originally from the Lanquín region of Alta Verapaz, who came to the Candelaria area in the late 1960s. They were followed by other natives of the highlands in search of land, who were attracted by the hot lowland climate that allows for the cultivation of two corn crops per year. At about the same time, a French speleologist, Daniel Dreux, arrived to explore various caves in northern Alta Verapaz, including the Candelaria system. Dreux has frequently been credited with having 'discovered' the Candelaria Caves. He later returned to the region to purchase land from residents of Muqb'ilha' who lived near the entrance to one of the caves, and in 1990, he established a hotel and eco-tourism complex that caters primarily to foreign tourists.[8] Since then, Dreux has employed inhabitants of Muqb'ilha' in the hotel and as cave guides. He also runs a private school for a selected group of the village's children in which he encourages principles of environmental conservation. Dreux's past relationship with residents of Muqb'ilha' can be characterized as amicably paternalistic. However, since the formation of the community tourism project, a series of conflicts has ensued between Dreux and his associates and members of ASIQMUC (Q'eqchi' Indigenous Association of Muqb'ilha'), the local entity that manages tourism and agricultural projects in the village. In addition, a rift has developed between the eight families who continue to work for Dreux and the rest of the community's families, who participate in the new tourism enterprise.

Before the construction of the gravel road, the only access to the community was via footpath. Although the new road is accessible to vehicles (mainly four-wheel drive), there is no regular transport, so residents must walk 2 kilometers to the main highway that leads to nearby towns, as well as south to the departmental capital of Cobán or north to the department of the Petén (see figs. 1 and 2). Although the village has electricity, there is no running water or cell phone service, the lack of which continues to isolate the community despite its burgeoning tourism project. There is no secondary school in the village, which means that the few youths who study beyond sixth grade must commute to the larger towns of Chisec or Raxruhá. In addition to today's lack of educational opportunities, 80 percent of adults who live in Muqb'ilha' have no formal education, and many older women are mono-lingual Q'eqchi' speakers (MICUDE 2003: 21).

In 1999, Guatemala's Ministry of Culture designated the Candelaria Caves as Cultural Patrimony of the Nation[9] based on their "archaeological, natural, scientific, and speleological value" (MICUDE 2003). The protected area includes the caves, river, and surrounding forest, and occupies 25 percent of Muqb'ilha' property, as well as 10 percent of that of the adjacent village, Candelaria Camposanto (ibid.). In early 2004, the presidents of the community associations of Muqb'ilha' and Candelaria Camposanto signed an agreement with the Ministry of Culture and Sports for the co-management of the natural and cultural resources associated with the Candelaria Caves. A few months later, the communities were officially opened for tourism. Although the project is in its initial stages, tourism in Muqb'ilha' has grown steadily: in 2004, the community had 200 visitors, a number that increased to 1,300 in 2005 and more than doubled again in 2006.

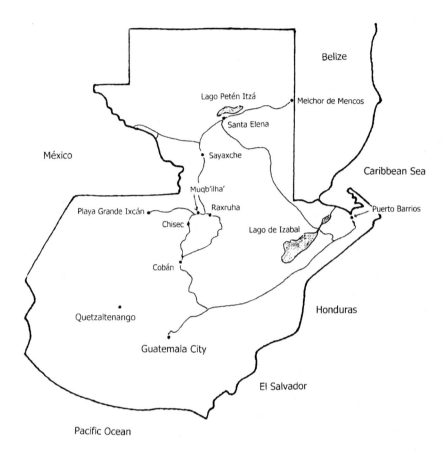

FIGURE 1 Map of Guatemala and Main Roads Linking the Chisec Region to Guatemala City, the Petén, and the Atlantic. Map by author.

The community tourism enterprise was established in 2004 with the help of various international development organizations. The tourism complex serves as the hub of activity for tourists who come to visit the caves or go river tubing, but residents of Muqb'ilha' commonly refer to this side as *el otro lado* (the other side) in Spanish, or *le'* (over there) and *junpak'al* (on the other side) in Q'eqchi'. The reference to the tourism complex as the 'other' side highlights the contrasts between the developed side and the 'lived' side, where the community is located. On the side geared toward tourism, stones delineate gravel paths and carved wooden signs mark the way to the caves, river, and community; bathrooms are equipped with running water and ceramic toilets; and residents keep lush subtropical vegetation in check. The visitor center serves as the site for meetings with development agents and workshops on environmental conservation, money management, and streamlining the organization of the community association. Upon crossing the bridge that connects the two sides, both landscape

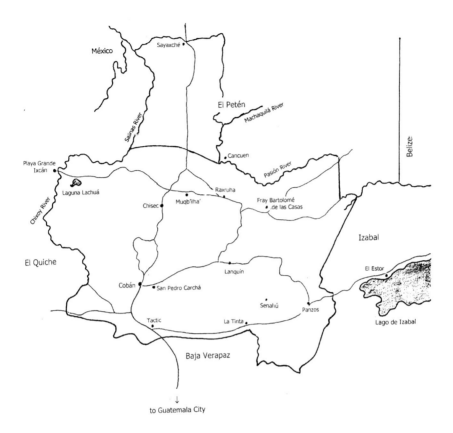

FIGURE 2 Communities and Major Roads in Alta Verapaz. Map by author.

and ideology change: village paths are strewn with trash and become slippery mud bogs during rainy season, bathrooms consist of rudimentary latrines, meetings occur in the open field or outside the schoolhouse, and women must haul water from the river for household use. The ideals associated with the developed side are at odds with the reality of inhabitants' daily life, symbolically illustrated by women washing clothes in the river in spite of the ecological conservation principles emphasized in the visitor center above them.

El otro lado

Residents of Muqb'ilha' take pride in their Maya heritage and local natural resources, a sentiment that has been largely informed by outsiders' knowledge via training workshops and that is generated and enacted on the other side. According to scholars, caves have long been considered to be sacred portals to the underworld throughout Mesoamerica (Byland and Pohl 1994; Demarest 2004: 202–204; Schele and Freidel 1990). Caves continue to be used today as sites for Q'eqchi' rituals such as the *mayehak*, which is carried out before planting. In this ritual, the Tzuultaq'a, or mountain-valley spirit, is petitioned for permission to plant or hunt through an offering as a reciprocal exchange. The ritual often takes place in caves within the mountain and consists of offering the Tzuultaq'a copal *pom* (incense), candles, cacao, tortillas, and the meat and blood of birds (Hatse and de Ceuster 2004; Siebers 1999: 66). The Tzuultaq'a is considered to be the owner of the land and all of its resources and is associated with a specific mountain in each community (Wilson 1995: 50–51). Thus, displacement and migration can affect a community's interaction with its Tzuultaq'a and the caves with which it is associated. Richard Wilson writes that practitioners of traditional religion lost their relationship with their local Tzuultaq'a during Guatemala's civil war, when many Q'eqchi' and other Maya communities were destroyed: "Followers of the mountain cult would not enter just any cave they encountered, according to one elder, 'because we do not know its name'" (1995: 225; see also Wilson 1991). Perhaps as a result of their relatively recent migration from highland areas and the increasing prevalence of evangelical religions that look down on such ritual practices, residents of Muqb'ilha' say that they did not have a strong relationship with the caves until development agents emphasized their natural and cultural value. With the exception of the first settlers who used the caves for shelter until they had constructed their homes, many inhabitants of the village had not entered the caves, and few had seen or practiced rituals in them before the advent of the tourism project.[10]

In the last few years, scientists and NGO representatives have explained to local guides the archaeological and historical significance of the ceramic artifacts and obsidian blades found in caves throughout the Chisec region. Cave experts have emphasized the delicate nature of the stalactites and stalagmites, have taught guides the names of various cave formations, and have designated which caves should be open to tourists and which should be off-limits in order to preserve them. Guides now communicate this knowledge to tourists, including nationals, local Q'eqchi' speakers, and foreigners, as well as to other community residents. One of the caves, referred to by inhabitants as Cueva de Ceremonias (Ceremonial Cave), has been designated for ritual use by pilgrims. According to guides, the cave was chosen as a site for ceremonies based on evidence of ancient use, including the blackened roof and the presence of ceramic shards.

The importance given to Maya history and culture by development agents and scientists, as well as pilgrims' veneration of the caves, has generated a sense of local pride that has been further bolstered by government recognition. In particular, the government's designation of the area as Cultural Patrimony of the Nation drew residents' attention to the significance of their community, in the broader context of Maya history and culture, and highlighted the value of the community's natural resources. One of the village's two park rangers says that before attending conservation workshops, he and other residents did not appreciate the caves, subtropical forests, river, or wildlife and thus did not take care of them. He explains that due to their lack of knowledge about the local ecosystem, in the past residents did not think twice about planting corn in the forest above the caves, which can destabilize the caves. Although there is some resistance, rangers and some community members now discourage inhabitants from cutting the forest or killing wildlife in the protected area. Valuation of the community's resources was further strengthened through an agreement made between the community and the Ministry of Culture and Sports (MICUDE 2003: annex 5). This agreement represents a unique conservation strategy in which an indigenous community shares responsibility with the government for the protection of natural and cultural resources and follows sustainable approaches to development that attempt to address critiques of top-down development by including local populations (Campfens 1997).

Residents' pride in their heritage and local natural resources translates into a sense of optimism that prevails in the context of *el otro lado* and that is furthered by the learning, entrepreneurialism, and change of pace from subsistence-based agriculture associated with this side. In the context of the limited educational opportunities in the village, the tourism complex has become important as a site of learning and knowledge. Development workers conduct training workshops here, and posters written in three languages (Q'eqchi', Spanish, and English) inside the visitor center offer a brief introduction to Maya history and culture, describe the creation of the caves, and promote conservation, as do the guides and leaders of the community association. Beyond formalized instruction, *el otro lado* also provides a space in which locals may experience alternative ways of thinking through their interaction with community outsiders, as well as a diversion from daily routines. Organized social events in the community are generally limited to church meetings that occur almost nightly in the two evangelical churches and three nights a week in the Catholic Church.[11] Residents describe Semana Santa (Holy Week, and one of Guatemala's peak tourism periods) as one of the happiest times of year due to the bustle of activity in the tourism complex. During this week, most members of the community spend at least part of the day on the other side, watching tourists come and go. Local children play with the children of tourists who spend the night or with the baby *pizote* (coatimundi, a member of the raccoon family native to lowland rain forests in the Americas) brought by development workers as an example of protected local fauna. Some enterprising families set up posts to sell drinks and snacks along the entry path, which tourists encounter before they reach ASIQMUC's store in the visitor center. The association of *el otro lado* with learning, optimism, and change leads to its conceptualization as the door, both literally and figuratively, to opportunities beyond the village.

The Lived Side

Compared to the positive attitude that dominates in the tourism complex, residents express greater indifference and less hope on the lived side. The members of one family, who dedicate much of their time to tourism and agricultural projects, claim that they never have time to repair the slippery, muddy path that leads up the hill to their house. Although learning is emphasized in the visitor center, many parents do not oblige their children to arrive at school on time or, in some cases, to attend school at all. Because the communal salon has fallen apart, any meetings held here occur in the open field under the hot sun or in the shade outside of the small schoolhouse. And on this side of the river, *pizote* is a delicacy eaten in soup or used to flavor tamales.

A Caritas[12] worker who is a native Q'eqchi' speaker from Cobán observed that members of the community have devoted so much of their time and energy to activities associated with tourism that they have "neglected their homes and their health." He described the indifferent attitude of residents in Muqb'ilha' as a reflection of the Q'eqchi' ability to adapt, which he views as a tendency toward passivity. His assessment was echoed by a tour operator from Guatemala City, who expressed surprise at the impoverished conditions of the community (which he described as "another world") when he crossed the bridge for the first time. Development workers dedicated to health care and social issues claim that Muqb'ilha' community associations, COCODE[13] and ASIQMUC, do not cooperate with them because they are more interested in working on the projects directed toward tourism, cash crops, and land titling in which they are already involved. When one of these workers arrived to the community for a scheduled meeting to perform an assessment of basic needs he was conducting for the municipality, he was informed that the president of ASIQMUC had called a communal workday to cut back growth alongside the entrance road for the upcoming holiday weekend, and so the meeting had been canceled. This prompted the development worker to complain that his services are in high demand in other villages in the region, yet the community associations in Muqb'ilha' barely recognize him. The number of NGOs working in this village allows its residents to exercise local control in the implementation of development, which they do by choosing to place NGO-managed development programs associated with tourism ahead of those directed toward basic needs.

Recent improvements to the road that leads to the community also point to residents' focus on tourism development. In September 2006, the national government sent machinery and workers to Muqb'ilha' to widen and level the road so that vehicles without four-wheel drive could enter. The improved road would provide greater access to local transport, meaning that residents would no longer have to walk the 2 kilometers from the main road, carrying goods and anything else that they bring to the community. But residents were most enthusiastic over the prospect that the improvements will allow tourists greater access to the community.

Inhabitants of Muqb'ilha' clearly recognize the lack of change on the lived side compared to that of the other side. Most residents state that the construction of the visitor center, bungalows, and road has made little difference in the community over the last few years. The biggest change they cite is the initiation of the process to obtain a communal land title, which should be complete within the next few years.[14] Other significant changes include the construction of the primary school, the establishment of a privately run corn mill in the late 1980s, the donation of water collection tanks by APRESAL (Support Project for Health Sector Reform), and the installation of electricity. Beyond these infrastructural improvements, many residents claim that life is much the same as it was when they settled here: there are no telephone lines (and only spotty cell phone service), they wash clothes in the river and live in wooden houses with earthen floors, they must travel to Raxruhá or Chisec to receive medical attention or to go to the market, and then they must carry any purchases they make the 2 kilometers to the village. Why do the residents of Muqb'ilha' invest so much time in tourism projects while seemingly neglecting more basic needs?

Local Ends and the Search for 'Projects'

Several factors figure into residents' differential investment between the lived side and the developed side: the recent proliferation of development programs and NGOs in the Chisec region, the immediate economic benefits brought by participation in the tourism enterprise, and the social and human capital associated with development agents. Because a number of NGOs have approached the community in a short period of time, local leaders have at times brushed off organizations directed toward basic needs as indicated by the above example. Dedicating time to activities associated with the tourism enterprise (e.g., construction and maintenance of the site and the road, guiding, cooking) is more attractive than participating in other programs because individuals either receive income for the services they provide or will soon benefit from attending training workshops. ASIQMUC employs 26 guides, a large number when compared to the other villages with tourism enterprises; for example, Sepalau, a larger community, has only 8 guides. Guides work according to a rotating schedule, earning approximately $4 (Q30) each day that they are scheduled, whether or not tourists arrive. Therefore, in Muqb'ilha', each guide is scheduled to work approximately one day per month, whereas guides in Sepalau work up to four days per month. During high tourism periods, additional guides are called in to work, so that during the week of 10 to 15 individuals who cooked, cleaned, or oversaw tourism activities. As a result, income from tourism is widely but thinly distributed in Muqb'ilha'.

This distribution of tourism income is attractive on the individual level, as there are more people in the community who go home with a small amount of money. Yet the downsides are that not everyone has equal access to participation in the tourism enterprise (and its profits) and that few funds remain in ASIQMUC's treasury to invest in the community.[15] Several families in the community are not active in the association and so receive no direct economic benefits. Some of these people choose not to participate in the tourism enterprise or agricultural programs, yet others complain that they are not advised of meetings or training workshops and, as a result, do not have a chance to work. The wider distribution is not necessarily at odds with program agendas, which emphasize the supplementary nature of tourism income and insist that it is not a replacement for subsistence agriculture. But development agents advocate the reinvestment of funds toward future community projects, a recommendation that the other five communities have followed.

In contrast to Muqb'ilha', other Puerta al Mundo Maya communities have used funds from tourism in ways that bolster tourism infrastructure and that benefit the community at large. For example, the community of Candelaria Camposanto used income generated from tourism during Semana Santa in 2005 to fund 75 percent of the construction of a hotel in their community (the other 25 percent was donated by INGUAT, Guatemala's National Institute of Tourism). In Sepalau, income from tourism was utilized to reconstruct the roof of the schoolhouse when it was destroyed in a storm last year, and La Unión employed income earned from transporting tourists to the archaeological site of Cancuén to establish a credit-lending program within the community. According to models of sustainable development, the reinvestment of capital generated through tourism decreases reliance on external funding as the latter two communities illustrate. Yet this reinvestment does not necessarily satisfy local needs for cash or infrastructural changes in the lived area of the village that inhabitants deem important.

Residents of Muqb'ilha' desire specific changes in their community, such as the establishment of a secondary school, running water, cement houses, and household *pilas* (concrete wash basins). Their expectation that these improvements will be achieved through outside aid is captured in a common dialogue about the need for a 'project'. Key to the concept of project is the involvement of an outside entity, either an individual or an NGO that provides not only financial aid but also know-how and social connections. For example, the director of the village youth group hoped to reorganize the group, which fell apart after its young president's untimely death in 2004. Peace Corps volunteers had previously helped him run the group, and now he felt that he could not revive it without first obtaining a project. The expectation of obtaining outside funding (and its frequent availability) also translates into an uncompromising attitude with regard to local agendas. One of the leaders in the village obtained some funding from the Peace Corps for the construction of a communal *pila*, but the community rejected it as it was not enough to cover the cost of the individual household washbasins they desired.

Development agents working in Muqb'ilha' also reinforce the importance of external aid by engaging in project dialogue. They emphasize the need not only for more funding but also for more training and workshops, to the point that this becomes the local focus. Describing the "development apparatus" as a modernist doctrine responsible for the idea of the Third World, Escobar (1995, 2005) argues that development discourse disempowers local populations, who internalize the idea that they are 'underdeveloped', and thus strengthens dependency on non-local entities. Yet while there is a clear expectation of outside aid in Muqb'ilha', residents take an active role in obtaining it. A few more educated residents of the community have taken projects into their own hands by writing proposals to seek funds from the national government and international NGOs. One of the guides in the community artfully employed the conservation of natural resources as the justification for the construction of new houses for all of the community's families. He asked development workers for guidance on writing funding proposals and then sent a petition to FOGUAVI (Guatemalan Housing Fund, the government's housing institute), arguing that because the terms of the Cultural Patrimony declaration prohibit residents from cutting trees or collecting *manaco* leaves in the protected area, the government should provide them with materials and funds to construct concrete (block) homes. Even though development programs aim to establish sustainable enterprises that will generate income for such projects, this man applied conservation rhetoric and technical knowledge that he had learned via such programs toward the direct achievement of local ends. This petition is still pending, as is another in process for submission to the Spanish Agency for International Cooperation, but in other cases residents have successfully obtained what they want. A private high school in Guatemala City donated T-shirts and school supplies to the community in early 2006 after receiving a request from a resident, and in September, Caritas supplied half of the families in Muqb'ilha' with household *pilas*.[16] A few members of the community spend more time attempting to obtain funds than learning management skills, thus developing a different skill set that is not necessarily an end goal of the development programs. In addition to learning skills, they utilize their association with development agents working in their communities toward establishing direct connections to other NGOs in Guatemala. Thus, the act of seeking projects satisfies local ends to improve community infrastructure, even though development programs aim to establish sustainable enterprises to generate income for such projects.

Beyond Material Gain

The concept of project entails a powerful social dimension as it implies a human component. In addition to seeing them as facilitators of economic aid, inhabitants of the larger Chisec region look to outsiders (whether they be ladinos from Guatemala City, non-local native Q'eqchi' speakers working in Chisec, French, or North Americans) as a source of knowledge. In part, this perspective has its roots in colonial and development discourse that values Western know-how over other forms of knowledge (Gupta 1998), but it is also based on the actual role outsiders have in communities in Chisec, where they serve as teachers (in the most general sense), medical practitioners, and agronomists. In the vacuum of educational opportunities, these outsiders offer skills and expertise otherwise unavailable to locals: principles of nature conservation, first aid techniques, money management, and cultivation methods. Outsiders are also respected because of the access to opportunities that they can furnish locals, thus increasing the latter's social and human capital (Bourdieu 1986; Coleman 1988; Portes and Landolt 2000). In the Puerta al Mundo Maya communities, this has played out in terms of experiences and opportunities offered by development agents to some individuals. In 2004, a few guides from Candelaria Camposanto and

Muqb'ilha' were selected to visit Belize to study existing cave tours, and on another occasion, members of each community were chosen to spend a week at Ak' Tenamit, where they learned to make handicrafts and met representatives from other Q'eqchi' communities.[17] In 2006, as part of their training, guides from various communities received weekly English classes, developing a skill that can be applied to other employment contexts in the future. Association with outsiders can bring status as well as lead to job opportunities, as illustrated by a resident of Muqb'ilha' who established a friendship with Peace Corps volunteers. He was recommended for a temporary job conducting surveys for a land-titling project and later received training to give regional workshops on nature conservation, which provides him with an additional source of income. Not only has he benefited economically, but his position has increased his standing in the eyes of the community.

The interchangeable nature of the various forms of capital (Bourdieu 1986) suggests that the desire to associate with outsiders represents a rational decision on the part of locals to increase their economic capital in the long run, as experience and educational opportunities can be translated into obtaining jobs. But the appeal of interacting with non-locals cannot be viewed solely as a means of increasing capital. Arjun Appadurai (1996: 4) suggests the importance of the role of the imagination in today's globalized world that arises through the connectivity created by electronic media and the mobility of individuals: "[F]ew persons in the world today do not have a friend, relative, or coworker who is not on the road to somewhere else or already coming back home, bearing stories and possibilities." Just as Guatemalan and foreign tourists are interested in Q'eqchi' culture and life-ways, locals express curiosity about tourists. Due to economic and political inequities, they rarely have the opportunity to travel, but they can have first-hand experiences through their interactions with outsiders on the other side of their community. Development agents and tourists offer a glimpse of these new perspectives (not necessarily always positive), and for youth, these individuals embody opportunities and possibilities for the future. This association of the other side with such potentials is strengthened by the fact that the other side is actually the gateway to secondary school in Chisec or Raxruhá, to work in fruit plantations in Belize or Mexico, or to Guatemala City. In this view, the appeal of the other side is linked not necessarily to outsiders themselves but rather to their representation of the globalized world and the potentials it holds, whether imagined or real.

Conclusion

For residents of Muqb'ilha', *el otro lado* symbolizes a door to a world associated with higher education, jobs, entrepreneurialism, material goods, and novel experiences. The pull to this side of the river indicates residents' desire to explore new ideas and possibilities not available in their community. But residents do not view these opportunities as a way to escape their village; rather, they invest much of the knowledge and experience they gain, and even the new possibilities they imagine, in their community. Inhabitants of Muqb'ilha' claim that their village has all that one could desire: fresh air, a healthy forest, fruit trees, the possibility to plant two crops of corn a year, a river, and family and friends. Young people express a desire to know new areas of Guatemala and perhaps beyond, but most say that they would like to live in Muqb'ilha' and raise a family. The community-run tourism enterprise in Muqb'ilha' represents an effort by civil society to improve local economic conditions; however, its benefits are not equally spread among community members. In contrast, individual members of the community undertake projects that produce improvements on the lived side and benefit the community at large. This difference reflects the strong desire on the part of residents of Muqb'ilha' to do things according to their own terms. They take advantage of the know-how accorded to outsiders through participating in civil society development programs situated on the other side, and so gain knowledge and connections that allow them to obtain support independently for the basic projects they desire. Thus, local ends are ultimately directed toward gaining skills that allow residents to direct processes of change in their own community.

Acknowledgments

The author wishes to thank Ted Fischer for the opportunity to participate in this project and for his valuable guidance. She also thanks the members of the community of Muqb'ilha' for their time and generosity towards her; Carlos Girón, who provided insights during fieldwork and helped with the maps; and anonymous reviewers for their comments. Research was funded by a Dissertation Research grant (#0450980) from the National Science Foundation.

Avery Dickins is a doctoral candidate at Vanderbilt University. She completed her dissertation research in the Chisec region of Guatemala in September 2005. Her dissertation uses social and cultural capital to explore the articulation of individuals with development programs and their representatives in Q'eqchi' Maya communities. She has also conducted a small study on the security guard industry in Guatemala and participates in Vanderbilt's Center for Americas work group that seeks to establish social indicators in the context of sustainable forestry certification programs. She is currently writing her dissertation in Nashville, Tennessee.

Notes

1. The name of the community is registered as 'Mucbilha I' or 'Mujbilha' in government documents.
2. This average is based on demographic data collected by the author in Muqb'ilha' in 2006. The average represents 25 families in which the mother is over 35 years old and includes only the number of living children. If the number of children that have died in infancy or early childhood (an average of 1.3 children per family) is included, the average number of children per family is 8.1.
3. In addition to the lack of secondary schools in most villages, the only track available to students in the Chisec municipality who want to study beyond ninth grade is the *magisterio*, which trains students to become primary school teachers. This track is offered only in the town of Chisec, the municipal seat.
4. Although there is a growing sense of Q'eqchi' and pan-Maya identity in Alta Verapaz, especially through the efforts of the ALMG (Academy of Mayan Languages) in Cobán, it has little presence in rural communities such as Muqb'ilha'.
5. The village of El Zapote is located on the northern side of the Pasión River, which forms the departmental border between Alta Verapaz and the Petén. Although El Zapote actually belongs to the department of the Petén, it is closely tied to these communities in northern Alta Verapaz.
6. SANK (Saaq' Aach'ool Nimla K'aleb'aal, or Harmony in Our Community) is a Chisec-based NGO that helps Q'eqchi' communities resolve land conflicts and promotes environmental education. Founded in 2002 as an outgrowth of Chisec's youth group, Mojuchi (which was established in 2000 by Peace Corps volunteers and a municipal worker), SANK is now run entirely by Q'eqchi' native to Chisec. It currently manages a scholarship program for local children to attend secondary school, conservation projects in the Sierra de Chinajá, and Proyecto Tzuultaq'a, which promotes forest conservation through land titling in 20 communities in the Chisec region. SANK receives funds from USAID and the European Union and works closely with Veterinarios Sin Fronteras and Counterpart International.
7. Although Peace Corps volunteers are trained and funded by the US government, they work side by side with NGO development workers in local communities, and thus they blur the line between governmental and non-governmental representatives at the ground level.
8. Dreux's purchase has been questioned, as members of the community did not own titles to the land at the time that he paid them for it. He is also said to have purchased a plot of land that is smaller than the plot on which his hotel was built.
9. The Candelaria Caves were declared Cultural Patrimony of the Nation under the Ministerial Accord 188-99.
10. Some Q'eqchi' believe that women should not enter caves or express fear of caves, as they are considered to be powerful and potentially angry. However, these beliefs are not necessarily held by all Q'eqchi' today. Five of the guides in Muqb'ilha' are women, and one guide's mother, whom I accompanied when she entered the caves for the first time, expressed amazement and curiosity but not fear.
11. Entertainment options also include nightly movies shown by a family that owns a television set and DVD player. They charge Q1 to view the movie in a room of their home; the audience is generally limited to young men.
12. Caritas is a non-profit charity organization aligned with the Catholic Church that is dedicated to the relief of poverty. Founded in 1961, Caritas Guatemala conducts a variety of agricultural, alimentation, and livestock programs in small villages throughout the country. Caritas projects in the Chisec region include tilapia production, food supplements for families with children under three years old, and education programs on hygiene.
13. In rural villages, COCODE (Consejo Comunitario de Desarrollo, or Community Development Committee) serves as the local level of the government; each COCODE reports to the municipal government. It is also the body that manages property claims, debts, and

titles within the community. Residents of each community compose the officers of its COCODE, and elections are held every two years.

14. Because some of the community's lands were located within the protected area, the declaration of the region as Cultural Patrimony of the Nation initially worked against residents of Muqb'ilha' area, which led to setbacks in the land titling process (del Cid and García 2004).

15. Mismanagement of income has been a problem in all Puerta al Mundo Maya communities, which accounts in part for the lack of surplus funds in ASIQMUC's coffers.

16. The *pilas* were designated for families with children under three years old who participate in the alimentation program sponsored by Caritas.

17. Ak' Tenamit is a Q'eqchi'-run non-profit organization located in the department of Izabal. Dedicated to promoting health care, education, agriculture, and eco-tourism in Q'eqchi' villages, the organization trains community representatives at its project site on the Rió Dulce.

References

Adams, Abigail E. 2001. "The Transformation of the Tzuultaq'a: Jorge Ubico, Protestants and Other Verapaz Maya at the Crossroads of Community, State, and Transnational Interests." *Journal of Latin American Anthropology* 6, no. 2: 193–233.

Appadurai, Arjun. 1996. *Modernity at Large: Cultural Dimensions of Globalization.* Minneapolis: University of Minnesota Press.

Bourdieu, Pierre. 1986. "The Forms of Capital." Pp. 241–258 in *Handbook of Theory and Research for the Sociology of Education*, ed. John G. Richardson; trans. Richard Nice. New York: Greenwood Press.

Byland, Bruce, and John Pohl. 1994. *In the Realm of Eight Deer: The Archaeology of the Mixtec Codices.* Norman: University of Oklahoma Press.

Campfens, Hubert, ed. 1997. *Community Development Around the World: Practice, Theory, Research, Training.* Toronto: University of Toronto Press.

Coleman, James. 1988. "Social Capital in the Creation of Human Capital." *American Journal of Sociology* 94: S95–S120.

del Cid, M. and D. R. García. 2004. "Cuevas candelaria: Desmitificando la participación comunitaria en la conservación del patrimonio." Paper presented at the Simposio de Arqueología Guatemalteca, Guatemala City.

Demarest, Arthur. 2004. *Ancient Maya: The Rise and Fall of a Rainforest Civilization.* Cambridge: Cambridge University Press.

Escobar, Arturo. 1995. *Encountering Development: The Making and the Unmaking of the Third World.* Princeton, NJ: Princeton University Press.

_____. 2005. "Imagining a Post-Development Era." Pp. 341–351 in *The Anthropology of Globalization: From Classical Political Economy to Contemporary Neoliberalism*, ed. Marc Edelman and Angelique Haugerud. Malden, MA: Blackwell.

Foster, Vivien, and Maria Caridad Araujo. 2004. *Does Infrastructure Reform Work for the Poor? A Case Study from Guatemala.* World Bank Policy Research Working Paper 3185. Washington, DC: World Bank.

Grandia, Liza. 2006. "Unsettling: Land Dispossession and Enduring Inequity for the Q'eqchi' Maya in the Guatemalan and Belizean Frontier Colonization Process." PhD diss., University of California Berkeley.

Gupta, Akhil. 1998. *Postcolonial Developments: Agriculture in the Making of Modern India.* Durham, NC: Duke University Press.

Gwynne, Robert N., and Cristóbal Kay. 2000. "Views from the Periphery: Futures of Neoliberalism in Latin America." *Third World Quarterly* 21, no. 1: 141–156.

Hatse, Inge, and Patrick de Ceuster. 2004. *Cosmovisión y espiritualidad en la agricultura q'eqchi'.* Cobán, A.V., Guatemala: Ak'Kutan, Centro Bartolomé de las Casas.

INE (Instituto Nacional de Estadística). 1973. *Censos nacionales de población y habitación.* Guatemala City: Republica de Guatemala.

_____. 2002. *Censos nacionales de población y habitación.* Guatemala City: Republica de Guatemala.

King, Arden. 1974. *Coban and the Verapaz: History and Culture Process in Northern Guatemala.* New Orleans, LA: Tulane University Middle American Research Institute.

MICUDE (Ministerio de Cultura y Deportes). 2003. *Plan maestro parque nacional cuevas de candelaria.* Guatemala City: Republica de Guatemala.

Pérez, Francisco J. 2005. "Effects of Land Legalization in the Agrarian Dynamics of the Indigenous Communities of Alta Verapaz, Guatemala." MA diss., Ohio University.

Portes, Alejandro, and Patricia Landolt. 2000. "Social Capital: Promise and Pitfalls of Its Role in Development." *Journal of Latin American Studies* 32, no. 2: 529–539.

Schele, Linda, and David A. Freidel. 1990. *A Forest of Kings.* New York: W. M. Morrow.

Siebers, Hans. 1999. *'We Are Children of the Mountain': Creolization and Modernization among the Q'eqchi'es.* Amsterdam: Center for Latin American Research and Documentation.

Wilson, Richard. 1991. "Machine Guns and Mountain Spirits: The Cultural Effects of State Repression Among the Q'eqchi' of Guatemala." *Critique of Anthropology* 11, no. 1: 33–61.

_____. 1995. *Maya Resurgence in Guatemala: Q'eqchi' Experiences.* Norman: University of Oklahoma Press.

Chapter 9

THE POLITICAL USES OF MAYA MEDICINE
Civil Organizations in Chiapas and the
Ventriloquism Effect

Pedro Pitarch

In 1989, when I began my fieldwork in the village of Cancuc, the indigenous people were pleasantly surprised that, unlike civil servants and political and religious activists, I had come not to try to teach them something but rather to learn from them. Seventeen years later, the situation has changed radically. Now, the indigenous people ask for—or rather, demand—aid and 'cooperation'. Relations between the indigenous communities of Chiapas (the southernmost state in Mexico) and the rest of the country have been transformed, and civil organizations have played a decisive part in this transformation process. As in other parts of Mexico and Latin America (Avritzer 2002; Méndez 1999; Olvera 1997), the growth of associative ties has strengthened civil society. In the past, the Mexican state was characterized by a system of patronage that controlled society through a mixture of personal ties and vertical relationships. Civil

Notes for this chapter are located on page 205.

organizations had to subsume themselves into this patronage system or be relegated to the margins of public life. However, now the control and subordination that the Mexican state, and to a lesser extent the Catholic Church and leftist parties, imposed on the indigenous population has given way to a more complex, plural, and in some ways confusing type of relationship.

The general effect has been positive. While civil organizations are still very dependent on federal and state governments, there is no doubt that they have played a crucial role in supporting indigenous groups as they are gaining more political independence in their dealings with public powers. Naturally, the fact that the central Chiapas region is mostly indigenous means that civil society there takes on a unique form. In this type of civil society, indigenous communities are locked in a complex relationship with activists, advisers, and non-indigenous civil servants based on cooperation and mutual dependence, as well as on mutual prejudices, conflicts of interest, and politically motivated symbolic co-optation. This set of circumstances is common to all regions of Mexico with an indigenous presence, but these pressures are especially intense in Chiapas. For more than a century, this region has been seen, rightly or wrongly, by the rest of Mexicans and foreign visitors as the quintessentially 'Indian' region of the country (even as the meaning of the designation has changed over time). As a result, starting in the 1940s, the region became a laboratory for indigenous policies that were to be applied later in other areas, making Chiapas especially attractive to social scientists and political activists. The Zapatista rebellion of 1994 and the immense national and international interest that followed only intensified the image of Chiapas as an indigenous place.

Chiapas civil society, therefore, is wrapped up in a very politically and symbolically charged atmosphere. This determines the somewhat peculiar way that things work there and creates specific problems as well. For understandable reasons, studies concerned with civil organizations in the indigenous context tend to focus on the conflict between indigenous peoples and the state. These studies generally assume that such civil organizations represent the indigenous population, with non-indigenous actors and political activists limited to the role of transmitting and facilitating indigenous interests. In other words, civil society tends to be seen not as problematic in and of itself. Compared with the wide range of difficulties faced by indigenous groups, the issue of how civil society is organized and how it functions is of secondary importance. However, if we momentarily leave aside the question of indigenous-state tensions to concentrate on the internal workings of civil society, the image of civil society as homogeneous, focused, and representative becomes problematic.

For the purposes of this chapter, it is especially significant that not all of the organizations make civil use of the resources of civil society. This is to say that there are associations whose activity and internal organization, instead of fostering more plural and open relationships, create authoritarian projects that lead to a climate of incivility and confrontation within civil society (Pérez-Díaz 2003; Putnam 1995). Therefore, it is not enough to speak of civil society in the abstract, as if by being 'civil' any possible complications would be avoided. Rather, it is essential to understand the type of framework that underpins civil society. The work of civil society organizations has tangible, significant effects on the situation of indigenous peoples. Are these organizations centered on promoting liberty and a civic conversation between indigenous peoples and the rest of Mexican society, or, conversely, are they shadowy, authoritarian organizations? Do indigenous peoples have access to the leadership and do they have the ability to define the activities undertaken, or are these centers fundamentally controlled by non-indigenous activists? Do these groups recognize a variety of points of view and interests, or do they try to present a single legitimate and authorized indigenous voice? These are but a few of the questions about civil society that in other situations are considered routine, but when applied to indigenous contexts somehow become irrelevant or inconvenient. As the indigenous public space expands and matures, judging its basic, internal quality is crucial.

I approach these questions through an examination of the organizations of 'indigenous doctors'. To be fair, this is only one possible choice among the panorama of civil associations in Chiapas. Nonetheless, an analysis of the uses and definitions of 'indigenous medicine' as employed by these organizations reveals a number of contradictions of civil society. The political value assigned to indigenous medicine may be attributed to the fact that medicine is a key link between indigenous communities and public institutions (governmental and non-governmental). From an indigenous perspective, medicine occupies a broader and more elaborate domain than it does in the Western viewpoint. Among indigenous peoples, sickness and treatment seem to provide a moral language through which social, political, and religious relations can be expressed and issues of conflict can be settled. Moreover, this language encompasses relations with the non-indigenous world. From the perspective of non-indigenous organizations, medicine also represents one of the poles around which interactions with the indigenous world gravitates. In a way, it also constitutes a 'language' through which relationships can be established with indigenous people. A logical first step toward understanding this language would be to explore the powerful symbolic attraction that indigenous shamans exercise on the Western imagination, a topic I will return to below. On the other hand, at an institutional level, one finds the commitment of Western society to extend public health care to indigenous population as part of cooperation and development programs.

The central region of Chiapas and its neighboring area, with an indigenous population of close to a million, has become a densely populated center for the activities of medical organizations. It comes as no surprise that official Mexican institutions (the Mexican Social Security Institute, Red Cross, the National Indigenous Institute, among others) and also the largest international organizations (International Red Cross, Doctors of the World, Doctors without Borders, etc.) are on hand. However, the presence of a wide range of smaller organizations (the Catholic Church, evangelical churches, Mexican and international NGOs), whose activities include medical training and treatment programs, may be of even more importance. There is probably no other place in the world that has gathered in such a small space so many and such different medical organizations, each with its own style and political agenda.

Over the years, these organizations have been careful to recognize to some degree the importance of indigenous medicine and to pursue at least nominal cooperation with indigenous medical systems. In the end, however, they have encountered difficulties in establishing cooperation with indigenous healers and have ultimately failed, in my opinion, in the exchange of medical knowledge. Yet the reasons for this failure are not the subject of this chapter. Rather, my focus is on the organizations' political role and particularly their unforeseen influence on the genesis of indigenous medical associations. It can be said that the appearance of indigenous medical associations resulted from the policy of official non-indigenous institutions to recognize and collaborate with indigenous medicine. In the 1980s, Mexican medical institutions began to follow the recommendations of international organizations (United Nations, Food and Agriculture Organization, World Health Organization, United Nations ICEF) with respect to strengthening the practice of primary health care. Furthermore, the Alma Ata Declaration of 1978 pointed out that the coverage of local medical services could be augmented by providing "persons that practice traditional medicine" with "the proper technical training." Between 1979 and 1994, the National Indigenous Institute of Mexico (INI) and the Mexican Social Security Institute (IMSS) initiated in Chiapas, with international financing, a series of programs directed at linking 'indigenous healers' with the local medical healthcare practice, essentially as assistants to Mexican doctors. The assumption was that implementing truly effective health and epidemiological projects required the help of indigenous specialists.[1] In part, these projects reflected a growing tendency in Mexico to recognize indigenous culture differences, but they also fundamentally (if less explicitly) represented a test case for reducing costs in the public health system as part of a general project of neo-liberal reform. These reforms would eventually lead, during the presidency of Carlos Salinas de Gortari, to the privatization of numerous public enterprises (see Rus 1995). The various programs of medical cooperation concentrated on three general areas: first, locating indigenous specialists and trying to recruit them; second, botanical identification of the medicinal plants they used and the creation of herbariums near health clinics; and, third, training bilingual indigenous young people to serve as cultural translators and health 'promoters' (Aguirre Beltrán 1986; Freyermuth Enciso 1993).

Around 1985, some of these programs of collaboration with indigenous medicine were discontinued, while others suffered internal conflicts, leading to the creation of the Organization of Indigenous Doctors of the State of Chiapas (OMIECH). For the most part, OMIECH's founders were Mexican doctors, who played the role of 'advisers' to the organization, and a group of young, bilingual indigenous staff from the previous programs. The objective of OMIECH was basically to continue the work begun by the government programs, but to do so as a civil organization capable of obtaining national and international financing on its own (Freyermuth Enciso 1993). The first half of the 1990s saw the rise across the indigenous regions of Chiapas of between 10 and 15 new organizations dedicated to indigenous medicine. In some cases, these were local offshoots of OMIECH, and in others, they were new organizations promoted by official programs of INI and IMSS, which by this time were directly involved in setting up and financing such organizations, as well as providing them with technical assistance. The reasons for this growth of organizations were twofold. First, the seeds sown by the rhetoric of cultural recognition had taken root. Second, the process of economic liberalization of the Salinas de Gortari government was in full swing, and liberalizing measures in the health-care system were being implemented. Later, the Zapatista rebellion of 1994 created various kinds of difficulties for these organizations. Today, with the possible exception of two or three that are capable of attracting public or international financing, the organizations of indigenous medicine are mired in a state of lethargy or have simply disappeared. Deceptively, the initials of these organizations' names seem to live on after the groups themselves, for all intents and purposes, cease activity.

This chapter is presented in three sections, each of which is dedicated to examining a specific type of organization of indigenous medicine. The first section deals with OMIECH, the oldest and largest of such organizations in Chiapas.[2] In some ways, OMIECH has become the standard-bearer of indigenous medicine. My interest in this organization is not so much its internal composition as the way it presents itself, especially with respect to a rather ambivalent attempt to construct a 'Maya medicine'. In the end, I find that OMIECH's view of Maya medicine turns out to something conceptually equivalent to European medicine. The second section concerns a small organization of indigenous physicians in a Tzeltal-speaking village (Cancuc) in which the indigenous people have for the most part maintained control over Maya medicine. Here I pay close attention to the meaning that indigenous people attach to the organization, which is markedly different from the presuppositions that public institutions and political activists make about such organizations. The third and final section examines the case of a council of indigenous doctors—the Council of Traditional Indigenous Doctors and Midwives of Chiapas (COMPITCH)—whose objective, when put into practice, consisted of recruiting doctors and promoting indigenous medicine as a means of political mobilization. What interests me about this case is the 'ventriloquial' use that the non-indigenous advisers make of the indigenous medicine organization.

In the Museum of Mayan Medicine

OMIECH's Center for the Development of Mayan Medicine (CEDEMM) has its headquarters in the city of San Cristóbal de Las Casas, a place that just a few decades ago was practically off-limits to indigenous people but where today perhaps half the inhabitants are of indigenous origin. In fact, the city has become the main center of political organization and exchange of products and ideas for the indigenous population in the state of Chiapas. CEDEMM is located on a portion of the land that made up the Tzeltal-Tzotzil Coordinating Center, famous for being the first such center founded by the INI in the entire country and for serving as a laboratory of indigenous policies from 1953 onwards. Nevertheless, shortly after the Zapatista insurrection of 1994, the INI center ceased to exist in any practical sense. Its installations and the large plot of land it owned on the outskirts of the city were taken over by different semi-official indigenous groups, including indigenous immigrants who occupied land and set up home there.

CEDEMM, which defines itself as a "model for medical attention," consists of five sections referred to as services: the House of Healing, the Administrative Center, the Museum of Mayan Medicine, the pharmacy, and the medicinal herb garden. The Administrative Center is composed of offices, a meeting hall for the members of OMIECH, and, most importantly, an Agreement Liaison Office, which manages the acquisition of Mexican and international financing. In the medicinal herb garden, experiments are conducted with the region's medicinal plants. In the pharmacy, medicinal plants gathered or cultivated by indigenous people of the region are prepared and sold to customers from the city or tourists; there is a laboratory, curing areas, and an archive of medicinal plants. In 1996, when the center began operation, the House of Healing was planned as a place for shamans from the rural communities of the region to treat patients, both indigenous and non-indigenous. Sebastian Luna, the technical staffer who showed me around the center, imagined it as a hospital with beds that, over time, would function as a training center of a future school of indigenous medicine. However, at present it still does not offer medical attention. The Museum of Mayan Medicine, on the other hand, has been relatively successful with the public and has received an official museological award. The center (see fig. 1) is visited by some urban indigenous people—mostly schoolchildren—and by tourists who are charged admission to the museum and who sometimes makes purchases in the pharmacy.

This center's organizational structure results from the confluence of various points of view and interests. In theory, it is a center of indigenous doctors, that is, people designated as shamans in the ethnographic literature, but who, in practical terms, have only a minor role. The shamans that participate in the organization have, following the Weberian distinction, formal authority but no effective power. They have been given honorary positions in the organizational chart of OMIECH, but the real power is held by the advisers and technical staffers. The advisers are for the most part Mexican physician-activists, only some of whom are employed full-time by the organization. The technical staffers are urban-dwelling indigenous people, usually quite young, who generally work full-time for the center. The organization's original members came from institutional programs of collaboration with indigenous medicine developed during the 1980s.

In the organization, it is the advisers and staffers who have the power to decide how indigenous medicine is presented. The vehicle to exhibit indigenous medicine is the Museum of Mayan Medicine. What follows is a quick tour of what the museum offers.[3] At the entrance, one reads: "Indigenous people have always had ways to prevent and cure the illnesses of our people. Like our ancestors, we do this with prayers, plants, candles, stones, incense, and

FIGURE 1 Entrance to the Center for the Development of Mayan Medicine

medicinal drinks. Our oldest ancestors taught their children, who taught their own children, and so on, and in this way their knowledge was handed down to us: pulse healers, midwives, healing with herbs, setting bones, and shamans who went off to the hills to pray ... We are the ones responsible for taking care of the health of our communities."

The first room of the museum represents the central square of an indigenous village in the Chiapas highlands. Its walls are covered with informative murals. On one of them, five traditional medical specialties are portrayed in the Tzotzil language: *ilol* (prayer healer), *rezador de los cerros* (healer who performs prayer rites in the hills), *tzak bak* (bone setter), the midwives, and *ak' womol* (herbalist). The next room is a chapel with an altar on which there is an image of Christ and four saints. On the other side of the room there are mannequins representative of a shaman and his family, arranged in the pose of asking for permission to cure. The third space represents an open space in the woods, and in front of a small hill with three crosses is the mannequin of a *rezador de los cerros*. On the walls are photographs of plants and animals with medicinal uses. On one of the walls there is a large mural in red and black depicting Emiliano Zapata, who is shown embracing the mountains and forests of Chiapas (this mural was painted by Chicano muralists who have done other works in San Cristóbal). In the next room, the interior of an indigenous house made of adobe is represented: on one side there is a belt loom, on the other are chicken coops. In this room, mannequins represent a woman giving birth (see fig. 2), attended by her husband and a midwife, while in the foreground are some household articles. In an adjoining room,

FIGURE 2 Representation of Childbirth in the Museum

there is a display of the traditional techniques for making candles and the manu-
facture of indigenous tobacco, both items used in therapeutic rituals. The last area
of the museum is a conference room and theater for audio-visual projections. On
my last visit, in 2006, a video on traditional treatment during childbirth seemed to
make a great impression on several European couples who watched it.

In 1996, when I asked Sebastian Luna, the indigenous technical staffer of
the organization, about the significance of the museum, he replied:[4]

> The museum is to compile a history of traditional medicine. To show that the
> indigenous traditional medical customs have not disappeared completely, we
> seek to recover and preserve those things that are our customs. We want to
> show that it is not true what they say in the [rural] communities that we are
> not indigenous people anymore, that we have become modernized. That isn't
> true ... The museum shows that, yes, we are indigenous people, but that does
> not mean that we are against other medicines, that there isn't mutual respect
> between the different medicines. So the indigenous children who study in school
> learn how our grandparents and great-grandparents lived, what they did to try
> to heal the sick before they knew about other medicines or the hospital. The
> reason for the museum is not just to teach indigenous people but other people

[Mexican and international tourists] as well about how we lived before, as the original people. That way, if the institutions cut the financing, the tourists can help us with their money.

CEDEMM shows a certain unresolved ambivalence in the fact that the museum is designed primarily to be interesting, useful, and meaningful both to the indigenous as well as to outsiders. The display style shows this attempt to try to capture the attention of people with different interests and aesthetic tastes—on the one hand, a diverse group of indigenous people (traditionalists, evangelicals, rural and urban people) and, on the other hand, foreign tourists, local residents, international financing agencies, and Mexican public health institutions. Hence, the museum exhibits a mix of aesthetic, geographic, and temporal differences that produce an odd effect when combined into a collage. To the extent that it is oriented toward the indigenous population, the museum has a historical bent, showing 'things as they were'. The houses are old-fashioned and lack such common modern objects as radios, televisions, and Coca-Cola bottles (which for several decades now have been used by shamans in rural communities to make offerings), and the activities shown, such as candle making, have fallen into disuse. Luna underlined the historical character of the museum in his reference to indigenous children learning what their grandparents and great-grandparents "did to try to heal the sick, before they knew about other medicines or the hospital." The key word here is "before." The medicine on display in the museum is presented as something that is old and disappearing, and therefore something that the children ought to learn. In a more subtle sense, the museum defends the traditionalness of the city-dwelling indigenous people as compared with the more pure rural communities. According to Luna, the indigenous in the rural communities accuse urban indigenous of forgetting their traditions, but the museum and CEDEMM show that traditional medicine has not disappeared in the city, even if it has different forms and meaning.

The Museum of Mayan Medicine also seeks to interest visitors from outside the Chiapas community. This side of the museum has a distinctly ethnographic character—'things as they are now'. As with any ethnographic museum, it is possible to assume that there is a certain temporal difference between the representation of traditional objects and what is occurring at present with the natives' contact with 'modernity'. Overall, the premise of the museum is to show authentic Maya medicine. The fact that it is termed 'Maya' (a conceit that, unlike in Guatemala, is not generally used in the region or in Mexico, except in the technical sense or to refer to the indigenous people of the Yucatan) emphasizes the extent to which the museum and the center are directed toward foreign visitors—by linking contemporary indigenous medicine with the prestige of ancient Maya civilization. The target audience of non-indigenous people whom the center seeks to attract is, nevertheless, heterogeneous. There are the non-indigenous inhabitants of the city, who occasionally buy the herbal medicines in the pharmacy. There are the tourists attracted by the presence of the indigenous population of the region and especially those in search of the esoteric—in spite of the fact that the center is hardly exotic, located as it is in a suburb of the city, and considering that tourists can go to the nearby town of Chamula where shamans practice their craft inside a church and there is no doubt as to the authenticity of their rituals. However, Mexican institutions, persons in charge of international organizations, and members of NGOs are the center's main audience. To this end, the museum presents indigenous medicine 'just as things are now' but at the point of disappearing—especially if recognition and adequate financing are not forthcoming.

Nonetheless, taken together, all the parts of the museum and CEDEMM are designed so that indigenous medicine will constitute a subject in and of itself. The museum is based on the type of display that Kirshenblatt-Gimblett (1991) calls in situ: mimetic art that—whether it be in the form of period rooms, re-created environments, re-enacted rituals, or photomurals—places objects (or replicas of them) in situ. "In situ approaches to installations enlarge the ethnographic object by expanding its boundaries to include more of what was left behind, even if only in replica, after the object was excised from its physical, social and cultural settings" (ibid.: 389). Nevertheless, in situ installations, no matter how mimetic, are not neutral: "They are not a slice of life lifted from the everyday world and inserted into the museum gallery, though this is the rhetoric of the mimetic mode. On the contrary, those who construct the display also constitute the subject" (ibid.).

If the museum is meant to define Maya medicine, it does so in such a way that Maya medicine appears symmetrical to Western academic medicine. CEDEMM maintains something like a hospital (the House of Healing), a pharmacy, an experimental garden of medicinal plants (the equivalent of a laboratory), and a network of administration and services. The presentation of the museum responds to a scheme that is functionally similar to the European medical model: a field in which there exist specialties and specialists (diagnostics, prayer, botany, midwifery, etc.), a canon of knowledge, standard therapeutic methods, and so forth. In this sense, the museum displays not only so-called indigenous medicine but also indigenous medicine that satisfies the requirements of 'authentic' medicine. Although the museum's presentation of indigenous medicine shows a mix of different interests and emphases, possibly due to the participation of Mexican doctors and urban indigenous staffers, on the whole, a vision of the European medical model predominates. It is true that the museum pays a certain amount of attention to 'non-empirical' facets and the ritual nature of the region's medicine, such as shamanic chants (communing with spirits), but this does not go far in establishing the uniqueness of indigenous medicine. For all practical purposes, CEDEMM clearly favors activities that have a chance of being recognized as medically useful from the academic point of view. In the final analysis, the predominant idea is that there is an empirical basis underlying 'magical' activities that can be mined from the scientific viewpoint. This explains the importance of the work with medicinal plants (something that does not alienate the Catholic and evangelical indigenous people, who consider traditional rituals to be diabolical by nature) and the emphasis on the organization and instruction of female midwives. Thus, CEDEMM is a direct product of the medical programs based on 'collaboration' between public medicine and indigenous medicine, and ultimately its work depends on the criteria of utility employed by the cooperating institutions.

The Local Use of an Organization of Indigenous Physicians

The Organization of Traditional Doctors is a local organization in the municipality of Cancuc, a Tzeltal-speaking indigenous village in the highlands of Chiapas, a few hours away from the city of San Cristóbal. The organization began its work in 1991, shortly after I had finished the fieldwork for my doctoral thesis. At that time, in spite of the fact that a good portion of my work was with shamans, some of whom later participated in the organization, I had not heard about the need to create such an organization. The impetus to found it came once again from the programs collaborating with indigenous medicine through the INI and the IMSS. However, indigenous healers gave their own meaning to the organization.

In 1991, INI organized a 'workshop' in the recently created Cancuc House of Culture. The director of the House of Culture was Miguel Gómez, a young, educated indigenous man who had lived in the city and who had a lot of initiative and interest in traditional indigenous culture. As Gómez explained, during the entire day of the workshop, an anthropologist explained to them what culture was. This somehow led to the idea of creating an organization of the shamans of the municipality. A year later, the first meeting of indigenous medical practitioners was held, during which they were to explain their way of working and their needs. Gómez remembers that the principal difficulty lay in identifying the true "traditional doctors," an issue that was ultimately left up to the authorities in each village. Convincing the shamans to attend also posed an additional difficulty. They were able to attract 42 shamans, although, according to Gómez, not all were "complete" experts; some were knowledgeable only about herbs.

Indeed, it is not easy to calculate an approximate number of the medical specialists who practice in Cancuc. Among other reasons, there is the problem of how to define the category. Simplifying greatly, we can differentiate three types of experts (see Pitarch 1996). The *ch'abajometik* specialize in negotiating with the sacred through ceremonies of a preventative character or negotiating with spirits, for example, to recover kidnapped souls. The *poxtaywanej* (literally, agents of medicines) use medicine to extract pathogenic substances introduced into the body magically by aggressive spirits. They may do this with medical plants through shamanistic chants that are considered medicines in their own right. Finally, there are the *pik'abaletik*, who specialize in medical diagnosis through pulse reading. In practice, however, it is normal for *ch'abajometik* also to be *pik'abaletik*, and often *poxtaywanej* as well. Surely, it is such a combination that Gómez considers the "complete indigenous doctor." I calculate that in Cancuc, out of a total of 30,000 inhabitants, they number no more than 200, including both men and women.

Three years later, with INI financing, the organization put up a small building for gatherings, with offices, an altar, and a garden for growing medicinal plants. At the behest of INI, the organization was legally constituted with formal leadership positions and statutes. In retrospect, it is said that the organization was founded to defend itself against possible attacks from indigenous people converted to Catholicism or evangelical religions. This was not actually an imminent risk in Cancuc, a traditionalist municipality where converts had no political control. However, in neighboring municipalities, especially the Catholic ones, some shamans had been murdered during the previous decade, and shamanist activities had practically been outlawed. The existence of an organization of doctors seemed to prevent aggression, even on the part of traditional indigenous people who, as it often happened, suspected the shamans of bad practices (given the morally ambivalent character of the shamans). In becoming part of a legally recognized group, the shamans now seemed fit to act as interlocutors with public institutions and churches. The indigenous doctor's organization in Cancuc was most active from about 1992 to 1995, concentrating primarily on obtaining funding and technical assistance from INI, constructing the House of Indigenous Physicians, and setting up the garden of medicinal plants. But the number of indigenous doctors who belonged to the group was always small, and their involvement was generally sporadic. During those years, only three shamans participated in a relatively consistent manner, principally by attending indigenous patients from other villages in the region.

There are circumstantial reasons that explain this low participation. For shamans, generally older men and women, traveling to town required too much time and effort; even the offer of gifts in the form of machetes, axes, and metallic roofing sheets was not sufficiently enticing. However, a more profound reason for the low participation had to do with the nature of shamanic practice itself. Tzeltal shamanism is in essence an individual and solitary activity. This aspect characterizes initiation into the vocation as well as its therapeutic activities. Shamans do not consult each other, nor is there any more or less public sphere in which they can exchange knowledge and discuss techniques of their specialty. Where there is a relationship between shamans, it is usually based on competition rather than cooperation, which is easy to understand if we consider that other shamans are among their multiple potential enemies. In a way, an organization of shamans is a contradiction in terms. In other words, the Organization of Traditional Doctors was a group with hardly any medical practitioners and little actual therapeutic activity. However, this was not considered a significant problem by the indigenous people with whom I spoke and was in fact to be expected. It is evident that this organization of indigenous doctors was not thought of as a center of therapeutic activity or as a professional association, although it undoubtedly served these functions to some limited extent. In reality, it had a different significance, to which I return below.

Starting in 1995, the activity of the Organization of Traditional Doctors progressively declined. This was due in part to the fact that Miguel Gómez, its main local booster, had to devote himself to other tasks. However, there were two other significant reasons. First, INI indigenous medical programs abruptly closed down. A rethinking of official policies toward indigenous people—mostly as a consequence of the public success of the Zapatista Army of National Liberation (EZLN), which had led the revolt in Chiapas in 1994—made the existence of INI politically inconvenient, and the institution ended up being eliminated. The second reason had to do with attempts to recruit indigenous medical organizations to participate in activism of an openly political nature. It is clear that the Zapatista rebellion created a climate of political effervescence in which some organizations and activists, often drawn from other parts of Mexico or abroad, tried to get indigenous medical organizations to commit to anti-governmental and generally anti-establishment political activity. As happened in other parts of Chiapas, the result in Cancuc was that shamanic activity receded farther into the shadows. We will see in the following section that the interest of these new activists tended toward questions of biodiversity, and the role of shamans became circumscribed to emblems of authenticity.

The reasons behind the decline of the Organization of Traditional Doctors reflect what the group meant to the indigenous people of Cancuc. The organization is not thought of as something that depends primarily on its relation with the rest of the indigenous community. Instead, its value lies in its ability to give voice to a sector of the community—indigenous doctors—in their dealings with external institutions. When these institutions disappear, as in the case of INI, or when they become inappropriate, as in the case of political activism, the usefulness of the organization disappears. Surely, this is a common characteristic of any organization, official or civil, that operates among indigenous populations. But in the case of an organization of shamans—which as we have seen, does not represent shamans so much as shamanic activities— this attempt to articulate with the outside world seems particularly appropriate. There and across the Americas, the principal role of the shaman is to serve as a communicator with the spirit world, a sort of ontological translator between different planes of existence. Thus, in the case of Tzeltal shamans, their actions have been key in the ordering of the relationship between the indigenous and the Mexican and European worlds. Elsewhere, I detail how shamanic activity represents a discourse and an interpretation of the historical relationship between indigenous peoples and Europeans (Pitarch 1996). It would be going too far to assert that, from a political point of view, shamans represent a fundamental part of the relation with the Mexican world, especially if we compare their role with that of bilingual schoolteachers, representatives of political parties, and leaders of cooperatives. However, from the indigenous perspective, the shaman's position, while lacking ordinary power, continues to occupy a central place in the relationship with the non-indigenous world.

Indigenous Medicine as Political Ventriloquism

Let us now turn to an organization dominated by non-indigenous advisers whose objective, in practical terms, is to use indigenous medicine as an instrument to influence Mexican politics. Founded in 2000, the Council of Traditional Indigenous Doctors and Midwives of Chiapas (COMPITCH) seeks to represent all of the organizations concerned with indigenous medicine in Chiapas. The public aims of this organization—"to recover, defend, disseminate, and advance traditional medicine," listed on a now defunct Web site—are relatively easy to comprehend. However, the group's internal mechanisms have a more secretive character, no doubt due to its militant stance. What I know about this organization is gleaned in part from oral accounts circulating in San Cristóbal but above all from what I have been told by indigenous Tzeltals who have had dealings with it. In particular, I have learned a great deal through conversations with Juan García (a pseudonym), who, as a delegate from his small organization of indigenous doctors, collaborated with COMPITCH from its founding.

The history of COMPITCH may be traced back to 1998, when a group of academics and activists in the city of San Cristóbal proposed suspending the Bioprospection, Conservation of Biodiversity, and Sustainable Development in the Chiapas Highlands project, known as ICBG-Maya, directed by US anthropologist Brent Berlin.[5] As in other places in Mexico (Hayden 2003), the opponents to the project argued that because Mexico had no national law regulating access to plant and genetic materials, the licenses offered by federal agencies to bioprospectors were invalid. The conflict affected most of the organizations of indigenous doctors in Chiapas and led to the creation of COMPITCH. Juan García participated from the beginning of the process as a delegate of his organization. He remembers those years as an exhausting period but also as a great learning process, as it informed him about international legislation and biodiversity. Two years after the ICBG-Maya project had been suspended, the protest attracted the attention of activists from Mexico City who joined as 'outside advisers' to COMPITCH. More radical and combative, these new activists eased out the original group and effectively took control over the organization, probably as part of a more general strategy of the Mexican far left to introduce themselves into organizations connected to the indigenous world and to place themselves provisionally at the service of the Zapatista movement. Juan García describes this change of course:

> Then the new advisers arrived to take power, they wanted to control everything, all the organizations, but they had a different idea of what traditional medicine is. They began to mobilize the people, they took them to marches, everything was protests, congresses, marches. They didn't ask "What do you people think?" No, they only said we have to support this or that group, the marches in favor of women, against racism, and I don't know what else, things outside Mexico too. Their ideas were related with Zapatismo, that's where things began. They used the image of the Zapatistas, the leaders felt as if they were Zapatistas, they came to form their own crews. Some indigenous people defended themselves, they weren't going to let themselves be used so easily, but they [the advisers] weren't interested, they wanted power.

In spite of presenting itself as a council of organizations of traditional indigenous doctors and midwives, COMPITCH places its focus on problems with bioprospecting policies, not so much for environmental protection reasons but as a form of anti-capitalist struggle. The adviser-leaders, as Juan García observed, have been able to form a small group of indigenous youth (the 'multipliers') trained in these issues, who, according to COMPITCH, will begin "a great political and social reflection to construct, in an objective way, their proposal of long-lasting and grass-roots development." Meanwhile, the participation of indigenous doctors (and attention to their concerns) is practically non-existent. In fact, Juan García thinks that what he understands to be traditional medicine has been abandoned by COMPITCH in favor of political activism and that this trend has accelerated with the decline of the indigenous physician organizations. In his words:

> What is COMPITCH's policy? It is the defense of natural resources, mixed with marching, with rallies. A complete change in course has occurred, traditional medicine was ignored; next, they removed some indigenous thinkers who did not agree with their ideas. For example, giving a workshop on international legislation to an indigenous doctor is difficult; they don't need to know that, they don't need bibliography. I feel that you shouldn't fool around with traditional medicine, because you can't convert traditional doctors into politicians, I feel that the ideas should come from the region itself, the community, the organization, with their own doctors.

Conversely, COMPITCH is very interested in the activities of midwives. This is partly because midwives' practice seems more justifiable from the standpoint of the empirical perspective on health care. But there are also other reasons. COMPITCH has made concerted efforts to introduce itself into the regions of Chiapas where the Zapatista presence is the largest. Nevertheless, the majority of the indigenous Zapatistas are committed Catholics and reject traditional medical practices as 'witchcraft'. Yet the technical training of midwives, together with the administration of medicinal herbs absent any accompanying ritual, is religiously acceptable. It cannot be a coincidence that among the recently approved public objectives of COMPITCH is the "development of a model of community self-sufficiency, based fundamentally on traditional midwives and herbalists, that rises in response to the crisis of the policies as regards public health," without any mention of what they consider indigenous doctors to be.

Nevertheless, although they occupy no formal role in the organization, indigenous doctors are necessarily its central figures. The shamans are the symbol of tradition that is ultimately necessary to justify COMPITCH's existence and activities. Everything is based on the premise—sometimes tacit, sometimes explicit—that indigenous doctors are guardians of a natural inheritance, standard-bearers of local knowledge, and the deed holders of the rights to the biodiversity of the region. In this logical scheme, COMPITCH would represent the politically organized response of indigenous doctors to defend their natural inheritance. By presenting itself as a voice of indigenous physicians—and not simply as the voice of midwives and multipliers—the organization acquires the symbolic capital and the national and international financing necessary to develop its political agenda.

I have termed this practice 'ventriloquism', that is, the art of giving a voice different intonations and modifying it in such a way that it seems to originate from indigenous people (Pitarch 2004). The best example of political ventriloquism in Chiapas is Subcommander Marcos, the leader of the Zapatista Army.

In his speeches, he projects his own interests and strategies, but he does so using certain stylistic devices and shared thematic areas to make it appear as if they come from the indigenous population. Due to Marcos's great success, numerous political actors related to the indigenous world in Chiapas and throughout Mexico followed his example as a means to project legitimacy. In this case, the Mexican advisers of COMPITCH not only 'represent' the indigenous physicians but also 'speak' for them in what appears to be the indigenous voice. Part of the ventriloquial effect involves mixing into Spanish supposedly indigenous words that the Mexican, and above all the international community, take to be genuine. This is the type of language that Marcos improvised with great mastery and that some of the non-indigenous activists adopted. A COMPITCH communiqué might reflect this 'Indian' language (although, in contrast to Marcos, with little imagination or literary sense) as follows:

> We were born among the flowers and the heat of the sweat baths; we learned to walk the mountain and to find water among the stones; we prayed to the hills and we celebrated with the sky; and the things that were born only one thing, we were able to make into many things. The forests that remain, their flowers and their animals remain where our men and women walk, where our men and women live. We know of what we speak because our knowledge walks what we talk; it is not only that which is written, not only that which is seen, it is first and foremost what is walked. It is in this way that our memory is born and becomes strong, and in our steps together the community guards and transmits it.

Such texts would be combined with passages of conventional language of the revolutionary left, for instance: "Modern biotechnology, developed by capital and today consolidated in sectors of profits propelled by accumulation, marks the beginning of a new industrial era in the production of manufactured goods. Vital to this new era will be the accumulation and patenting of genetic resources of commercial interest that are located on our lands."

Another example shows this ventriloquial use of indigenous medicine. On 15 September 2002, *La Jornada*, a Mexican newspaper with a nationwide circulation, reported on a meeting of indigenous doctors held in the town of San Pedro Atlapulco (see fig. 3). The news item stated that traditional doctors, in addition to opposing the commercialization of medicinal plants, insisted that the Mexican government accept a series of demands by the Zapatista Army as a condition for restarting peace talks and also that the government adopt the San Andreas Accords as the Indigenous Constitution.[6] The story also reported on a lecture by an economics professor who denounced globalization for destroying indigenous lands and traditions. More than the news itself, what most attracted my attention was the photograph that accompanied and illustrated the news story. The picture shows four indigenous physicians praying. The second from the left is Sebastian Bok, a shaman from Cancuc whom I had known for some time. When I bumped into him a year later, he told me that he had been sent by COMPITCH, that it had been a meeting about medicinal plants, and that he knew nothing about the measures demanded in favor of the Zapatistas reported in the article.

14 POLÍTICA • DOMINGO • 15 • SEPTIEMBRE • 2002

■ Exigen el cumplimiento de las tres señales del EZ para la reanudación del diálogo

Médicos tradicionalistas adoptan los acuerdos de San Andrés como *Constitución indígena*

■ Manifiestan su oposición a que trasnacionales se apropien de la sabiduría de las etnias

Médicos chiapanecos, durante una ceremonia en el Foro Nacional de Defensa de la Medicina Tradicional, en San Pedro Atlapulco

ROSA ROJAS
ENVIADA

SAN PEDRO ATLAPULCO, OCOYOACAC, MEX., 14 DE SEPTIEMBRE. Al inaugurarse el tercer Foro Nacional en Defensa de la Medicina Tradicional, unos 500 participantes de 29 pueblos indios de 20 entidades del país desconocieron la reforma constitucional "indigenista" del 28 de abril de 2001 y declararon que, "ante la quiebra del estado de derecho", reconocen como "única constitución en materia indígena la que se contiene en los acuerdos de San Andrés".

la reforma agraria"- y borrar la discriminación "frente a nuestro gobierno, que no le veo directriz para llevarnos hacia el futuro".

Teresa Zurian, indígena zoque, y Francisca Pérez, tzotzil, ambas médicas tradicionales de Chiapas, así como Antonio Hernández, señalaron que debe evitarse que las empresas trasnacionales sigan robándose la sabiduría de los pueblos indios en el uso curativo de las plantas a cambio de una bicoca, aprovechándose de la miseria de la gente. Doña Teresa, quien

Hernández López subrayó que los pueblos indios se oponen a que las compañías trasnacionales patenten los conocimientos indígenas para beneficiarse, pues esta sabiduría, que incluye "la curación de las enfermedades del alma", debe ser patrimonio de la humanidad.

En defensa de la tierra

Mario Flores, presidente del comisariado de bienes comunales de Atlapulco, destacó que el propósito del foro es acordar la defensa de la tierra y los recursos naturales

FIGURE 3 Front Page of *La Jornada*, 15 September 2002

Paradoxically, Sebastian favored the party that until then had governed Mexico, the Institutional Revolutionary Party (PRI), and was against the Zapatistas. So here we have a situation where an indigenous doctor went to demonstrate his knowledge about herbal medicine, of which he was proud, and he ended up, without knowing it, declaring support for the Zapatistas against neo-liberalism, the Puebla to Panama Plan, and other things about which he knew nothing.

In reality, the entire effort by radical left-wing organizations to recruit shamans—a symbolic co-opting of all things Indian to their cause—is based on an odd contradiction. For historical reasons that are in part related to the complex relationship between the Mexican state and the indigenous population, the great majority of shamans are politically conservative and tend to associate the government and official institutions with respect for their therapeutic practices. In an inverse way, they feel that left-wing revolutionary organizations and the Catholic Church, which in this region is associated with liberation theology, oppose their practices. And they have good reason to believe this. For example, although the bishopry of this region nominally supports indigenous medicine organizations, in practice indigenous Catholics have harshly repressed shamanic activities in those villages where they exercise political control. When the Zapatista Army revolted in 1994, they expelled several shamans accused of witchcraft in the areas that they controlled.[7]

All in all, the political alliances of the extreme left-wing organizations that call themselves pro-indigenous often reveal an opportunistic character that supersedes ideology. In 2005, COMPITCH, which for years had given political support to the Zapatista Army, made an abrupt about-face and began to support Andrés Manuel López Obrador, the left-wing candidate for the presidency of Mexico, who eventually lost the elections of 2006. From one day to the next, COMPITCH advisers went from glorifying Subcommander Marcos to making extremely violent accusations against him. Under certain circumstances, such a change, while surprising, might be understandable. But in this case, the shift in the organization's alliance seemed all the more drastic as Marcos was deeply and personally opposed to López Obrador. In the game of political alliances, support for López Obrador was equivalent to betraying the Zapatistas. This is how Juan García remembers the arguments that the advisers used to convince members: "They said that López Obrador was going to be a good president, that he was going to do a good job, that he was director of the INI in I can't remember what part of Tabasco, that he was a humble person, that he had a small automobile, a Nissan, and no bodyguards. But this thing about López Obrador, so, what did it have to do with traditional medicine?"

Conclusion

The growing number of civil society organizations in the center of Chiapas concerned with indigenous issues has led to a much needed strengthening of public space in the region. Taken together, these organizations have helped accomplish such things as safeguarding human rights, improving economic opportunities, defending indigenous culture, and limiting the abuses, corruption, and political violence of the public powers. They have often done so at great sacrifice and with considerable personal risk to their members. But not all of these organizations make civil use of civil society. We have examined three organizations of indigenous doctors that represent a certain degree of civility and diverse pluralism. The Organization of Indigenous Doctors of Cancuc, a small organization controlled by the town's indigenous people themselves, is characterized by common accord and local control over the meaning of indigenous medicine. In the Organization of Indigenous Doctors of the State of

Chiapas (OMIECH), indigenous people partially control the organization, but non-indigenous advisers have a central role in the definition of the organization's activity, as we have seen with regard to the Museum of Mayan Medicine. Lastly, in COMPITCH, non-indigenous activists run and define the organization with an aggressive style, while a small number of indigenous collaborators are limited to the role of assistants.

In cases such as that of COMPITCH, there is a lack of meaningful dialogue with the indigenous population based on respect and plurality. The dealings of this organization are not that different from those of the Spanish friars of the sixteenth century. COMPITCH aspires to dominate the mediation between the indigenous population (in this case, indigenous medical specialists) and non-indigenous sectors and institutions, and ultimately to monopolize the representation of the indigenous world. The goal is not for indigenous people to participate institutionally, but rather for the organization to be recognized as the only legitimate indigenous representative in dealings with public powers and the international audience.

The effect on civil society of this type of organization is uncivil and results in serious damage to liberty and to the possibilities for expansion. It suppresses recognition of the rich diversity of interests, points of view, and organizational experiences of indigenous society. The diversity of the indigenous world should not be interpreted as division but instead as a sign of maturity (Ekern 1998). To think that indigenous people can speak with one voice is absurd. However, what gives COMPITCH a measure of credibility is the romantic supposition that the indigenous world is dominated by a homogeneity of interests and opinions and that matters of legitimacy and representation—basic in other contexts—create no major problems. Historically, the indigenous population has had great difficulty being admitted to the public space of expression, and organizations have tried to monopolize the 'indigenous voice' and exclude alternatives, thus prolonging and compounding this difficulty.

Nonetheless, in the case of organizations such as COMPITCH, non-indigenous activists do not so much monopolize the indigenous voice as supplant it. This is ventriloquism: taking the stage and speaking in a way that urban and international audiences expect Indians to think and express themselves. This symbolic association with Indianness permits them to intervene successfully in the political debate in arenas that under other circumstances would be inaccessible. It is possible that an element of ventriloquism appears in the policies of indigenous identity in other regions of Latin America, but my impression is that the degree to which it is employed with respect to the indigenous people of Chiapas is a characteristically Mexican phenomenon. Since the revolution, the Mexican state has dominated representation of the indigenous population through various types of corporative organizations whose leadership is historically non-indigenous. There is therefore a long tradition of accepting (and considering quite normal) that non-indigenous representation speaks for the indigenous peoples and of supposing that indigenous people have some basic difficulty expressing themselves. Hence, it is assumed that they need non-indigenous spokespeople. Perhaps only in Mexico could a personality like Subcommander Marcos have emerged who speaks not only for the indigenous in his organization but also for the indigenous of Chiapas and Mexico in general without any serious question of his legitimacy. Often, the oddity of this paradox is forgotten. When Juan García, the young indigenous man who was a member of COMPITCH, attended a meeting on indigenous culture celebrated in Quetzaltenango, Guatemala, he was shocked to see that the meeting was designed and directed—in fact and not just in name—by indigenous people. For him, this experience was decisive in his rethinking of the way that indigenous civil society should be organized.

For the ventriloquial effect to be politically useful requires using a stereotyped image of the Indian that can be easily recognized and not signal contradictions. Regarding indigenous medical organizations, the ventriloquial activity requires the creation of the category 'indigenous medicine'. For indigenous medicine to be used as a weapon in the North-South struggle, it must first be constituted as real medicine—something that is conceptually equivalent to European medicine, perhaps different in some superficial features but similar at the core. The result of this type of operation is to make something strange and foreign into something close to Western logic. The indigenous difference is suppressed in favor of the creation of an artificial but less troublesome indigenous culture. As Ramos (1998: 275) observes, the indigenous functions here as a simulacrum, that is, in the Baudrillardian sense, the operation that provides all the signs of the real without any of its contradictions or nuisances: "It is a model that molds the Indian's interest to the organization's shape and need." The multicultural rhetoric that is employed—in my opinion, often for opportunistic reasons and without conviction—as a factor in the delegitimization of the state by some left-wing activists ends up being a retrograde discourse. This is so because the Mexican state, starting especially in the 1990s, has adopted more liberal policies toward the indigenous population and is comfortable with the new situation that frees it from its previous social obligations. However, in a more general way, it is also retrograde discourse because, under the pretext of valuing and dignifying indigenous culture, the activists' strategy and language operates to identify and assimilate. Deep cultural differences remain hidden, while a type of difference that is purely folkloric and ultimately in accord with neo-liberal logic is highlighted.

In this context, it is particularly admirable that the indigenous people of Chiapas have begun to adopt an attitude of critical distance toward non-indigenous leaders and that they are asking for greater freedom of ideas and organizations. More and more, the indigenous population shows that it is conscious of and opposed to the pressures to participate in authoritarian organizations and to be used in ventriloquial fictions. Speaking about the organization of indigenous doctors, Miguel Gómez expressed this with complete clarity: "For example, in the case of the traditional medicine in Cancuc, [we] have different ideas, [but] since the organization was formed, we have been very plural. In other words, we respect each other's way of being, our differences. I think that is the key of the community [of our organization], that is why it works. It makes no difference that a person belongs to the PRI or the PRD. The main thing is that we are traditional doctors, that we help indigenous medicine, that is what is important to us."

Acknowledgments

The author would like to thank Ted Fischer for coordinating this volume and for the invitation to participate. Thanks are extended also to Miguel Gómez Gómez for sharing openly his opinions on the topic of Indian medicine and for enabling the conversation on which this chapter is to a great degree based.

Pedro Pitarch is Professor of Anthropology at the Universidad Complutense de Madrid. He has worked with indigenous speakers of Tzeltal in Chiapas, Mexico, where he has focused on local concepts of personhood. He is the author of *Ch'ulel: Una etnografía de las almas tzeltales* (1997), and he has also edited, among others, the volume *Los derechos humanos en tierras mayas: Política, representaciones y moralidad* (2001) with Julián López García.

Notes

1. Proyecto de Medicinas Paralelas del Instituto Nacional Indigenista: 1979–1985; Modelo Alternativo de Salud, Secretaria de Salud: 1983–1985; Programa de Interrelación de la Medicina Tradicional, IMSS, 1982–1992 (Freyermuth Enciso 1993; Page Pliego 2002).
2. For more information about OMIECH, see http://www.medicinamaya.org.
3. More detailed description and analysis can be found in Pitarch (1999). Ayora Díaz (2002) also has written about the museum. See also Castañeda (1996).
4. The transcribed interviews with Tzeltal speakers have been edited to facilitate fluid reading in English.
5. The conflict that this project inspired was relatively well-publicized, including in academic literature; see, for example, *Current Anthropology* 43, no. 3 (2002).
6. The San Andreas Accords were negotiated between the Zapatistas and the Mexican government, and in the end, the former accused the government of not recognizing them.
7. According to what I was told by various shamans from Cancuc. See also Leyva (1995).

References

Aguirre Beltrán, Gonzalo. 1986. *Antropología médica*. Mexico City: CIESAS.

Avritzer, Leonardo. 2002. *Democracy and the Public Space in Latin America*. Princeton, NJ: Princeton University Press.

Ayora Díaz, Igor. 2002. *Globalización, conocimiento y poder: Médicos locales y sus luchas por el reconocimiento en Chiapas*. Mexico City: Plaza y Valdés.

Castañeda, Quetzil E. 1996. *In the Museum of Maya Culture*. Minneapolis: University of Minnesota Press.

Ekern, Stener. 1998. "Las organizaciones mayas de Guatemala: Panorama y retos institucionales." *Mayab* 11: 78–104.

Freyermuth Enciso, Graciela. 1993. *Médicos tradicionales y médicos alópatas: Un encuentro difícil en los Altos de Chiapas*. Tuxtla Gutiérrez, Mexico: Gobierno de Estado de Chiapas-CIESAS.

Hayden, Cori. 2003. *When Nature Goes Public: The Making and Unmaking of Bioprospecting in Mexico*. Princeton, NJ: Princeton University Press.

Kirshenblatt-Gimblett, Barbara. 1991. "Objects of Ethnography." Pp. 386–443 in *The Poetics and Politics of Museum Display*, ed. Ivan Karp and Steven D. Lavine. Washington, DC: Smithsonian Institution Press.

Leyva, Xochitl. 1995. "Catequistas, misioneros y tradiciones en Las Cañadas." Pp. 375–405 in *Chiapas, los rumbos de otra historia*, ed. Juan Pedro Viqueira and Mario Ruz. Mexico City: UNAM-CIESAS-CEMCA-UDG.

Méndez, José Luis. 1999. "Civil Organization in Mexico: Recent Evolution and Prospects." *Voluntas* 10, no. 1: 93–99.

Olvera, Alberto. 1997. "Civil Society and Political Transition in Mexico." *Constellations* 4, no. 1: 105–123.

Page Pliego, Jaime Tomás. 2002. "Medicina indígena y política sanitaria dirigida a los pueblos indígenas." *Anuario de Estudios Indígenas* 7: 34–78.

Pérez-Díaz, Victor. 2003. "De la guerra civil a la sociedad civil: El capital social en España entre los años treinta y los años noventa del siglo XX." Pp. 427–489 in *El declive del capital social*, ed. Robert Putnam. Barcelona: Galaxia Gutenberg.

Pitarch, Pedro. 1996. *Ch'ulel: Una etnografía de las almas tzeltales.* Mexico City: Fondo de Cultura Económica.

_____. 1999. "En el Museo de la Medicina Maya." *Mayab* 12: 79–92.

_____. 2004. "The Zapatistas and the Art of Ventriloquism." *Journal of Human Rights* 3, no. 3: 35–63.

Putnam, Robert D. 1995. "Bowling Alone: America's Declining Social Capital." *Journal of Democracy* 6, no. 1: 65–78.

Ramos, Alcida Rita. 1998. *Indigenism: Ethnic Politics in Brazil.* Madison: University of Wisconsin Press.

Rus, Jan. 1995. "Local Adaptation to Global Change: The Reordering of Native Society in Highland Chiapas, 1974–1994." *European Review of Latin American and Caribbean Studies* 58: 71–89.

INDEX

Printed in the United Kingdom
by Lightning Source UK Ltd.
134159UK00001B/130-168/P